The TEMPLARS and the GRAIL

Knights of the Quest

KAREN RALLS

Quest Books
Theosophical Publishing House

Wheaton, Illinois ♦ Chennai (Madras), India

The Theosophical Society acknowledges with gratitude the generous support of the Kern Foundation for the publication of this book.

First Quest Edition 2003

The Theosophical Publishing House
P. O. Box 270
Wheaton, IL 60189-0270

Cover art, book design, and typesetting by Dan Doolin

Library of Congress Cataloging-in-Publication Data

Ralls, Karen.
The Templars and the Grail: knights of the quest / Karen Ralls.—1st Quest ed.
    p.   cm.
Includes bibliographical references and index.
ISBN 0-8356-0807-7
1. Templars. 2. Grail—Legends—History and criticism.
3. Arthur, King. 4. Rosslyn Chapel (Roslin, Scotland) I. Title.

CR4743 .R35 2003
271'.7913—dc21   2002036906

5 * 04 05 06 07 08

Printed in the United States of America

CONTENTS

Foreword
by
John Matthews

Two of the most enigmatic and enduring mysteries in the world are dealt with in this book. The history of the Order of the Poor Knights of Christ and the Temple of Solomon—better known as the Knights Templar—remains an entangled and often impenetrable array of fact and supposition. Ever since their foundation in 1119, debate has raged over their true purpose, their beliefs, and above all the nature of certain documents or objects of great power that they may, or may not, have possessed. One of these objects represents the second great theme of this book—a relic once considered the most sacred artifact in the Christian world—the Holy Grail.

The story of the Grail is one of the crowning glories of the Western imagination. No one can say precisely from where, or even when, it emerged. Indeed, it seems to have always been present, hidden in the deepest recesses of the human soul, continuing to exact a powerful fascination over all who come in contact with it. Nor is this surprising, since it deals with so many themes that are as important today as they have always been—the search for absolutes, the quest for healing, and the unending quest for the truth.

The Grail has been described as many things: as a stone, fallen from the crown of the Angel of Light during the war in Heaven; as a cauldron of Celtic antiquity sought after by heroes; as the cup used by Christ to celebrate the Last Supper and the first Eucharist. But, more than the sum of its parts, the Grail is really an idea representing the presence of a numinous, mystical link between the sacred and the secular. It remains, to this day, a focus for search and a provider of wonder amid the often drab world in which we live our lives.

The story of the Templars and the quest for the Grail have long been associated in both history and tradition. The great medieval poet Wolfram von Eschenbach called those chosen to guard the Grail

Templiesen; however, the exact relationship between these guardians and the historical Order of the Templars has still to be resolved. Some believe that Wolfram modeled his Grail guardians on the actual Templars, others that they are a purely fictional invention by the poet, while a third group believes that Parzival refers to the Order itself. In their own time the Templars were believed to have come into the possession of something of great power and importance—something which, whatever it may actually have been, almost certainly contributed to the sudden and disastrous destruction of the Order in 1307. Before that moment the Templars were one of the most powerful organizations in the world—rich, influential, and highly respected. Almost overnight they became the focus of a highly orchestrated attack that presented them as heretics, sodomites, devil worshipers, and murderers. In a series of dramatic trials their leaders, together with a large number of their members, were forced under torture to confess to the most unspeakable acts. In a historical instant the Order was swept away—though, as Karen Ralls notes in this book, they by no means vanished utterly but rather were absorbed into other Orders or continued to function under other names. To this day, and increasingly over the past ten years, a huge amount of new research has been undertaken by both academic and popular researchers, and a great deal has come to light that points to the Templars as guardians of an esoteric knowledge of tremendous importance to the world.

Was that knowledge simply a body of ancient wisdom or the actual vessel of the Grail itself? We may never know, but we can continue to keep an open mind and to weigh the many conflicting accounts of the Templars and the Grail against the more sober judgment of medieval history. On the one hand, we must consider the sources of the vast literature of the Grail, indissolubly interwoven with the myths of Arthur and his court, which stretched from the ninth century to the fifteenth century and has continued to resurface ever since. On the other, we need to acknowledge the vast body of tradition, much of it orally transmitted, that has kept the mystery of the Grail fresh and in the forefront of modern research. Above all, as is the case in Karen Ralls's book (something of a Templar tour de force itself), we need to apply a widely interdisciplinary approach to subjects of this kind, which can only wither and die if left solely to those who seek to codify and quantify the deepest mysteries of life.

The oldest references to the Grail come from a ninth-century Welsh poem: the *Prieddeu Annwn*. After this we hear virtually nothing more of its story until the beginning of the twelfth century, when a French court poet named Chrétien de Troyes (Troyes being an area with significant Templar associations) composed a poem that he called *Perceval*, or *The Story of the Grail*. It told the story of a search, undertaken by a simple youth, brought up away from the ways of men, for a mysterious object known as a *graal*. But Chrétien left the poem unfinished—and in so doing created a mystery that has stirred the imagination of seekers ever since.

Over the next hundred years the story was told and retold, each author adding his own touches, deepening and building upon hints offered by Chrétien's poem. The Grail itself went through a number of transformations—a factor that became part of its nature, proving that it could not be codified or pinned to a single image or idea. In the versions that followed it acquired a family of guardians, and out of this arose the idea of the search for the castle where the miraculous vessel was kept. Among those who sought out this mystical place were the Templars, though whether they discovered it or not remains a mystery that is only now, in books like the one you are holding, receiving the attention it deserves.

The Grail can be many things; indeed it can manifest in almost any number of ways. It may have more than one form, or no form at all— it may not even exist in this dimension. Yet it provides us with an object of personal search, a quest from which may come personal growth and the restoration of the spirit. Karen Ralls's meticulously researched book is a significant addition both to the history and myths surrounding the Templars and to the highly esoteric literature of the Grail. In this work Dr. Ralls has created an important bridge between these two extraordinary and long-lived themes.

ACKNOWLEDGMENTS

I gratefully acknowledge the many Grail scholars for their inspiring academic work through the years—Harald Haferland, Helen Adolf, Jessie Weston, Willem Snelleman, Jean Frappier, Richard Barber, Roger Sherman Loomis, Jean Markale, Emma Jung, Marie-Louise von Franz, Glenys Goetinck, and Alfred Nutt, to name but a few. Similarly, as any book on the Templars must be examined in a wider context, the works of leading Crusades historians such as James Brundage, August C. Krey, Richard Kieckhefer, Denys Pringle, Jonathan Riley-Smith, Malcolm Barber, Helen Nicolson, Bernard Hamilton, Charles Beckingham, Judi Upton-Ward, Marie Louise Bulst-Thiele, Alan Forey, and Norman Housley have been helpful at key junctures in the process of writing this book.

I would also like to thank the librarians and curators at the following institutions for their kind help with specific research questions: British Library; J. P. Morgan Library; Bodleian Library, University of Oxford; British Museum; Smithsonian Institution; American Academy of Religion; Austrian National Library (Vienna); U.S. Navy Department Library at the U.S. Naval Historical Center; Association of Research and Enlightenment Library; the Medieval Institute at Western Michigan University; Harvard Divinity School; the Warburg Institute Library; School of Oriental and African Studies at the University of London; the Labyrinth Project (Medieval Studies

Program) at Georgetown University; Graduate Theological Union, University of California, Berkeley; and the Joseph Campbell and Marija Gimbutas Library, Pacifica Graduate Institute, Santa Barbara.

The following organizations and individuals have also been of assistance in various ways: the Society for the Study of the Crusades and the Latin East; Society of Antiquaries (U.K.); Mr. Robert Brydon, Templar historian and owner of the Brydon Collection; Mr. Stuart Beattie, Director, Rosslyn Chapel Trust; Mr. Alan Bain, President of the American-Scottish Foundation (N.Y.); Ordo Supremus Militaris Templi Hierosolymitani (OSMTH) and its International Grand Commander, RADM James J. Carey, GCTJ, GMTJ; the Grand Priory of the Knights Templar in England and Wales and its Grand Prior, Rev. John Bernardi; Sir Roy Redgrave; the Templar Pilgrimage Trust (U.K.); Dr. John Algeo, International Vice-President, The Theosophical Society; Capt. Howard Sartori; the Philosophical Research Society; the History of Science Society (U.S.A.); the British Society for the History of Science; the Science and Medical Network; the Folklore Society (U.K.); Rev. Dr. Matthew Fox; Denys, Barbara, and Simon le Fevre; Bill Chapman; Stella Bernardi; Stephen Dafoe; the Joseph Campbell Foundation; the Prince Henry Sinclair Society; Ward Ginn; Clan Sinclair U.S.A.; Niven Sinclair; Steve Britt-Hazard; Professor Jocelyn Godwin; the editors of *Parabola Magazine*; Mythic Journeys; David Fideler; Professor Arthur Versluis; John and Caitlin Matthews; Fred Steadman-Jones; Marian Green; Michael and Seza Eccles; Margo Fish; Dame Erika Barty-King; Mara Freeman; Kate Dixon; Jeremy Naydler; Claudine Glot of the Centre de l'Imaginaire Arthurien (Brittany); Professor Philippe Walter, University of Grenoble; the New York Open Center; the Association for Humanistic Psychology; the Institute of Transpersonal Psychology; and the International Arthurian Society; the Jupiter Trust; and Peter and Sarah Dawkins.

Many thanks must also go to my editor, Carolyn Bond; to the staff at Quest Books, especially Sharron Dorr; and to Dan Doolin, whose inspiring painting of a Knight Templar graces the cover of this book. I also extend great thanks to Mr. Stuart Beattie (Rosslyn Chapel Trust) and Mr. Robert Brydon (The Brydon Collection) for permission to use the special photographs in this book.

In addition to the inspiration I have found from my colleagues, past and present, at the Oxford University and the University of

Edinburgh, and from friends here and abroad, I would certainly like to give very special thanks to my husband, Jon, for his encouragement, patience, support, and overall faith in this project—truly "chivalry in action."

And finally, a tribute to the last Templar Grand Master, Jacques de Molay, and all those who have shown remarkable courage and perseverance in the face of seemingly impossible odds.

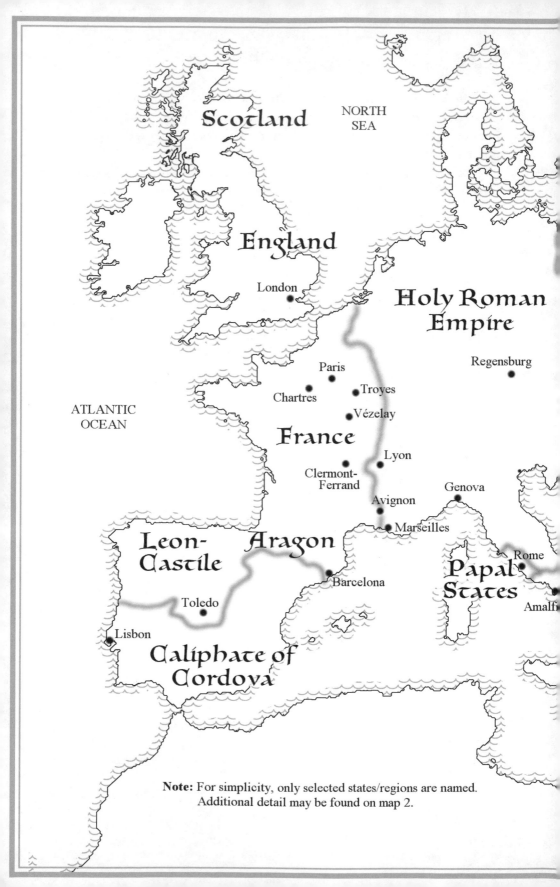

Scotland

NORTH
SEA

England

London

ATLANTIC
OCEAN

Holy Roman
Empire

Regensburg

Paris

Chartres

Troyes

Vézelay

France

Lyon

Clermont-
Ferrand

Avignon

Genova

Marseilles

Leon-
Castile

Aragon

Papal
States

Rome

Barcelona

Toledo

Amalfi

Lisbon

Caliphate of
Cordova

Note: For simplicity, only selected states/regions are named.
Additional detail may be found on map 2.

INTRODUCTION

In 1340, a German priest on pilgrimage to the Holy Land, while walking along the shore of the Dead Sea, came upon two elderly men who turned out to be former Knights Templar. At the time of the Templar arrests in 1307, these knights were already languishing in prison, having been captured after the city of Acre's tragic fall to the Saracens in 1291. After their release, they had "roughed it" in the mountains for years. They had seen no one from Latin Christendom for some time and were astonished to learn—thirty-three years after the fact—of the French king's attack on their great Order, its subsequent suppression by the Pope, and the dramatic burning at the stake of their beloved Grand Master, Jacques de Molay.

These two Templar knights may be emblematic of how—like the warriors of the film *Highlander*, who live forever—the memory of the Knights Templar lives on, even today. During the time of the Templars (1119–1312), "history" and "myth" concerning the Order were already becoming intertwined. Legendary accounts about the crusaders and their miraculous feats occasionally made the rounds. Back then, too, some whispered that the Templars may have found the gold of Solomon's Temple or ancient scrolls, or may even have possessed the Ark of the Covenant. Since then, stories about the knights have grown considerably.

After the suppression of the Order (1312) and the death of Jacques de Molay, its last Grand Master (1314), the factual history of the Order ended—and its powerful mythos began. A mythos is a belief system or cluster of archetypes that forms around an idea or person through time, like a type of "mystical aura." It has a life all its own. In the long run, the Templar mythos seems to have had as much power and influence in Western culture as the Order itself—if not more. Not only the Order's overall mythos has survived for centuries; so has the individual mythos surrounding Jacques de Molay. Places, too, can have a powerful mythos relating to the Templars—for example, Rosslyn Chapel in Scotland. This became apparent to me during my tenure as Deputy Curator of the Rosslyn Chapel Museum exhibition, a period concurrent with my time as Postdoctoral Fellow at the University of Edinburgh—an experience that started me on the in-depth research that eventually led to this book.

Many questions about the Templars focus on the idea of a quest: Did the Templars actually find something in the Holy Land? If so, what was it and where was it taken? Or did the Templars undertake a quest of another nature: Were they magical adepts of the highest order, custodians of secret knowledge? Does their quest continue today, however secretly? Is a quest associated with the Templars less a matter of gold and treasures and more of a spiritual pursuit—as many are beginning to realize?

Asking constructive questions is at least as important as presuming answers. For instance—as many wonder—why did the medieval Grail romances reach the height of their popularity during the heyday of the Templar Order? Many questions about the Templars are as yet unresolved. With so heavily romanticized a subject, historians often have difficulty sorting fact from fiction, especially concerning events after 1314. In this regard, the central Templar archive's disappearance—or destruction—in late medieval times has proved an incalculable loss. Nevertheless, Templar documents are being discovered all the time, so the factual history of the Knights Templar is gradually becoming clarified. We can also learn much from exploring the motives, beliefs, and circumstances of both the Templars and their contemporary chroniclers. Furthermore, until quite recently, historians and archaeologists have interacted very little, and academic and popular authors have rarely spoken to each other. Fortunately, more interdisciplinary research is taking place today, which some feel will encourage the flow of ideas and perhaps help to shed further light on the history of these enigmatic knights. It is in this spirit that I adopted a more interdisciplinary approach to the scholarly research methodology for this book.

Much has been written about the Templars, ranging from the soberly academic to the wildly sensational, especially in recent years, when interest in the Knights Templar has never been greater. Both their history and their mythos have sometimes been misunderstood or misrepresented. Recent historical and archaeological research shows that certain previously "assumed facts" as well as "presumed myths" about the Templars were unfounded. For example, contrary to popular belief, it is *not* true that no written sources about the medieval Templars exist; nor is it true that their Order was found guilty as charged by Pope Clement V and the papal commission on 5 June 1311. But it *is* true that Templar novices, upon reception into the Order, made solemn pledges "to God and the Blessed Mary," as their Rule states. It is also true that the Templars were very practical men—trusted diplomats, accountants, farmers, business managers, and navigators, and bankers to kings and Popes—a point that is often overlooked today, given their glamorous role as spiritual warrior monks. Another truth to keep in mind is that there is no incontrovertible evidence suggesting the Templars excavated beneath the Temple Mount in Jerusalem.

It is also true that the enigmatic "graffiti" carved by Templars on the walls of Chinon Castle's prison tower, where sixty Templars were imprisoned in 1308, remain undeciphered today. These carvings—which include heart-shaped patterns, geometrical grids, and what we now call the Star of David—have generally been ignored by academics and other researchers, partly because they are so puzzling. Yet we know for certain that some of these sixty Templars did carve these images and that some of those imprisoned at Chinon held high offices in the Order. These carvings clearly deserve more serious attention than they have received to date. Moreover, important questions remain about the Templars' possible knowledge of geometry, their known use of codes and biblical ciphers, their skills in building and masonry, and certain details of their controversial trial by the Inquisition.

Many medieval historians, including this one, are being asked more and more questions about the Templars. People say they are tired of wading through various theories without knowing what is credible and what is not, or how to distinguish between fact, sensationalism, and honest, informed speculation. This book aims to make the academic material accessible as well as to take a fresh, up-to-date look at a selection of theories. Thus it falls into two divisions: part 1, which is a factual history of the medieval Templar Order based on academic sources (chapters 1–4); and part 2, which presents the Templar mythos in a tripartite manner—showing how the Order's factual history has frequently become intertwined with elements of the Grail legends (chapter 5), speculations about the Order and events after its suppression (chapter 6), and the symbolism at Rosslyn Chapel in Scotland (chapter 7).

This is not merely a "one theory" book; instead, many points of view are presented, and the reader is then free to make up his or her own mind. In part 2, I present certain accepted academic viewpoints as well as several popular theories as, in the true spirit of the Round Table, every well-thought-out opinion deserves a fair hearing. A particular theory's inclusion in this book does not mean I believe or endorse it. Many viewpoints about the Templars have been presented over the centuries; in my opinion, none has proved itself incontrovertible. Like any good scientist, a historian may form any number of hypotheses, based on available evidence and educated guesswork, but must be careful not to draw conclusions unless—and until—there is indisputable evidence to support them.

Also included here are an extensive bibliography, a chronology of events during the Templars' era, two maps, information on the U.K. Templar Sites Project, and exclusive photos regarding Rosslyn Chapel in Scotland. As this book focuses on the medieval period, it does not include information about modern-day neo-chivalric Templar Orders or accounts of the numerous eighteenth- and nineteenth-century neo-Templar revival Orders.

Whatever their views on the Templars, nearly everyone seems to agree on one point: the memory of these famed warrior-monks of the Crusades has a staying power second to none. The Knights Templar seem to live on, regardless. Umberto Eco wrote in a famous 1986 essay that ever since medieval times Western culture has been "dreaming" the Middle Ages, and that our current fascination with the Templars, the Cathars, Arthurian legends, and other medieval traditions is part of a modern-day quest for our Western roots.[1] It is my hope that this book will further the reader on his or her own quest.

PART
I

A History
of the
Knights Templar

CHAPTER

1

WARRIOR-MONKS of the MIDDLE AGES

ho were the Knights Templar? Were they ever the guardians of something extraordinary, perhaps the Holy Grail or the Ark of the Covenant? Why were they suppressed for alleged heresy in 1312, after rising to the heights of wealth and power? Did the last Grand Master, Jacques de Molay, know in advance about their planned downfall? And did they really survive in secret afterwards? Such questions have surrounded the historical Templar Order through the centuries; they both fuel and are fueled by the Templar mythos. As this book unfolds, we will examine various theories. But let us begin with a history of the Order at the height of its power.

A new species of knighthood

The Knights Templar, best known today as fierce warriors of the Crusades, were a devout medieval military religious Order that uniquely combined the roles of knight and monk in a way the Western medieval world had never seen before.[1] In a famous letter, *In Praise of the New Knighthood*, written to his colleague Hugh de Payns, St. Bernard of Clairvaux elevated the Knights Templar Order above all other Orders of the day, including its main rival, the Knights

Hospitaller. This letter established the image of the Templars as a fierce spiritual militia for Christ. As medieval historian Malcolm Barber explains, St. Bernard regarded the Templars as a new species of knighthood, previously unknown in the secular world, pursuing a double conflict against both flesh and blood and the invisible forces of evil. "Strong warriors, on the one hand, and monks waging war with vice and demons on the other . . . A body of men who need have no fear . . . these men had no dread of death, confident in the knowledge that in the sight of the Lord they would be his martyrs."[2]

As a holy militia fighting for Christ, the Templars were willing to put aside the usual temptations of ordinary secular life for a dedicated life of service. They accepted many sacrifices, such as living by a strict religious Rule apart from secular society, giving all of their personal property to the Order, not shaving their beards, as well as having no ornamentation on their clothing, no luxurious foods, no women, little meat at meals, and the like. They were something like a spiritualized version of modern-day elite military special forces—such as the famed U.S. Navy Seals, the Marines, or the British SAS—who live by far more rigorous standards than other soldiers. They were elite special forces for Christ, the most disciplined fighting force in western Europe.

Contrary to popular belief, the Templars were not monks—though they did take the three monastic vows of poverty, chastity, and obedience. They "were religious people who followed a religious Rule of life and wore a distinctive habit, but who, unlike monks, did not live in an enclosed house."[3] The main purpose of monks who lived in an enclosed community was to pray and to fight spiritual battles. But from what we know of the Templars from the history of the Crusades, they also fought many bloody physical battles in the defense of Christendom.

Not everyone agreed initially with St. Bernard's idea of combining spiritual devotion with physical fighting. Some churchmen saw these two functions as simply incompatible because there was great concern about sins and souls in medieval society. Even St. Bernard himself struggled with some of these issues. The Byzantines, too, were "deeply shocked to see in the Crusader armies so many priests who bore arms" and went into battle.[4] But by and large the Templars gained much respect as they demonstrated their battle skills and won victories. The power of the New Knighthood concept was so strong that even the older religious institution, the Order of the Hospital of St. John of Jerusalem, also known as the Hospitallers or the Order of St. John, had to adapt by adding to their official Rule a new knightly monastic ideology. This new idea "fused two current ideals of medieval society, knighthood and monasticism, into a code for a community of warrior-monks."[5]

St. Bernard himself led a strictly ascetic life. "He fasted so much that he ruined his health . . . A little cubicle beside the stairs, more like a closet than a room, served as the abbot's cell . . . Here he slept at night, with a straw-covered block of wood for a pillow. And thus he lived for thirty years."[6] Such a near-anorexic lifestyle was not unusual in medieval times, but St. Bernard's was unarguably one of the most austere. Martin Luther thought highly of St. Bernard: "I regard Bernard as the most pious of all monks and prefer him to all the others . . . He is the only one worthy of the name 'Father' and of being studied diligently."[7] Quite a compliment, especially coming from the man who started the Reformation!

Bernard's powers of persuasion were extraordinary, and his dedication to the idea of a "new knighthood" was unflinching. Part of his insistence was in reaction to what he considered the excesses of secular knights. He often complained about their idle words; immoderate laughter; playing of chess and dice; hunting and hawking; going to soothsayers, jesters, or storytellers; and staging plays. He especially criticized their pomp and pride and said that these were to be avoided by monastic knights. The Templars, in his view, combined the best of both the practical and the spiritual—"lions in war, lambs in the house."[8] He would refer to the monastery at Clairvaux as the entrance to "the heavenly Jerusalem" and "the fortress of God," and many suggest this was because of his close association with the early inner circle of the Knights Templar, who defended and won "fortress Jerusalem" for Christendom in 1099.[9]

Among other things, the Templars were to protect pilgrims in the Holy Land and defend the Christian holy places there against the growing Muslim presence. Ironically, their adversaries, the Saracens, were also expertly trained to be martyrs and not fear death; and although the two faiths were very different, some of the underlying principles in their training were similar. It is well known that the Templar leadership regarded Saladin, the leader of the Saracens, with respect on a number of occasions and that certain Muslim chroniclers at times referred to Templar leaders in equal terms, even when they were fiercely at war. Thus the myth that the two sides never honored one other is simply not true. In fact, the Templars may have learned much about mathematics, architecture, and sacred geometry from their alleged enemies. It is known that the Templars hired Arab interpreters and scribes—filling a rather obvious need during the Crusades, though it led to later accusations of fraternizing with the enemy. And on the island of Majorca, the Templars employed Saracens to help farm the land, much to the chagrin of the papacy.

There is evidence of medieval Templar links with the Muslim world, especially with the Nizari Ismailis, a religiopolitical Islamic group that still flourishes under the leadership of the Aga Khan. The Nizari Ismailis, also known in medieval times as the Assassins, were trained as holy warriors—not unlike the Knights Templar. Christian crusaders had some contact with the Assassins at the beginning of the twelfth century, even before the founding of the Templar Order in 1119. The medieval mission of Hasan-i-Sabah, Arab chronicler of the Crusades, to the Ismailis of Syria resulted in the early European contact with the Assassins during the Crusades. "The mythical Old Man of the Mountain...was the Syrian chief of the [Assassin] Order...The first documented contact between the Assassins and the Crusaders took place in September 1106. Tancred, prince of Antioch, attacked the newly acquired Nizari castle of Apace outside of Aleppo. The Christians defeated the Nizaris and leveled a tribute against the sect. Tancred captured the new Syrian chief *dai*, Abu Tahir, "the Goldsmith," and forced him to ransom himself. In 1110, the Nizaris lost a second piece of territory to Tancred."[10]

Despite their losses, the Syrian Assassins were able to expel crusader troops from various castles and strongholds, something that the Seljuk Turkish princes had been unable to do.

In the beginning of the fourteenth century, the world explorer Marco Polo fueled European fascination with the Assassins when he compiled many legends about them into a collection, adding embellishments of his own. In the classic account of his travels, Polo described tales of "a magnificent enclosed garden hidden at Alamut in which all details corresponded to Muhammad's description of Paradise."[11] Since then, legends about both the Templars and the Assassins have been plentiful.

The Templars as empire-builders and financiers

The Knights Templar were more than spiritual special forces for Christ. They were also highly practical, being diplomats and trusted advisors to kings and Popes; special guardians of a number of royal treasuries; maritime and seafaring experts; major property developers; caretakers of land and animals; agriculture experts; and business experts in commerce, trade, markets, and fairs.

Indeed, the Templars became one of the wealthiest and most powerful organizations the Western world has ever known. During the twelfth and thirteenth centuries, the Order acquired extensive property not only in the West, especially France, but also in the crusader states of Palestine and Syria. It developed a network of hundreds of preceptories and commanderies throughout Europe and the Latin East. Aristocratic families, kings, and fallen soldiers gave the Order thousands of properties—churches, farms, mills, villages, monasteries, ports, and so on—to assist the knights in their crusades. Within just ten years or so of their official founding, they held donated lands in nearly every part of western Europe and beyond—a truly spectacular rise to power that has hardly been seen before or since. And the more popular they became, the greater their wealth and the number of new recruits.

The extent of the Templar empire at its height was probably unknown, even to certain kings. Templar wealth was spread widely across numerous commercial activities and subsidiaries and supported by diverse elements, so it would have been hard to specify the precise location and form of all their assets. With such an extensive empire, the Templar Order was similar to a modern-day multinational corporation. Indeed, Masonic Knights Templar Grand Historian Stephen Dafoe and Alan Butler refer to this vast medieval web of connections as "Templar, Inc."[12] However, unlike in a corporation, much of the Templars' wealth donated by individuals remained in their treasuries and could not be moved without the owner's permission.

The Templars were known to have had tremendous stores of gold and money in their treasuries, a subject about which there tends to be misconception and even wild speculation. They lent great sums of money, not only to kings, but also to Popes and prominent merchants.

In fact, some believe that a number of their business methods were the prototypes for some of our modern-day banking practices. They originated the concept of a letter of credit, for instance, and for very good reasons:

> Travel in the 12th c was extremely dangerous. Bandits occupied every forest, and even controlled many towns and villages. It was therefore perilous enough to get oneself safely, from one part of the region to another, let alone to consider transporting large amounts of money . . . The Templars solved this problem . . . For example, a merchant from Bristol in England, who wanted to undertake a financial transaction in Paris, would simply deposit a prescribed sum of money in the Templar establishment in his own town. In exchange for the money, he would be supplied with a promissory note written in cipher—an item that would have been of no use to a potential robber. Our merchant would then travel to Paris, unencumbered by the cash, and go immediately to the Templar headquarters in Paris. On production of the note, and proof of his identity, he would be given his money in the local currency less (and this is the most important part) a handling fee. The fee was not large; certainly a good investment in terms of insurance for the safe arrival of the money.[13]

At the time, Church law forbade the practice of usury, lending money for interest. So the Templars had to recover their administrative costs in other ways, mainly by adding a service charge, instead of charging interest directly. Sound familiar? This is much the same basic procedure as with traveler's checks today. So when traveling abroad and using traveler's checks, we can be mindful of their medieval Templar origins.

There are few complaints on record concerning how the Templars handled other people's money, even huge transactions for kings. They were generally regarded as extremely trustworthy. Rare accusations that they were greedy did not usually refer to their loan practices. Templar loans from southern France did include a clause about a fixed fee due the lender, which may have caused some resentment. British Templar historian Helen Nicolson explains that these loans included a clause in the loan agreement that if the coin depreciated in value between the time of the loan and the repayment, then the borrower must add a fixed sum to compensate the lender. As the fixed sum would remain the same however much the coin depreciated, it is likely that an interest charge lay buried in this fixed sum. Again, if land was given as the pledge for the debt, it might be stipulated in the loan conditions that the produce from the land did not count towards the repayment of the loan.[14]

So what had started out as basic financial services provided to pilgrims—a sideline to crusading—developed into a full-scale financial empire. In the twelfth century, crusading loans were the Templars' most common financial transactions, but by the thirteenth century the Templar empire had grown considerably, becoming a key part of the European financial system. Barber describes:

> The most basic facility (and probably the most widely used) was the use of Templar houses for protection of important documents (including treaties, charters, and wills) and the guard of funds and precious objects, all of particular concern to the pilgrim or crusader who might be away for several years... [and] the Templars held documents associated with forthcoming Crusades, perhaps left as security for a loan which made the expedition possible in the first place, or as a pious donation, always in the forefront of the mind of the departing crusader who wished to set in order his relationship with the ecclesiastical world.[15]

In other words, noble and peasant alike were inclined to leave their valuables with the Templars, where they knew they would be kept safe and in good condition, even for a number of years. They also tended to put their earthly affairs in order before they left, in case they would die in the Holy Land and never return. Many crusaders made out a will, if they did not already have one.

The Templars' wealth was distributed throughout their vast empire. Butler and Dafoe comment:

> If we stop for a moment to consider the implications ... to service such a network, Templar wealth, at least in terms of gold, must have been constantly redistributed throughout the many preceptories and certainly the ones in the larger and more popular cities of western Europe ... Much of the Templars' wealth was constantly moving about, and was being used to make more money, thickening out the services on offer and expanding the business empire ... to finance bigger and better ventures.[16]

This sounds similar to how corporations and banks operate today: major urban offices usually have more assets than smaller branches in outlying areas, so many of these assets are put to use in other investments.

However, it is important to reiterate that much of the Templars' wealth could never be moved at all, due to their strict policy of storing the owner's money and goods in a secure box within their various treasuries, where it could not be accessed without the owner's permission.[17] This is not unlike bank policy today regarding safety deposit boxes. So no doubt the assets from other Templar enterprises—and not the valuables deposited with them by individuals—made up the capital that was "kept moving."

Since the Templars were the trusted guardians of wealth for so many people—royalty, nobles, and peasants alike—their storage practices have fueled many unanswered questions: Inasmuch as the French Templars ran their central Paris treasury, how much gold or treasure was in it at the time of their arrests in 1307? And where did it all go? Others wonder if the Templars really did find anything in the Holy Land, and if so, what was it? Did the Templar Order hold such sacred treasures in their treasuries—in France and elsewhere?

It is doubtful, however, that the Templars kept all of their wealth in one place. Such a practice is not advisable even now—much less in the dangerous political and economic climate of medieval Europe—and the Templars were especially adept at finance, enterprise, and investment. They diversified their holdings, as did a number of other religious Orders of the times.

As the Templars were a religious Order, they strictly avoided conducting business on major Christian feast days of Easter, the Ascension, and Christmas, the three feast days of the Virgin, the Feast of St. John the Baptist, or on saints' days of particular interest. Barber tells us that "November, December, and July were the busiest months, when the Templars were receiving deposits collected . . . near All Saints' Day (1 November) and the Feast of St. John the Baptist (24 June), the days most frequently designated in charters . . . and [in] surveys for payments."[18]

The Templars as trusted advisors and diplomats

Members of the various military Orders were advisors to popes, kings, and other rulers, and the Templars were no exception. In 1177, for example, King Henry II chose "Brother Roger, the Templar"—as the man was officially known—as his almoner. And Aymeric St. Mawr, the Master of the Knights Templar in England, was advisor to King John and at his side as he signed the Magna Carta in 1215. From the time of Pope Alexander III on, a Templar and a Hospitaller routinely appeared as papal chamberlains, attending to the Pope in his private chambers.[19] This meant they often had coveted private access to the Pope himself. At the papal court the Templars served as treasurers, papal messengers, judge-delegates, marshals, and porters—holding positions of great trust. Secular rulers, too, made frequent use of the Templars' reliable services. Nicolson writes:

> The Templars had permanent representatives at the papal court from the 1230s, while the kings of England had since the 12th century provided for the upkeep of a knight of the Order at their courts, with horses and servants, . . . But Templars could also advise about secular matters. King Henry II relied on their advice during his dispute with Thomas Becket, archbishop of Canterbury. King John of England (1199–1216) stated in his will that the Master of the Temple in England . . . was one of those men whose advice he trusted and followed.[20]

The Order became practically an arm of the royal government in England and France, due to the many services the Templars provided. It had various legal privileges, such as not having to pay taxes on much of their trade within England, which Richard I granted in October 1189 to help the Templars save money for the Crusades.

The Templars also served as judges. In England, for example, high-ranking Templars presided in criminal matters, except for cases involving major crimes punishable by hanging or mutilation, which went to the king's courts. Many a medieval common thief was probably tried by the Knights Templar.

Because they acted inconspicuously as monk-messengers for kings, nobles, and Popes, the Templars were ideally suited for functioning as spies: "Templars and Hospitallers were always on the road, preaching and collecting alms from the faithful, and because they were religious men they were less likely than secular messengers to be stopped by an enemy and searched or even imprisoned."[21] Yet since the Templars were entrusted with great power and the secrets of those in power, they occasionally aroused suspicions, warranted or not.

The enigmatic capture of King Richard I

King Richard I—the famous "Richard the Lionheart"—certainly had Templars in his entourage when returning from the Third Crusade in the fall of 1192. Legend has it he may have disguised himself as a Templar to evade his enemies. Historical accounts tell us he was captured by the troops of the Austrian Duke Leopold V, with whom he had quarreled on crusade. Precisely what they argued about is open to question, but the usual version—that it was simply over whose standard could be raised where on the battlefield—seems trivial and hard to believe. In any case, the Duke turned Richard over to the German emperor Henry VI in January 1193, and Richard was imprisoned for ransom—an extraordinary event, for a *king* to be held prisoner. Scholars doubt the Templar-disguise legend, but they do acknowledge that there were Templars close to Richard and present in his court, so it is a possibility. And they also know Richard was captured and held for 150,000 marks—a great fortune in those days.

What role, if any, might the Templars have had regarding Richard's ransom?

> The ransom money was to be collected by a levy of twenty shillings on all property and income of the laity and clergy in Richard's dominions, and all privileges were suspended. This included those held by the Templars. They also had to pay a tax on the land they held as knights fee, and a 25 percent tax levied on all ecclesiastical foundations would have netted about £1,000 from them . . . There is no evidence regarding the Templars' role in the collection of Richard's ransom. We can only surmise that they would have remained loyal to Richard as an anointed king and a fellow crusader

who had fought beside their brothers. Nevertheless, when Richard died in 1199 and was succeeded by his brother, the time-serving John, the Templars were quick to ingratiate themselves with him, giving him a palfrey and paying him £1,000 for the confirmation of their rights and privileges.[22]

Certain aspects of Richard's captivity, including details about the accounting records, are still unclear. Apparently the precise location of his imprisonment in Germany was not known for some time. According to legend, he was finally found by his faithful troubadour Blondel, who sang a musical phrase Richard recognized and sang back, thus pinpointing his location. Other aspects of his captivity remain unresolved today.

The Templars as agricultural experts

For some time it seemed that nearly every noble and king was giv-ing property to the Templars. Aristocratic families left them entire parcels of land, soldiers left their estates, and kings even split their domains to assist the illustrious "militia of Christ." A number of these lands were completely undeveloped; in fact, donors often gave prop-erty they could not afford to work themselves. To the Templars' cred-it, they were able to make these lands fertile and productive, partly because they had the cash and the labor to develop them. Whatever lands they didn't cultivate themselves they let out to tenants for a tithe—usually one tenth of all produce. Renting land saved the expens-es of cultivation, "but in a period of inflation such as the late twelfth and early thriteenth centuries, the value of rents fell rapidly and it could be more cost-effective to cultivate the land directly."[23] As a result, the Templars became "farmer monks," too, in certain areas. Their barns at Cressing in Essex, England, for example, illustrate their prosperity. They still survive today, having been recently restored.

The Cistercian monks, with whom the French Templars were intimately associated, were the most famous recipients of marginal land, which they often used to support huge flocks of sheep.[24] Sheep proved to be a brilliant investment for the Templars, too, and a very lucrative one:

Virtually all Cistercian wool, and particularly that from both Britain and northern France, ultimately found its way to the area around the city of Bruges, in what is today Belgium. There, the local populace was skilled at rapidly turning the wool into cloth, and it was this cloth that ultimately found its way to the Champagne fairs. We can therefore see how important these Fairs were to the Cistercians and the Templars . . . Templar money was involved in the financial transactions at every stage, and it is quite likely that they were also responsible for transshipping much of the wool to the ports of Flanders.[25]

Mills were particularly profitable for the Order, as wherever the Templars produced grain they needed mills to grind it. As few mills existed in the twelfth century, the Templars could charge a fee to others. The mills were mostly water driven, and there are records of the Templars and the Hospitallers fighting fiercely over water supplies, even to the extent of sabotaging one another. The Templars also participated in coal mining and the extraction of ores such as silver, gold, and copper,[26] which has led to speculation about their having extensive knowledge of precious metals, especially gold, and about where they may have hidden their treasures.

The Templars and the Champagne fairs

The famous Champagne fairs began as a result of the increased trade traffic during the High Middle Ages between Europe, the Mediterranean, and the Middle East. The fairs were exciting, colorful events. The quality of the merchandise, especially the exquisitely woven cloth, was very high, attracting expert buyers from as far as Italy. The fairs' prominence did not begin to wane until into the fourteenth century. Rarely acknowledged, yet worth noting, is that the period of their greatest success corresponds exactly to the era of the Templar Order (1119–1312). Moreover, Champagne, especially the area around Troyes, was the early Order's spiritual heartland. The Templars had strong links with Burgundy/Champagne; they received one of their earliest grants at Barbonne, near Sezanne, in October 1127.[27] A number of the Order's founders were of the old Burgundian nobility and came from what is now Champagne. At the time of the First Crusade (1095), however, Champagne's boundaries were not as we know them today, and Troyes was only a larger city in Burgundy.

At their height, there were six annual Champagne fairs—one each at sponsoring towns such as Lagne and Bar-sur-Aube and two each at Provins and Troyes, each running for forty-nine days—quite a festival! The Templars' preceptory in Provins, in Champagne, was one of their most important in northern France, and by the end of the twelfth century they had two houses there. And Troyes was central to the Templar Order.

We know that Templar influence was behind these popular fairs. In a fascinating 1883 study, Cornelius Walford, then vice-president of the Royal Historical Society of London, tells us that the French King Philip of Valois granted the privileges of the Champagne fairs to the Templars. The Order often received rights connected with trade, such as that to hold weekly markets and annual fairs on Templar lands and elsewhere. In this instance, at the fair in Provins, Templars were allowed to levy certain tolls on produce. Walford comments on the great importance of the fairs and on the origins of the "Troyes weight" measure:

> A lasting record of the importance of the dealings is handed down to us in the form of *the Troy (Troyes) weight*, used in connection with dealings with precious metals. It is said that this system of weights was brought from Cairo by the crusaders, and was first and permanently adopted as the standard of weight in the dealings of the fairs of Troyes . . . Goods sold at the fairs were exempted from all customs outwards, local dues excepted, under certain restrictions . . . It is recorded especially of these fairs, that [there were] those whose duty it was to examine the quality of goods exposed for sale, and to confiscate those found unfit for consumption.[28]

The Templars' commercial privileges and great success sometimes caused disputes, however, as in one case at Provins in the 1260s. Along with the king, the Counts of Champagne had also given the Templars the right to levy tolls on produce entering the town, but some merchants felt the members of the Order were charging too much, reducing trade. This led to a major dispute, whereby the merchants wrote a letter of complaint to the then Count of Champagne—whose response, unfortunately, has never been found.[29]

Needing money for the Crusades, the Templars, nevertheless, steadily increased their share of the taxation levied on sales at these fairs, gaining rights on wool and yarn in 1164; on animals destined for slaughter in 1214; and, probably most valuable of all—given the large-scale tanning industry of thirteenth-century Provins—on hides in 1243. Their presence was evident almost everywhere in the town.[30] Interestingly, the tanning guilds helped sponsor some of the earliest Templar buildings in Paris. In fact, it was not at all unusual for guilds to have connections with the Order.

An early form of the letter of credit was employed at the fairs:

> One peculiarity of these fairs was the use of letters that promised full payment of a particular debt, at the next fair. In this respect, the fairs showed the first appearance in Europe of the use of "credit transactions." It is hard to believe that such practices had not been introduced by the Templars, or more likely, by the institution that stood behind the Order. It is also certain, that the Templars gained a great deal from the fairs, either by acting through agents, as suppliers of merchandise, or as shippers and transporters of the various goods on offer.[31]

The Templars traded in many other locations as well. For instance, they were granted the right to hold weekly markets and annual fairs at many of their commanderies in England, including at Witham in Essex. This widespread involvement affirms that trade was an important financial source for their institution in funding the high expense of the Crusades, the military Orders being in constant need of men, equipment, horses, and supplies.

The Templars as maritime experts

The Templars' empire expanded not only on land but also on the seas. They required ships to carry money and supplies from the West, where the money and goods were made, to the East, where they were badly needed for the Crusades:

> The Templars needed ships to carry their coin, as well as agricultural produce, horses and personnel for the east. They also provided a secure carrying service for pilgrims—safer and cheaper than hiring a commercial carrier. These would have been heavy transport vessels rather than warships. Much of the surviving evidence for Templar shipping comes from the relevant port records or royal records giving permission for the export of produce...[For example] the records of the port of La Rochelle show that the Templars were exporting wine by ship...The hierarchal statutes attached to the Templars' Rule, dating from the 12th century...refer to the Order's ships at Acre (section 119), but do not state how many ships the Order owned.[32]

The Templar Rule shows that both horses and food were regularly imported from Europe, as were other pack animals. A steady supply of fresh horses for warfare was especially necessary. Any Templar who wounded or killed a horse or mule risked being deprived of the habit (mantle) of the Order—a serious punishment second only to outright expulsion. Documents from about 1207 on indicate that the Templars had their own ships and were starting to build their own fleet. They eventually possessed their own ports and shipyards as well.

The Templars' ships theoretically belonged to the Order, but in actuality they were run as individual units under Templar brothers who were experienced sailors. These ships usually carried pilgrims, cash, produce, wine, or other supplies. Nicolson tells us: "When they were not being used by the Order, for example for carrying pilgrims or produce, they engaged in privateering and other commercial enterprises. This was the normal method of organising ships during the Middle Ages. Ships were owned and run by their captains and hired by others as they were needed. Kings and others had no 'standing fleet' as such."[33]

The role of naval warfare in the Templars' strategies seems little acknowledged outside of specialists' circles. Yet we know that a number of savage sea battles took place and that naval operations grew in importance for the Templars, as well as for other military Orders. The first mention of an admiral for the Knights Templar Order appears in records in 1301, and for the Hospital in 1299.

Various medieval military Orders, including the Hospitallers (renowned for their naval fleet), engaged in what today we might politely call licensed piracy, and the Templars were no exception. Running into pirates, however unscrupulous or daring, was simply unavoidable in the course of doing medieval maritime business. Thus the high seas were a battleground in many ways.

Was Brother Roger "Jolly Roger"?

One story features the infamous Roger de Flor, one of the most successful pirates of his time:

> Roger de Flor, who founded the notorious Catalan mercenary company which terrorised the Aegean in the early 14th century, began his career working on a Templar ship commanded by a Templar sergeant named Brother Vassayll of Marseilles. When he was aged twenty, the Master "gave him the mantle" . . . and made him a sergeant-Brother. A little while later the Templars acquired from the Genoese a great ship, 'the biggest made in those times', called the Falcon . . . In this ship, Brother Roger made a lot of money for the Order . . . [His biographer] does not explain how and we may wonder whether Roger was engaged in the same sort of licensed piracy against the Muslims and those who traded with them as the Hospital of St. John later practised in the Mediterranean.[34]

Roger de Flor was a key player in the late-thirteenth-century naval scene and the only foreign-born man in Byzantine history to hold the title of "Caesar"—no small feat. He also commanded a vast army of mounted Catalan knights and various mercenaries renowned for instilling terror into their enemies. Brother Roger and the Templars evacuated the wealthy citizens of Acre, a major port city in the Holy Land, in May 1291, but unfortunately he also helped himself to their riches. Roger was accused of lining his own pockets with the proceeds of his maritime exploits, and Grand Master Jacques de Molay expelled him from the Order and denounced him as a thief. Roger immediately fled from possible execution by taking his ship to Marseilles, where he abandoned it. Thereafter he became one of the most successful, infamous privateers on the high seas. Even so, some believe that Roger had contact with the Templars later on; he worked as an admiral for Frederick III of Aragon, where he may have acted as a double agent, reporting back to the Templars and providing them with greatly needed intelligence. That is, perhaps he was too valuable an ally to lose. The Templars may also have wanted more influence in the Byzantine empire and regarded the powerful Roger de Flor as a necessary evil to help achieve that goal.

In 1301, after the major peace initiative at Caltabellotta, Roger was left unemployed. He had made contact, however, with thousands of soldiers who were in a similar position. Always enterprising, he gave his navy a new name, the Grand Catalan Company, and then contacted the Byzantine emperor Andonkios II and negotiated with him, married into the Byzantine imperial family, and gained the title *Megas Dux* ("Great Leader"). His Grand Catalan Company repeatedly defeated the Seljuk Turks in many battles and became renowned for its ferocity. A victim of some clandestine Byzantine political maneuvering, Roger de Flor was stabbed to death in 1305—only two years before the sudden arrests of the Knights Templar.

Some believe the French king and the Pope would never have dared make their move against the Templars before de Flor's death. We can speculate that the king and the Pope may have known more about events in Byzantium than the surviving record shows and so would have known about de Flor's powerful influence. Some speculate that had de Flor lived, he would have "gotten wind" of any plans to destroy the Templar Order, as he and his men had an extensive network of contacts in French port cities and elsewhere.

Interestingly, the story of Roger de Flor might be the origin for the famous skull-and-crossbones pirates' flag and its nickname, the "Jolly Roger." Often attributed to the sixteenth-century French buccaneer Bartholomew Roberts ("Jolie Rouge"), it is conceivable that the legend, if not the naming of the flag, may date back to the earlier renegade "Brother Roger." Others believe it was named after Roger II of Sicily.

Did some Templars
escape by ship in 1307?

Contrary to legend, the likelihood that a huge Templar fleet based at La Rochelle, a port city on the west coast of France, would have escaped with treasure after the arrest of the Templars in 1307 is very small. To begin with, the Templars probably wouldn't have kept so many of their main ships in one port. Such action would have been tantamount to risking political and economic suicide and contrary to normal practice, anyway, as many of their ships were galleys, perpetually on the high seas. We have no concrete evidence that a number of ships left from La Rochelle in 1307 after the arrests. Moreover, the French king and his men would certainly have kept a watchful eye on this major port.

Even if the fleeing knights did want to escape by sea, chances are that they would not have set sail from La Rochelle alone. In fact, it may have been one of the least likely places from which to attempt an escape. If anything, as some believe, this port may have served as a "decoy location," from which a few ships would have deliberately sailed to distract the king and his men. However, tangible proof is lacking, so no conclusions can be drawn.

If the knights did escape by sea, they more likely did so from Aragon, where they had advance warning in 1307, hearing of what had happened to their unfortunate brothers in France. They immediately swung into action and, in the words of one respected academic, "fortified castles, changed goods into gold which could be more easily concealed and, it was suspected, charted a ship in which to make their escape."[35] Though vassals of the French king in a nominal sense, certain areas of the Roussillon and Languedoc in the south of France, the island of Majorca, and so on, had closer ties to Aragon than to the French king, and for a time this area amounted to something like an independent Templar region.

Some have proposed, however wildly, that some of Roger de Flor's men—remnants of his Aragonese and Catalan army of privateers—might have been involved in a Templar escape from Aragon, as they were some of the most renowned men on the high seas. Roger was killed in 1305, but a number of his men survived through 1307; they had already been helpful to the Templars and also had strong connections to Aragon and Catalonia. Many of the Templar ships being galleys, they were ideally suited for piracy. And who would be better qualified to transport treasure by ship than professional pirates and privateers? Of course, this is only some researchers' speculation; no documentation to prove it has yet come to light.

CHAPTER

2

ORIGINS of
the ORDER

any historical accounts and legends suggest what may
have happened after the Templar Order was suppressed
in 1312—at its end. What isn't widely acknowledged is
that in some ways its beginning was even more enigmatic, and perhaps
more interesting. For example, why do historians still not know much
about the first Grand Master of the Templar Order, Hugh de Payns?
Why did so many of the early "key movers and shakers" come from
primarily the area we now call Champagne?

Developments leading to a major historical event are often just as
important as those following it; sometimes, even more so. Let us start
with an account of the first public emergence of the Templar Order in
1119. Then we will examine the developments that preceded it.

Official emergence in 1119

Following the First Crusade, which took place in the last decade
of the eleventh century, increasing numbers of pilgrims flocked to
Jerusalem from all over Europe, risking their lives in the process.
Judging from eyewitness accounts, protection of pilgrims in the Holy
Land was certainly needed. One such traumatized pilgrim in the first
decade of the twelfth century reported that "Muslims lurked by day
and night in caves in the mountains between Jaffa and Jerusalem, ready
to ambush Christians journeying to and from the coast."[1]

Similar frightening accounts kept arriving in Europe. Malcolm Barber graphically describes what many pilgrims encountered:

> In the early twelfth century, men could seldom be spared to patrol these pilgrim routes, nor to escort new arrivals from the ports. In 1102–3, the Norse pilgrim Saewulf, was horrified by the journey . . . to Jerusalem. Saracen robbers roamed the rocky mountains, waiting for bands of pilgrims. Stragglers were picked off and robbed and killed. Saewulf saw members of other parties lying unburied along the route, the corpses gnawed by wild animals. The ground was often hard and unyielding with little, if any, topsoil. Men did not linger to undertake the difficult task of burying . . . Instead, they passed on rapidly for fear of being attacked themselves. Little provision seems to have been made along the route to supply the pilgrim with food, and above all, water, and those who survived the journey seem to have arrived at Jerusalem in a severely distressed condition.[2]

Previously, Christian pilgrimages to Jerusalem had come under Islamic rule, and "for the most part the Islamic rulers, in accordance with the Prophet's instructions, were happy to allow their subject races to practice their religion without interference."[3] But there were still bands of robbers who terrified pilgrims along the way. And once the Christians had gained control of Jerusalem in 1099, the experiences of many pilgrims worsened—perhaps due to the inevitable Muslim retaliation.

An already tense situation thus became unbearable. At Easter in 1119, the Saracens killed three hundred pilgrims and took sixty prisoners. Obviously, the leaders of Christendom wanted to respond to this crisis, so the idea of an institution that combined a religious way of life with a military function was born. In 1119, the Order of the Poor Knights of Christ and the Temple of Solomon—better known as the Knights Templar—officially emerged, for the purpose of protecting pilgrims to the Holy Land.[4] Several of the original nine knights were related to each other. The Order thus began as very much "a family affair" of certain old Burgundian and Flemish families, based around the area of Troyes in Champagne, originally part of old Burgundy.

That there was a crying need for more policing of pilgrim routes by the early twelfth century seems indisputable. Many have wondered, however, how only nine knights could have taken on this immense job, even in a limited area in and around Jerusalem. On the other hand, the Templars were encouraged by both King Baldwin II, the Christian ruler of Jerusalem, and Warmund of Picquigny, the Patriarch of Jerusalem. Early Templars were probably seen as complementary to the Hospitallers, who were already caring for sick, exhausted pilgrims in their medical convent in Jerusalem. In two of the four charters drafted in the Kingdom of Jerusalem before 1128, the Templars are mentioned in connection with the affairs of the Hospitaller Order. The Church had recognized the latter Order as early as 1113, but it wasn't "militarized" until the 1130s. Scholars believe the Templars were very much welcomed in 1119, as more manpower was needed to help the increasing number of pilgrims arriving in Jerusalem.

Jacques de Molay, the last Templar Grand Master, regarded the missions of the Hospital and the Temple as fundamentally different. There is little doubt, however, that the charitable intentions of both were originally connected.[5] The famous will of Alfonso I of Aragon (1131) illustrates how the functions of various Orders were seen at the time. Being childless, he had left one third of his extensive lands to be divided between the canons of the Holy Sepulchre, who served and guarded the Holy Sepulchre in Jerusalem; the Hospitallers, who cared for the poor in Jerusalem; and the Templars, the "warriors for Christ" who defended the Christian name in the Holy Land. Barber comments that this makes better sense than historians have usually thought, "for the three elements of liturgical, charitable and military functions all stem from the same root, and thus offer the balanced rule of the true Christian kingdom."[6]

The Temple Mount area as the Templars' first home

If the Templars' original nine knights mainly guarded pilgrims' routes in the early years, then why, critics contend, did King Baldwin II give them such exclusive accommodation in his palace on the south side of the "Lord's Temple," just a few hundred meters away from what is known today as the Dome of the Rock? This palace was called the al-Aqsa Mosque; crusaders had earlier called it Solomon's Temple. The extensive tunnel system underneath it has prompted some to ask if the Templars were engaged in activities other than policing pilgrims' routes—perhaps even digging for something under the temple? If so, how did they know where to look, or what to look for? Speculation about possible Templar treasure—gold, scrolls, and the like—has reached epic proportions in our time.

Undeniably, the King of Jerusalem and the Patriarch of Jerusalem themselves sanctioned the first nine Templars from the beginning, directly helping them obtain food, shelter, and clothing. That the shelter of these poor knights was one of the most important and exclusive buildings in the Holy Land also seems clear. We know they received honor and official recognition from the Church at the Council of Troyes in Champagne (1129) and, as history shows, further glory as the famed warrior-monks of Christ.

During the first nine years of the Order (1119–28), the Templars wore simple, ordinary clothes, so when they were based at the Temple Mount area they would not have been wearing their famous white mantles. They began wearing white mantles after the Church Council of Troyes in 1129 when they were given a religious Rule and a white habit. The trademark red cross was added when Pope Eugenius III (1145–53) allowed them to wear it as a symbol of Christian martyrdom.

Helen Nicolson explains that, from the beginning, the Templars were considered devout men living a religious life:

> Archbishop William of Tyre, composing his history of the crusader states between 1165 and 1184, wrote that the first Templars were a group of noble knights, "devoted to God, religious and God-fearing" who entrusted themselves into the hands of the patriarch (Warmund of Picquigny, 1118–28) to serve Christ. They had intended to become regular canons—that is, priests following a religious rule and living a communal lifestyle in a religious house—and they took the three monastic vows of chastity . . . poverty . . . and obedience . . . William of Tyre stressed the Brothers' initial poverty and the fact that recruitment was slow: he wrote that after nine years there were still only nine Brothers.[7]

William, or Guillaume, de Tyre thus viewed the original nine knights as the equivalent of regular canons or priests living in a religious community. He said their military vocation was the creation of the

Patriarch and his canons of the Holy Sepulchre—the same individuals who had charged these knights with keeping the pilgrim routes safe.

Yet critics of this orthodox view say that Guillaume's description makes these nine early Templars appear more like "a private exclusive group" sanctioned by the Jerusalem king and the Patriarch as well as the canons of the Holy Sepulchre. They point out that the Templars do not seem to have made much effort to recruit others whose help they would surely have needed to police the pilgrim routes, especially given the growing numbers arriving in Jerusalem; so perhaps the knights' real purpose was something else. In fact, many scholars believe that the number of Templars did not begin to increase until around 1128; we know that by the 1170s there were about three hundred knights in the Kingdom of Jerusalem. Moreover, others contend, why would the first nine knights have been given a wing of the king's palace, of all places, as their home base? We know the Templars kept their horses in the spacious stables under Solomon's Temple—which had room for thousands—so some speculate that this provided an ideal "cover" for other activities, such as digging in the tunnels. Lacking access to more archaeological evidence, though, some scholars view the idea of excavation as theoretically possible, no one can determine whether this occurred during the Templars' first nine years, or whether they actually found anything (see chapter 6).

That the first nine Templar knights, during the Order's initial nine years, may have been engaged in other activities besides assisting pilgrims should at least be considered, since the evidence that they were helping pilgrims full time is as scanty as the evidence that they were digging for something. The truth is, there is not enough evidence or eyewitness testimony, especially regarding the Order's earliest years, to say anything definitive. According to Fulk de Chartres, royal historian of King Baldwin II, the Christian Franks did not have enough resources to maintain the Temple of Solomon properly for a period of years, and eventually the building became as run down as the knights' clothing. This description reinforces the early Templars' pious, humble image. Morale was reported to be quite low at times among the initial nine knights, arguing against the idea that they were finding treasure in the tunnels. But, as critics counter, perhaps they simply hadn't yet found what they were searching for! Whatever one's viewpoint, many questions remain.

Medieval chronicles disagree on the Order's beginnings

Even medieval chroniclers contemporary with the Order disagree about its beginnings. The work of Archbishop Guillaume de Tyre (William of Tyre) is the key accepted source, written between 1165 and 1184, on which many subsequent accounts have been based. Yet historians today, including the eminent Crusades scholar Sir Stephen Runciman, acknowledge that some of Guillaume's dates "are confused and at times demonstrably wrong."[8]

According to Guillaume's account, "the Order . . . was founded in 1118. Its founder is said to be one Hugues de Payen, a nobleman from Champagne and vassal of the Count of Champagne. One day Hugues, unsolicited, presented himself with eight comrades at the palace of . . . [the] king of Jerusalem, whose elder brother, Godfroi de Bouillon, had captured the Holy City nineteen years before."[9]

That King Baldwin II and the Patriarch of Jerusalem favorably received these initial nine knights is certain. In fact, they seem to have been very warmly welcomed—an interesting point, given that they are portrayed as unannounced visitors who arrived suddenly, without an appointment, as it were.

Nicolson writes of some of the earlier chroniclers and how their accounts often differ from that of Guillaume de Tyre:

> One Simon, a monk of St. Bertin . . . wrote in around 1135–7 that the first Templars were crusaders who had decided to stay in the Holy Land after the First Crusade instead of returning home . . . They had given up their previous lifestyle and taken vows which involved chastity and poverty. He believed that the secular nobles in the kingdom of Jerusalem advised this move, and he did not refer to any involvement by the patriarch of Jerusalem. The Anglo-Norman monk Orderic Vitalis (1075–c. 1141) . . . recorded in the 1120s or 1130s that Count Fulk V of Anjou (d. 1143) had joined the "knights of the Temple" for a while when he was on pilgrimage to Jerusalem in 1120 . . . Orderic said nothing about how the Order began, but his work showed that it was in operation by 1120.[10]

Even though the opinion of these and other writers of the period differed from those of Guillaume, unfortunately we have no more details about how the Order started. But nearly all agree that it was officially in operation by 1120. "We know that Fulk V, Count of Anjou (later Baldwin's successor to the throne of Jerusalem) lodged at the Temple while on pilgrimage in Jerusalem in 1120–21, and joined the Order as a lay associate."[11] The date that Guillaume provides—1118—has been the Order's assumed official starting date, but historians now recognize 1119 as more accurate. As Barber says, "Among the early grants to the Order was one by Thierry, Count of Flanders, dated 13 September 1128, which states that it was made in the ninth year from the Order's foundation," which means that the founding year was 1119.[12] Even Guillaume himself says, "the Council of Troyes, at which the Templars received official papal recognition, occurred in their ninth year."[13] This again means the Order began in 1119, which conflicts with his earlier mention of 1118.

Early Western chroniclers often got confused about the relationship between the canons of the Holy Sepulchre, who lived and worked in the Holy Sepulchre; the Templars; and the Hospitaller Order, which was "set up in the 1060s or 1070s to care for poor sick pilgrims to Jerusalem . . . The Hospitallers and the Templars [both] followed the liturgy of the Holy Sepulchre in their church services, and . . . the seal of the Master of the Temple bore the image of the dome of the Holy Sepulchre."[14] So it appears the Templars were, from the beginning, intimately connected with the Holy Sepulchre and the canons based there. Some contemporaries also called them the Knights of Solomon's Temple.

The nine founding knights

According to Guillaume de Tyre, the Order of the Temple officially began when two French knights, Hugh de Payns and Godfroi de St. Omer, led seven others to the Patriarch of Jerusalem, Warmund of Picquigny, and took vows of poverty, chastity, and obedience. Initially they were referred to as *Milites Templi Salomonis*, or "Knights of Solomon's Temple," and eventually simply as "Templars."

The original nine knights included the scions of several noble families. Hugh de Payns was a vassal of Hughes I, Count of Champagne. So was André de Montbard, the uncle of Bernard of Clairvaux—the Cistercian abbot, later canonized as St. Bernard, who had a major role in helping the Order get official papal recognition in 1129. Godfroi de St. Omer, of Picardy, was a son of Hughes de St. Omer. Two relatives of the ruling family of Flanders were also part of this initial group: Payen de Montdidier and Achambaud de St.-Amand. The others were Godfroi, Geoffroi Bisol, Gondemar, and Rossal—the last two being Cistercians—possibly from Seborga in northern Italy—who may have joined the new Order with St. Bernard's encouragement.

Hugh de Payns, the first Templar Grand Master, remains, ironically, an enigmatic figure. The accepted view is that he came from the village of Payens, or Payns, about eight miles north of Troyes. He is said to have been a vassal of Hughes I, whose court was centered at Troyes and who we know took part in the First Crusade. Moreover, Hugh was also related to Hughes I, being of a cadet branch of the dynasty of the Counts of Champagne.[15] Some speculate that Hugh married a Katherine de St. Clair, but nothing for certain is known of his wife or her lineage. Some believe he had a son (others say nephew) named Theobald, who became abbot of St. Columbe-de-Sens in 1139. Another key question concerns his name before he obtained his title. Canadian researcher Nicolas H. Mazet presents the following view:

> The only questionable entity seems to be Hughs de Payns. The area of Payns was, from 1095 to 1125, in the hands of Lorraine. And before being in Lorraine's hands, it was in the Comte of Angers' possessions, a vassal of the King of France, not Blois, the noble house from which Hughes de Champagne is said to have come from... Many authors have bypassed all responsibility by simply stating that the lands were given by the Comte de Champagne, which is, and is not, so. They were given to the Cistercians by the Comte de Blois, who also held the properties in Champagne, in 1132. The lands were given to the Comte de Blois in 1125, by the enigmatic Hughes de Champagne. They were not given to the Templars. The second problem is that the Abbey of Clairvaux was a field until 1132 when Thibaud, Comte de Blois AND Champagne gave the property to St. Bernard.[16]

Hence, according to Mazet, many authors have erroneously assigned a name to someone well after the fact; that is, "Hughs de Payns" was probably not the man's name in 1119, when the Order was founded, because he did not receive "Payns" as a title until at least 1125. Yet authors have assumed that his name was "de Payns" in 1119. We do know he was not officially known as "Master of the Temple" until 1125.

That the earliest chroniclers whose works we have did not start writing until later in the twelfth century compounds the problem. For example, Guillaume of Tyre began his chronicle about 1165—*after* Hugh de Payns would have received his title. So he naturally called him by that name. Mazet clarifies:

> Say for instance that John Doe goes off to war in 2000, and twenty years later, in 2020, he receives an honour of some kind that gives him a property called Thomas. From that point on, he is legally known as John of Thomas. Now in 2080, someone decides to write a biography of the man but makes the error of calling him John of Thomas at every turn. *Those readers would never know that his real name had been John Doe.* This is exactly what has happened with the major players in the mystery of the Templars . . . Hugh de Payens and Hughes de Champagne. For instance, Hugh de Payens received Payens as a title after 1128. What was his name beforehand?[17]

Who, then, was the real Hugh de Payns? Some scholars believe his name was Hugh de Pagens. Others insist that he was Hugh Peccator (Hugh the Sinner), author of a letter addressed to "the knights of Christ in the Temple at Jerusalem." Critics contend that because the letter has no date on it, and because the name on the manuscript is not clear, one cannot be certain. Mazet believes two other likely candidates are Hughes de Puiset, who was given the town of Jaffa in the Holy Land, and Hughes de Crecy, who was given the town of Corbeil along with its castle in France. He says: "Their families were heavily involved with the process of Templar establishment in both the Holy Land and on French soil. Their families were also very much involved in the mysterious transfers of land between Blois, the Cistercians, the Templars and Champagne, some of which ended up in Templar hands before Clairvaux was established."[18]

Champagne (old Burgundy) was the "headquarters" of this early group of interrelated families, dubbed the "Troyes fraternity" by some.[19] It was at that court that the medieval author Chrétien of Troyes wrote his famous Grail romances. In the treasury of the Cathedral of St. Peter and St. Paul at Troyes, the bones of St. Bernard of Clairvaux, along with a portrait, are venerated. Troyes was also the birthplace of one of the most brilliant Jewish intellectuals in Western European history—Rabbi Solomon ben Isaac, affectionately known as Rabbi Rashi. He was a frequently honored guest at the court of Hughes I—a court known to have been a haven for Jews and other non-Catholics who fled persecution. Rabbi Rashi started his famed Kabbalistic school, also based at Troyes, in 1070.[20] He was renowned for his expert translation skills and especially adept at translating Hebrew into other languages, including French. St. Bernard, the Cistercian abbot of Clairvaux, as well as abbots from other Orders, highly valued the skills of certain learned scholars in Champagne (and elsewhere) who were well versed in Hebrew, Greek, Latin, and Aramaic, some of whom stayed at various abbeys for long periods of time translating texts.

Events preceding the founding of the Order

The story leading up to the founding of the Templar Order may actually begin as early as 1071, when the Turks conquered Palestine and then turned their sights on Constantinople, threatening the stability of the entire Western world. Unfortunately, eastern Christendom emerged from this fierce battle with very little territory left, and had to accept downright humiliating peace terms and the possibility of future invasions. Times were insecure. It was into this climate that a third son, Hughes, was born in 1077 to Thibaud I, the Count of Blois, Chartres, Sancerre, and Champagne. Hughes was to become Hughes I, the Count of Champagne, one of the most powerful men in all of medieval western Christendom. He was also a key figure in the early developments of the Templar Order, although much of his influence was behind the scenes.

Hughes I was only nineteen when the First Crusade left for the Holy Land in March 1096. This entourage included his older half-brother, Stephen de Blois, who was married to Adele, the daughter of William the Conqueror.[21] Although Hughes was involved with an assembly of bishops and nobles in Reims who had discussed the crusade, he did not immediately set out with the others but came to Jerusalem later.

Pope Urban II preached the First Crusade at Clermont-Ferrand in the Auvergne in 1095. Another influential preacher of the First Crusade was an enigmatic figure who may have played an important role behind the scenes—Peter the Hermit. Probably one of the greatest popular orators of medieval Europe, Peter seems to have remained largely "low profile." When he did emerge, his influence was often dramatic, as he was able to rally large masses of people all over Europe to take up the cross, endure great sacrifices, and follow him to the Holy Land. As part of his recruiting effort among peasants and nobles alike, Peter visited some of the major titled families, especially in northern France, and probably met Hughes I. Many powerful lords took up the cross after hearing Peter's fiery sermons, giving all or part of their possessions to the cause. As Crusades scholar Jonathan Riley-Smith describes: "Peter the Hermit was active in Berry, northern France, and Germany . . . The response in them, which included men such as Geoffrey lord of Issoudon . . . the lords of Chatillon and Aigurande, and probably Arnold II, the castellan of Vierzon, was due to Peter's efforts."[22]

Albert of Aix, writing in the mid-twelfth century, composed a history of the Crusades to about the year 1120. Although he never visited the East himself, he based his chronicle on eyewitness accounts and written sources. Concerning Peter he writes:

> There was a priest, Peter by name, formerly a hermit. He was born in the city of Amiens, which is in the western part of the kingdom of the Franks, and he was appointed preacher in Berry in the aforesaid kingdom. In every admonition and sermon, with all the persuasion of which he was capable, he urged setting out on the journey as soon as possible. In response to his constant admonition and call, bishops, abbots, clerics, and monks set out; next, most noble laymen, and princes of the different kingdoms; then, all the common people, the chaste as well as the sinful, adulterers, homicides, thieves, perjurers, and robbers; indeed, every class of the Christian profession, nay, also women and those influenced by the spirit of penance—all joyfully entered upon this expedition.[23]

Many legends grew around Peter's amazing popularity. He would often travel from village to village on a donkey. Some accounts state that those fortunate enough to snatch a hair from the animal treasured it for years as a holy relic. Often dismissed as a mere eccentric, Peter the Hermit may have had higher-level contacts than is generally acknowledged. He was described as an unkempt, barefoot peasant, but what we know of him suggests that he might have been a more educated man who chose to appear that way. He was born in Picardy in 1050. Before becoming a monk he was a minor noble who owed his fiefdom to Eustace de Boulogne, Godfroi de Bouillon's father.

Sometime after 1070, Peter joined a monastery in the Ardennes started by a largely unknown group of monks from Calabria who were given land at Orval, near Stenay, by Godfroi de Bouillon's aunt, Mathilde de Toscane, the Duchess of Lorraine. Peter did well in this monastic community, eventually becoming, legends say, tutor to Godfroi de Bouillon, who would later become the hero of the First Crusade and first ruler of the Kingdom of Jerusalem.

Apparently, this was no ordinary monastery. The members, although not individually named, were thought to be part of a network of especially learned monks from Calabria, in southern Italy, interested in researching the bloodline of the Duke of Lorraine, Godfroi's family. Stenay was also widely known as an ancient place of importance to the Merovingian kings of France, and King Dagobert II had been murdered nearby in the year 679.[24] Godfroi de Bouillon is known to have paid special reverence to Stenay and to Orval Abbey, where the relics of Dagobert II were kept.[25] The abbey at Orval was built in 1070, the same time that the cultured Rabbi Rashi started his famed Kabbalistic academy at Troyes.

Unfortunately, the early history of this monastery and its founding seems to have been lost or removed from the historical record. But we know that these monks suddenly left their abbey, en masse, in 1108; that the land and abbey ultimately came into the possession of St. Bernard of Clairvaux; and that a Cistercian abbey was later built on the premises. It is uncertain where the earlier monks went, but some believe it was to Jerusalem, to the religious community on Mount Sion, or perhaps even back to Calabria.

Around 1080, Peter the Hermit left Europe for Jerusalem. He is thought to have stayed there until 1088, when he went to Rome to deliver a message from the Byzantine Patriarch of Jerusalem to Pope Urban II—certainly not a task entrusted to an insignificant peasant or an eccentric. Guillaume of Tyre writes:

A certain priest named Peter, from the kingdom of the Franks and the bishopric of Amiens, a hermit in both deed and name . . . arrived at Jerusalem . . . Hearing also that the Patriarch of the city was a devout and God-fearing man, he wished to confer with him . . . The name of the Patriarch was Simeon. As he learned from Peter's conversation that the latter was prudent, able and eloquent, and a man of great experience, he began to disclose to him more confidentially all the evils which the people of God had suffered while dwelling in Jerusalem. To whom Peter replied:

> You may be assured, holy father, that if the Roman church and the princes of the West should learn from a zealous and a reliable witness the calamities which you suffer, there is not the slightest doubt that they would hasten to remedy the evil, by both words and deeds . . . Write them zealously both to the lord Pope and the Roman church and to the kings and princes of the West, and confirm your letter by the authority of your seal. I, truly, for the sake of the salvation of my soul, do not hesitate to undertake this task.[26]

However, not all chroniclers say this about Peter, and certainly not all scholars agree as to whether he had such an important diplomatic role. But he does seem to have been persuasive with a number of prominent people—certainly a mark of diplomatic skill. Nothing more is known about his whereabouts until the winter of 1095, when he suddenly emerged to preach the First Crusade with Pope Urban II—again an obviously important function.

His contemporaries describe Peter as mesmerizing when he spoke, inspiring huge crowds to take up the cross and follow him. And many did. Long before the official departure date of 15 August 1096, Peter and his "peasant's army" left western Europe, ahead of the crusaders, on the long trek to meet the "enemies of Christ." This notorious "People's Crusade" unfortunately became an uncontrollable mob that engaged in some horrific, inexcusable behavior as their journey wore on. The huge ragtag group finally reached Constantinople in 1097, tired, hungry, and very unruly. They recklessly decided to attack the Turks, and most were killed in the ensuing fiasco. But as Peter had not agreed to plunge ahead with them, remaining instead in Constantinople, he lived, along with a few other survivors. Godfroi de Bouillon's massive army of crusaders then arrived, and Peter—and what little was left of his wild band—joined them, marching on to Antioch.

Interestingly, both Crusades scholars and Jewish historians tell of a notorious but small group called Tafurs who apparently survived the People's Crusade. Some among them, said to be starving after their attack on the Turks, were accused of all kinds of things, even cannibalism, by the emir of Antioch. John France writes in *Victory in the East: A Military History of the First Crusade* that the Tafurs "were a hard-core of poor men organised under their own leaders, whose name may be derived from the big light wooden shield which many of them carried, the *talevart* or *talevas*. These desperadoes seem to have been pre-eminently North French and Fleming in origin and to have represented a quasi-autonomous force within the army . . .

"The Tafurs were recorded to have resorted to cannibalism at the siege of Ma'arra; this was reported by Raymond of Aguilers, but not by other chroniclers of the First Crusade."[27]

Among this group was an inner core of leaders who had their own leader, King Tafur—a man whom even the crusade princes were said to approach with great reverence. Clearly, more research is needed on this controversial topic.[28]

When Godfroi de Bouillon, the leader of the First Crusade, left for Jerusalem with others in his family, he chose to give up his lands and sell all of his possessions. He fought courageously, and in July 1099, after a long and bloody battle, his armies took Jerusalem, regaining the Holy Land for Christendom. The Latin Kingdom of Jerusalem was then founded. Godfroi, with all humility, famously refused to accept the crown of Jerusalem, preferring instead the title "Defender of the Holy Sepulchre." As he died on 18 July 1100, his only official act as "king" and Defender of Jerusalem was to reapprove the charter of an abbey—located on Mount Sion, an imposing hill outside the city walls—which was rebuilt at his instigation on the site of an earlier, fourth-century Byzantine church. Many scholars think that monks present on the site in 1099 may have been Augustinian, yet the community was primarily known as the Order of Notre Dame de Sion, and their church dubbed "the Mother of All Churches." There is a charter signed by a Prior Arnaldus dated 19 July 1116.[29] Arnaldus's name shows up again on another charter dated 2 May 1125, this time in conjunction with Hugh de Payns, the first Grand Master of the Knights Templar.[30] Some accounts state that Peter the Hermit may have visited the site and that he knew the monks there, but details are sketchy at best.

In any case, it appears that this Order of Notre Dame de Sion was organized like others of its time, as was the Order of the Holy Sepulchre, which was associated with the monks and canons of the Church of the Holy Sepulchre, close associates of the original nine Templars. We know there was an abbey on the site by 1100 and that Godfroi de Bouillon was supportive of its community. In 1099, a powerful, yet clandestine, group of nobles and monks elected to offer Godfroi the kingdom of Jerusalem after his victory there. Sir Stephen Runciman tells us the group's identity is unknown, although Guillaume de Tyre does mention that the most important among them was "a certain bishop from Calabria" in Italy.[31] As Peter the Hermit was known to be in Jerusalem at this time, some historians conjecture that he may have been part of this conclave. Although this is a possibility, to date there is no documentary evidence to support it. After Godfroi died in 1100, he was succeeded by his brother Baldwin I, who gladly accepted the title King of Jerusalem. Godfroi has since become a figure of powerful legend in his own right, as the extraordinary leader of the First Crusade. In later medieval poetry he was commemorated as a descendant of the Swan Knight. He was included among the famous Nine Worthies, considered the greatest warriors of all time—three from the Old Testament, three pagans from the ancient world, and three Christian rulers (the other two being King Arthur and Charlemagne).[32] The Nine Worthies were featured on many tapestries, including those that the Burgundy nobles commissioned from Arras and Tournai. Many medieval tapestries and paintings featured scenes from the Crusades, and at least fifteen tapestries focused on Godfroi de Bouillon.

In 1100, Peter the Hermit returned to Europe—right after the crowning of Baldwin I—and became prior of the abbey in Huy, Flanders, "an institution which he personally founded on land granted by the family of Godfroi."[33] Again, a post involving such extensive administrative and leadership abilities is not entrusted to a "fanatic itinerant preacher." Later, Peter returned to Constantinople and apparently also revisited Jerusalem. Scholars believe that he spent his last years at Neumoustier, the Augustinian abbey near Huy dedicated to the Holy Sepulchre and St. John the Baptist. The community there claimed that Peter had founded it. A legend developed that if one could not fulfill one's vows to pilgrimage to Jerusalem itself, one could gain the same benefits by visiting Neumoustier; so the abbey in Huy became a popular pilgrimage destination. Peter died in 1115 and was buried in the church.[34]

The first
Cistercian monastery

In 1097, Hughes I, now Count of Champagne, spent Easter with a small group of associates at the monastery of Molesmes, south of Troyes. Its abbot was Robert, who belonged to the same family as Bernard of Clairvaux, and who, with his monks, lived a very austere life according to the Rule of St. Benedict. A few historians believe this initial visit by Hughes and his associates may have been a factor in the later split between Robert's especially austere group and the other monks at Molesmes, who refused to obey Robert and preferred to keep their titles and observe more liberal policies.

In 1098, Robert and his austere group of monks—which included Alberic and Stephen Harding, an Englishman from Dorset, both of whom would later play key roles—received permission to leave Molesmes and found a new monastery. Leaving Champagne for Burgundy, they founded the monastery at Citeaux, the "mother" of all later Cistercian monasteries and center of the new Cistercian Order. Its constitution, the *Carta caritatis*, was presented to Pope Calixtus II in 1119—the same year the first nine Templars announced themselves to Baldwin II. St. Bernard was also instrumental in this effort and the constitution was codified between 1119 and 1165.

In the spring of 1099, the same monks who had remained at Molesmes and adamantly refused to live by Robert's strict regime went to Pope Urban II in Rome. They said their monastery was now deprived of its abbot and other staff and they wanted Robert sent back. This was apparently a total *volte face* from their earlier position, and one wonders why. Some historians believe Hughes I may have been involved. Perhaps the powerful archbishop of Lyons had more to do with it. In any case, the Pope wrote to the church authorities in Lyons and ordered Robert back to Molesmes. Afterward, Robert seems to have acquiesced to the Molesmes monks' way of life, though he had sharply disapproved of it before.[35]

In the spring of 1101, Hughes I again visited Molesmes. His brother, the valiant Stephen de Blois, had returned from the Holy Land in 1098. After this 1101 meeting—and only three years after the new monastery was founded—the Citeaux monastery was moved half a league further south from its original location, ostensibly for better access to water. Stephen de Blois subsequently returned to the Holy Land, where the crusaders and Baldwin I, King of Jerusalem, favorably received him.

The Cistercian Robert of Molesmes later founded other monasteries, even after he was ordered to return to Molesmes. Meanwhile, Alberic became the new abbot of Citeaux, and after his death in 1109, Stephen Harding became abbot. A brilliant scholar, Harding consulted with Jewish rabbis and other learned men to better study the Hebrew of the Old Testament. He proved to be a very effective administrator. He also deserves credit for giving shape to the early Cistercian ideal, which combined practical daily work with a life of devout prayer, based on the earliest versions of St. Benedict's Rule and incorporating ideas developed by St. Basil and John Cassian.[36]

It was at Citeaux that Bernard de Fontaine, later canonized as St. Bernard, began his religious life before moving to Clairvaux. He arrived at Citeaux in 1112 with thirty nobles from the houses of Tonnerre, Montbard, and Burgundy—a number of whom were his relatives and all of whom were willing to give up everything, which for some even meant leaving wives and children—to join the austere Cistercians. That Bernard was only twenty-two years old and his relatives considerably older has often been regarded as a prime example of his extraordinary talents, piety, and ability to persuade others. Indeed, Bernard had great influence on the twelfth-century Church, exuding tremendous spiritual energy and inspiring many. However, recent researchers speculate that there was probably more to it: What could have so motivated these thirty nobles to join Bernard and the austere Cistercians, when apparently they didn't even consider joining another Order? Faith can certainly be a strong motivator. But all thirty? And all at once?

As we have seen, St. Bernard was also instrumental in getting official papal recognition for the Templar Order at the Council of Troyes in 1129. Historians know that, especially in northern France, the Templar Order and the Cistercians were closely associated. And both had connections with Troyes. These ties precede 1129 and involve a number of key family associations—for instance, André de Montbard being the uncle of Bernard. Possibly, something more was going on behind the scenes—perhaps "directed" from Champagne—that especially involved the First Crusade, Godfroi de Bouillon and his family, the old Burgundian nobility, the Cistercians, Troyes, and the first nine Knights Templar, all of whom had close associations of various kinds.

The buildup to the Council of Troyes (1129)

In 1104, Hughes I attended a synod in Troyes, at which many eminent people were present, to hear an abbot from Jerusalem whose name was not recorded. Matters in the Holy Land were probably discussed. A series of other meetings followed, instigated by Count Hughes. Hughes himself then left for the Holy Land, in 1104, returning to Champagne in 1108. In 1114, he again traveled to the Holy Land along with Hugh de Payns. In a letter Ivo, the bishop of Chartres, rebuked Hughes for leaving his wife as he made this second trip and referred to Hughes's having taken vows "to the 'knighthood of Christ' *(militi Christi)* in order to take up 'that gospel knighthood' *(evangelicam militiam)*, by which two thousand may fight securely against him who rushes to attack us with two hundred thousand."[37] St. Bernard would use the same imagery years later in support of the Order of the Temple, even though Ivo did not mention the Templars specifically in his letter.[38]

Historians have tried to determine what Ivo meant by Hughes's vows to this unspecified "knighthood of Christ." They have largely concluded that Hughes may have taken crusader's vows to go to Jerusalem, or he may have vowed to join a confraternity of knights formed to protect the Christian holy places in the Holy Land. Such knightly confraternities were "becoming common in western Europe during the 11th century (that is, the century before the First

Crusade)."[39] These were groups of wealthy warriors, though not necessarily nobles, who agreed to work together towards a common aim, such as defending churches against bandits. On the face of it, this explanation seems probable.

But, as others point out, someone as wealthy and influential as the Count of Champagne would more likely have joined an Order. We know it was not the Hospital or the Templars, so some conjecture that it was the Order of Notre Dame of Sion, on Mount Sion on the outskirts of Jerusalem. This Order also had monasteries and abbeys in other areas, such as Mount Carmel, southern Italy, and France. There are also a number of links between the Order of Notre Dame of Sion, the Carmelites, and Calabria in southern Italy. As we saw earlier, Godfroi de Bouillon's first major act as "king" and Defender of Jerusalem in 1099 was to order this abbey's repair and fortification and to reconfirm its charter. Precisely why he did so, other than simply to aid a devout Christian Order, remains to be clarified.

What we do know is that Hughes I did not officially join the Templars until late in 1125. As Count of Champagne he had donated the land on which the first Cistercian monastery, Cîteaux, had been built. Ironically, when he made his Templar vows, he had to pledge fealty to his own vassal, Hugh de Payns, who was the first Templar Grand Master. Hughes's willingness to do so shows that he believed wholeheartedly in what he was doing. And even though he joined at this rather late date, his behind-the-scenes influence seems to have been present in the early stages of the Order.

Some historians speculate that the Order of the Temple was created as an important "military arm" of the already existing Order of Notre Dame de Sion, and that Godfroi de Bouillon—and Baldwin I—both knew and supported this group of monks in Jerusalem. Scholars do know that both men showed support for the various Christian Orders present in Jerusalem, but details are scanty, consisting mainly of a few charters. Obviously, both Godfroi and Hughes I had connections to Troyes and Champagne/Burgundy, so a connection between the Templars and the already-existing Order of Notre Dame de Sion—however tenuous—is at least a possibility.

Others speculate the Templars may have been formed as an adjunct to the Order of the Holy Sepulchre, as their "knights," since some accounts—many undoubtedly legendary—claim the Order of the

Holy Sepulchre was founded by Godfroi de Bouillon. Yet no contemporary evidence exists that the canons of the Holy Sepulchre ever assumed a military function, or that a group of knights was associated with them to protect the Holy Sepulchre.

Researcher Nicolas Mazet believes the Cluniac Order, based at the powerful abbey of Cluny, may have been the influence behind the scenes:

> Since the Milice du Christ was the name of the crusaders as well as the name for the Templars some twenty odd years later, it is conceivable that both entities have been confused ... Given the cross-pollination professed by St Bernard of Clairvaux and others from 1090 to 1130, it is not only conceivable but also downright possible. And all of it points to Cluny. Not only did they have the money, but they also had the power, the lands, and the exemptions and last but not least, the Pope who called the Crusade. If there truly was a secret arm to the Templars, it was through Cluny and by extension through the house of Bourgogne (Burgundy).[40]

Many theories exist about the "Order behind the Order" of the early Knights Templar. Pope Urban II, who called the First Crusade, was a product of Cluny. The Cluniacs are interesting in other ways, too. Joint missions from Cluny and Chartres were known to have visited Saracen Spain and to have been well received in a fraternal manner. The Cluniacs greatly approved of the First Crusade; they were also instrumental in expanding the practice of pilgrimage to sacred places in medieval Christian Europe, from Portugal to Poland. Cluniac monks also made significant inroads into northern Spain and were presented by monarchs with monasteries along the lucrative pilgrimage route to Santiago de Compostela.[41]

Not much is known about Hughes I's activities in 1106 or 1107, or about his (or Hugh de Payns's) activities in the Holy Land during this time. Nearly four years later, in about 1108, Count Hughes returned to Champagne and met with the same group of nobles and clergy he had seen at Molesmes in 1104. As his signature is missing from all documents from 1104 to 1108, many historians believe that he, and Hugh de Payns were in the Holy Land then.

Yet strangely enough, chroniclers make no mention of the two men's activities in the Holy Land either, which seems unusual, given their prominence in western Christendom. So, where were they? Perhaps records have simply not survived; or perhaps their activities were not documented, for whatever reason. We do have the letter that Ivo, Bishop of Chartres, wrote to Hughes rebuking him for leaving his wife to return to Jerusalem in 1114. And we know Hughes returned to Champagne partly due to Ivo's pressure.

We also know that nevertheless, late in 1125, Hughes left his family for good to join the relatively new Templar Order, which at the time still had only nine knights. He stayed in Jerusalem for about two years, returning with the rest of the Templars in 1127. Barber notes that "since both William of Bures and Hugh de Payns were in Le Mans by mid April 1128, it is probable that the ... Templar group sailed together during the autumn passage of 1127."[42]

In early 1128—or according to recent scholarship, January of 1129—the Council of Troyes was held, after which the Templars received official papal recognition. St. Bernard was a key advocate in helping to launch the Templar Order as warrior-monks—an entirely new concept for medieval Christendom.

One wonders how such a tiny Order with only nine members not only managed to get official papal recognition but also grew exponentially in the next decade or so, becoming one of the wealthiest and most effective Orders in history. Henry I of England welcomed them with open arms, for example, and prominent nobles from all over Europe quickly flocked to join the Order and give the Templars lands, goods, money, and other support. Considering how long gaining such prestige could normally take, these extraordinary achievements were accomplished in a very short time. Historians acknowledge the Templars' spectacular rise as rare, hardly seen before or since. It may simply have been an example of St. Bernard's inspiring monastic evangelism in conjunction with the Templars' fame and the success of the First Crusade, or it may have had something to do with the small group of interrelated families that started the Templar Order—a group that included members of St. Bernard's family. Or it could have been both.

Whatever view one espouses, there is little doubt about what the Templars, as well as the Cistercians, exemplified—dedication, steadfast faith, perseverance, and unflinching faith in the face of incredible odds.

CHAPTER

3

ORGANIZATION
and BELIEFS

W e have seen how the Order of the Temple began, what led up to its founding, how its spectacular expansion took place after the Council of Troyes in 1129, and what its major achievements were. How, then, did these famed knights actually live? What was their daily life like? How did they so effectively combine a spiritual life with the life of a warrior?

The structure of the Templar Order

The Templar Order's administration was structured hierarchically, as in many other medieval military Orders. The Grand Master was based at the Order's headquarters in the Holy Land, along with the other major officers, each of whom had his own staff. In Europe, the Order's extensive territories were divided into provinces. Each of these was administered by an area commander who, in turn, oversaw the Masters who were responsible for running individual houses. The function of the houses in the West was to provide men, money, and supplies for the brothers fighting in the East, and a system of general chapter meetings kept the officials of the two regions in touch with one another.[1] Given the vast territory over which it spread, the Order would have had to deal with the challenges of multiple languages among its members.

The office
of Grand Master

A Templar Grand Master was elected for life. No longer an ordinary knight, too poor to keep sufficient horses and equipment, "he had become a great man, entitled to four horses and an entourage which included a chaplain, two knights, a clerk, a sergeant, and a servant to carry his shield and lance. He had, too, his own *farrier*, a Saracen scribe to act as an interpreter . . . and a cook."[2] When he traveled, a large staff accompanied him, and he received much respect on his journeys.

How was a Grand Master elected? After the funeral of the previous Grand Master, which was attended by many dignitaries and leaders in the Holy Land, all the provincial Templar officers in the East would meet in Jerusalem to appoint a Grand Commander to govern until a new Grand Master was chosen. Demonstrating respect for the international character of the Order, though without specifying national divisions, the officers from various countries would choose an electoral college of thirteen—who, after a night of prayer, would choose the new Grand Master. These thirteen—symbolizing Christ and his twelve disciples—consisted of eight knights, four sergeants, and one chaplain, as far as possible reflecting the diverse countries from which the membership was drawn. A majority decision was acceptable, having the usual aim of selecting someone already in Outremer, although the history of the Order shows that this did not invariably happen. When the name was announced, the new Master was acclaimed by the brothers and then, while the chaplains sang the *Te Deum*, they carried him to the chapel before the altar, as a means of offering him to God.[3]

In theory at least, these elections were structured according to the now-famous papal bull *Omne datum optimum* of 1139, which said that only a professed brother of the Order could be elected, chosen "by all the brothers together or by the sounder and purer part of them."[4] Incidentally, this papal bull also established the Templar Order as an exempt Order of the Church, which meant that from then on the Templars were answerable only to the papacy. The hierarchical statutes that set forth the procedures for the election give the impression—quite rightly—that it was more important to elect the right person than to elect someone quickly. But the process wasn't always so straightforward, because at least seven of the twenty-two Templar Grand Masters were appointed through the direct influence of a secular ruler.[5] According to policy, whatever occurred within the electoral conclave was supposed to be kept secret until the result was announced. This is reminiscent of how the Vatican selects a new Pope, which is done by a special conclave of Cardinals that meets privately, until the famous "puff of smoke" comes out the chimney, signaling to the world that they have made their choice.

Once chosen, the Grand Master had considerable power, within certain limits. As Malcolm Barber tells us:

> Major decisions over whether to make war or agree to a truce, whether to alienate land or acquire a castle, who should be appointed to positions of command . . . could only be taken in consultation with the Chapter . . . Similarly, although he [the Grand Master] was entitled to withdraw up to 3,000 *besants* from the treasury if he was intending to go to Tripoli or Antioch, he could do so only with the permission of the Commander of the Kingdom of Jerusalem, "who is Treasurer . . . and who should keep and guard the keys of the treasury."[6]

The Grand Master was spiritual head of the Order, and he would also lead the Templars into battle when he was present. He also had much to say about the distribution of funds. And being the main representative of the Order to the outside world, he had to possess political acumen and good diplomatic skills.[7]

Like the major officials of other military religious Orders, the Templar Grand Master had his own seal, which he used to validate approved documents:

> The Master of the Temple's great seal was double-sided and showed the circular dome of the Church of the Holy Sepulchre on one side and the Order's symbol of two knights on one horse on the other. There was also a smaller, single-sided seal, which showed the circular dome of the Holy Sepulchre. This is neither the Dome of the Rock which is octagonal, nor that of the Aqsa mosque, which stands on a rectangular base. The images on the seal reminded anyone who looked at it that the Templars defended the Holy Sepulchre and were the poor knights of Christ.[8]

Interestingly, a British Museum curator once told me that the Templar image of two knights on a horse may date back to Sumerian times, as some ancient Sumerian seals display similar iconography.

Probably the most famous Templar Grand Master was Jacques de Molay, the last Grand Master, who was unjustly burned at the stake by King Philip IV of France in 1314. We know that de Molay entered the Order of the Temple in 1265 at Beaune, in the diocese of Autun, and that he was received by Humbert of Pairaud, the Master in England, and also by Aimery of La Roche, the Master in France. He was probably from Burgundy—his birthplace the village of Molay in Franche-Comte. Not much else is known about his earlier years. We know he had one serving brother to harness his horses and care for his other animals, another to administer his household, and two more to guard his chamber. Horses were prized in the Crusades and were a symbol of rank and status. "When the Order received a fresh consignment of horses from the west, the Master was entitled to select any of them for himself, as well as one or two others."[9]

By the 1160s, the office of Grand Master held much power and prestige, especially among the crusading armies in Outremer (the "Latin East" in the Holy Land) but also among the Saracens and other leaders there. By the end of the thirteenth century, when de Molay served as Grand Master, there were at least 970 Templar houses, including commanderies and castles in both East and West, serviced by a membership of probably at least seven thousand, excluding employees and dependents, who must have been at least seven or eight times that number.[10]

Other offices of the Order

The Seneschal was the Grand Master's deputy, or "right-hand man." In ceremonies he carried the famed *beauseant*, the Templars' black-and-white banner. Chronicler Matthew Paris's thirteenth-century drawings show this banner as a simple oblong attached vertically to a pole or spear. Like the Grand Master, the Seneschal had his own staff and horses.

The Marshal was the chief military officer, responsible for the individual commanders and the horses, arms, equipment, and anything else involving military operations. He also had authority in obtaining, ordering, and distributing supplies, critically important at the time of the Crusades.

The Commander of the Kingdom of Jerusalem was the treasurer of the Order and was in charge of the strong room. He shared power with the Grand Master in a way that prevented either from having too much control over funds. The Grand Master, for instance, could keep a lockable strongbox in the treasury but was not allowed to hold the key to the room. And anything the Commander received was first seen by the Master and then recorded in writing, so that the list was available for inspection.[11] The Commander also oversaw all nonmilitary assets of the Order, such as pack animals, houses, villages, and the ships and storage vaults at Acre.[12]

The Draper issued clothes and bed linen and could also distribute gifts made to the Order. He was not only keeper of the famed white mantles but also ensured that every brother was dressed "decently," as the Rule put it.[13] The Draper could also remove items from a member—full knight or not—when he thought that person had more than was proper. In keeping with the New Knighthood concept of living more simply than secular knights, Templars were not allowed many personal belongings—and certainly nothing showy or ostentatious.

These four, along with the Grand Master, constituted the major officers of the Order, although there seem to have been local variations regarding the distribution of duties among them. "The Draper, for example, was obliged to obey the Commander of the Land of Jerusalem when that official required something from him, but he is also described as being 'superior to all other brothers' after the Master and the Marshal."[14]

Under these main five officers were other Templar commanders with specific regional responsibilities, such as the commanders of the cities of Jerusalem, Tripoli, and Antioch; a Commander of the Knights; the Turcopolier, in charge of light cavalry and scouts; the Under-Marshal, who managed craftsmen of the stable; the Standard Bearer, who was in charge of the squires; and the Infirmarer, who ran the infirmary for aged brothers. The Order "did not have a hospital at its central convent for poor pilgrims and the needy, although the brothers had to give alms to the poor."[15] It did maintain some hospices in Europe.

The men filling these positions seem to have come from the knightly class. The rank-and-file Templar army were either knights or sergeants, their status largely depending upon their social standing in secular life before entering the Order.[16] Even by the middle of the twelfth century "the Templar knights hardened almost into a caste. It was necessary to be of knightly descent to wear the white mantle."[17] The sergeants wore black tunics with a red cross on the front and back, and black or brown mantles. Among them there was a further division. The Templar Rule shows that they were intended to be part of the fighting force, but this apparently did not strictly apply to all of them, as some trial notaries described some among the sergeant ranks as "serving brothers," who were craftsmen, blacksmiths, masons, cooks, and so on.[18]

Barber comments on new members:

> New entrants handed over their outside clothes to the Draper and were then provided with a standard set of armour, clothing and equipment. For knights, armour ranged from a helmet and a mailed hauberk covering the head and body down to the iron hose and *solerets* which protected their legs and feet. The mail was reinforced by *espaliers* which appear to be metal shoulder protectors, and the whole outfit was worn over a padded jacket, probably made of leather.[19]

The new knight then received weapons—a sword, a shield, a lance, a "Turkish" mace, a dagger, a bread knife, a pocketknife—and basic simple clothes, including two white mantles and a heavy cloak. "Each knight was allowed three horses and a squire and, at the Master's discretion, an additional horse and squire."[20]

The Templars being a military Order, horses were key—all the military Orders, and especially the Templars, were reputedly skilled at mounted warfare. Not only would the knight himself have to be ready for battle at any time, but his horses, armor, and equipment had to be well maintained. Thus a squire was absolutely essential. When the Order was founded, squires were not members of the Order but outsiders hired for a set period.[21] Only later was this policy changed.

Daily administration of the Order's regional houses was governed by various officials called *bailies*, and the officer in charge was called the *baili*. Thus the Templar Order was made up of men in a variety of positions performing many different functions. It even hired some people from outside. Only a minority were full-fledged knights.

The black-and-white "beauseant"

The Templars so esteemed their famed black-and-white "piebald" banner, the *beauseant*, that in battle they placed a special guard of ten knights around it. They carried a second, folded banner to raise if anything happened to the first one.

> In no circumstances should it [the banner] be lowered to be used as a weapon; any Templar who did this ran the risk of losing the habit and being put in irons. No Templar should ever leave the field while the piebald banner was still to be seen, whatever the overall military situation . . . If the banner was eventually brought down, the Templars should seek to rally first to that of the Hospitallers and, failing that, to any Christian banner.[22]

Early portrayals show that the *beauseant* was divided vertically in some cases and horizontally in others, but it was always black and white. Symbolically, the black represented the darkness of sin that the Templars had left behind, and the white reflected the pure life of the Order. Interestingly, Wolfram von Eschenbach's *Parzival*, an important Grail romance, opens with a long passage showing that black and white are to be found in every action and life situation and arguing that, since every action has either good or bad repercussions, it is better to err on the side of the good. Even Parzival's half brother Feirefiz is unusually described as black and white, which many scholars believe to be von Eschenbach's metaphorical way of saying that Muslims, too, could have connections to the Grail—an amazingly ecumenical stance for a twelfth-century Christian author.

Some speculate that the *beauseant* may be connected to the black-and-white checkered squares of the chessboard—though Freemasons point out that the floor of a Masonic lodge is of similar design, as are other motifs in history. The crusaders had brought the Persian game of chess back with them to Europe. The chess player's "cry of 'Checkmate!' is a corruption of the Persian 'Shakh Mat!' which translates, 'the King is dead!'"[23] In Arabic-Spanish chess this means, more precisely, "the king is dishonored, defeated, or deposed."

The Templars were renowned as warriors who never left the battlefield. Even the Saracens were amazed at their sheer staying power, sometimes under impossible odds, as some Saracen chronicles show. Only after the *beauseant* and other Christian banners were brought down could a Templar knight retreat without fear of punishment in the Order.

Chapter meetings

Major meetings, called "general chapters," took place at the Order's headquarters or at one of its leading houses in the East. These were much like an annual general meeting at an international business conference today. Chapter meetings, not unlike modern company board meetings, were held in secret so as to keep all internal business within the Order.

Templar chapter meetings were also held in the West. These were chapter meetings of the Master and central convent and the leading officials of the Order from Europe. They were like the courts held by secular rulers, at which business was discussed and legal cases heard. "It is not known how frequently Templar general chapters were held . . . No procedure for holding the Templars' general chapters survives."[24]

We know from the Templar Rule that there were also ordinary chapter meetings held weekly. These began and ended with prayers led by the chaplain and were presided over by the Master of the house. Unfortunately, we have no records of these meetings, as the Order's central archive has been lost to posterity.

The central archive was originally held in Jerusalem, then at Acre, and after the fall of Acre in 1291, at Cyprus, as these were the locations of the Order's headquarters at those times. After the Order was suppressed in 1312, the archive was passed on to the Hospitallers. Scholars believe it was destroyed when the Turks captured Cyprus in 1571. The tragic loss of this central archive makes it difficult to determine, among other things, exactly what property and privileges the Templars held in the crusader states and in Cyprus. Moreover, it is one reason why there has been so much speculation about the Templars through the centuries.

The Rule of the Templars

During the twelfth and thirteenth centuries, the Order of the Temple developed a detailed set of regulations called the Rule. Written in French, it included a translation of the original Latin Rule that would not have been readily comprehensible, as many Templar recruits were not skilled in Latin. The Rule had seven main sections: the Primitive Rule, Hierarchical Statutes, Penances, Conventual Life, the Holding of Ordinary Chapters, Further Details on Penances, and Reception into the Order.[25]

Scholars believe the original manuscripts of the Latin Templar Rules were probably destroyed at the time of the arrests in France in 1307. Unfortunately, none have survived, so we must work from extant translations. The Primitive Rule was the result of the deliberations of the Council of Troyes (1129) and was based to an extent on previous practices. At the time of the Council, the Templars had been following the Rule of St. Augustine. This changed in 1129, with the influence of the Cistercian abbot St. Bernard of Clairvaux.[26] The Cistercians were reformed Benedictines, and one finds a number of similarities between the Rule of the Templars and the Rule of St. Benedict.[27] However, Bernard's specific influence is unmistakable, as other aspects were specifically modeled on the Cistercian Rule. (Notably, the Cistercian constitution was sent to the Pope for approval in 1119—the year the Templar Order was founded. Bernard was involved in both organizations, and both were dedicated to Our Lady, whom Bernard greatly revered.) By the mid-1160s, the Rule had also expanded into a military manual, although the knights' spiritual life and obligations were always the first priority.[28]

Any monastic Order requires strict rules, and the Templars, as warrior-monks, were no exception. There were penalties for a number of things, including revealing the Order's secrets, which has led to all sorts of speculation—even the idea of an inner circle, or "an Order within the Order." Major punishments, even the humiliation of "losing one's mantle" for a year and a day, were meted out when necessary:

There were two basic forms of punishment within the order. The first is referred to as "losing one's coat." Losing the coat (i.e., Mantle) of the Order was a penance of shame. Stripped from a guilty brother were his coat, weapons, and horse. He would be forced to eat from the floor, do menial tasks, and be generally separated from his brethren. Such penalties were imposed for infractions such as losing a horse through neglect, loaning Templar assets without the permission of the Order . . . Having sexual relations with a woman would also result in the losing of one's coat, but was not considered as serious as homosexuality, which resulted in expulsion from the Order, the harshest of all penalties.[29]

Ironically, although the inquisitors tried to use the charge of homosexuality as a major accusation during the Templar trials, we have little evidence that it occurred in the Templar Order. Knights were even required to sleep with candles burning to avoid the lust that darkness would supposedly bring—a common custom in many monasteries in the Middle Ages.

Other infractions of the Rule could result in outright expulsion from the Order, such as murdering a Christian, divulging to outsiders what went on in chapter meetings, committing an act of heresy or denouncing the Christian faith, conspiring to make false charges against a brother, leaving the Templar house for more than two days without permission, and—God forbid—leaving the battlefield while the black-and-white *beauseant* of the Templars still flew.[30] Many of these rules were similar to those of other military religious Orders of the time, such as the Hospitallers or the Teutonic Knights. But as Dafoe and Butler point out:

> There is one striking aspect of the Templar penal system . . . A Templar knight, upon being found guilty of an infraction punishable by expulsion from the Order, was not simply turned out into the street. By the very rule he had been read at his initiation, the expelled Templar was obligated to join another monastic order, in the hopes of saving his soul. It is very telling that the only religious order available to an erring and expelled Templar knight was that of the Cistercians. It is perhaps this fact, more than any other, which highlights the similarities and interdependence of the two institutions.[31]

The Cistercians and the Templars seem connected—especially in France—in a number of ways, not the least of which are certain important family links, such as the situation with André de Montbard: "one of the original nine knights and one of the . . . Grand Masters of the order. Upon joining the Templars, two of his brothers immediately joined the Cistercians at Citeaux, the same Citeaux that welcomed Bernard de Fontaine,"[32] later St. Bernard of Clairvaux.

For the most part, the Templars kept to their Rule. The Order's history includes no public sex scandals, unlike the histories of other medieval religious Orders, including the Hospitallers. And before the trial of 1307–12, the Templar Order had never been accused of outright heresy, again unlike other Orders—though there may have been the occasional errant individual, as in any large international organization. In fact, the Templars were generally viewed as more chaste than other religious men. One Salius, the son of a Muslim emir, even converted to Christianity and joined the Templars, so impressed was he with their piety.[33]

Even non-Templar witnesses at the trial in Cyprus testified that the Templars were devout, never missing mass, and so on. The medieval chronicler Walter Map, who was not much in favor of the military religious Orders and their behavior, tells the story of Aimery, a knight who had been on his way to a tournament but had turned aside to hear mass in a chapel of Our Lady. He missed the tournament, but Our Lady attended in his place and won the prize on his behalf. "Aimery was so struck by this miracle that he joined the Order of the Temple" in her honor,[34] for Our Lady was the patron of the Templar Order, and he knew of its sincere devotion to her.

There were other regulations that applied to the Templars in the Holy Land, especially inside the borders of the Kingdom of Jerusalem. The wandering Bedouin tribes are a case in point, as it seems they were under the jurisdiction of the King of Jerusalem:

> The Crusaders found a legal formula for these nomads. By definition neither city inhabitants nor . . . serfs, [the Bedouin] had a special legal status, by being the king's property. This meant that they paid for pasture rights probably in horses, camels, or sheep and were under royal . . . jurisdiction. This rule was well adapted to the mode of their existence as they moved from place to place: the

Crown . . . was the only factor that could assure them protection in every place . . . We do find Bedouin tribes in the possession of the Templars.[35]

So not only were the Templars responsible to their own Rule; they also took responsibility for other people, as well as for houses and lands, as they managed an extensive empire.

A day in the life of a Templar knight

A Templar's day began around 4 A.M., when he would rise for the day's first religious service, called Matins, during which he would be required to recite thirteen *Paternosters* (Lord's Prayers) and prayers to Our Lady. Matins was followed by Prime, at 6 A.M., and the hearing of Mass. Prime was followed by Sext at around 11:30 A.M.:

> By the time the Templars were ready for their first meal of the day, they would have recited a total of sixty Paternosters, 30 of which were spoken for the living and another 30 for the deceased. It was believed that the latter would ask God to deliver the dead from Purgatory and transport them to Paradise . . . For many people these days, the thought of a single prayer each day seems excessive, yet the Templars were so spiritually dedicated, that they would recite five dozen prayers before eating their first meal.[36]

Like their Cistercian and Benedictine counterparts, "the Templar knights ate their meal in absolute silence. The only speaking came from the Priest, who blessed the meal, and from the clerk who would give the Bible reading during the meal."[37] The Cistercian monks were totally vegetarian, but the Templars were required to eat meat—either mutton, veal, beef, goat, or fish—at least three days a week in order to remain "combat ready." The rest of the week they were served vegetables, cheese, and bread, as in other monasteries. They ate at least twice and sometimes three times a day.

After the afternoon meal, they would meet in the chapel to give thanks. Next came Nones at 2:30 P.M. and Vespers at 6 P.M. Vespers was followed by the evening meal, also eaten in silence. Compline was the last order of the day, and then the brethren would gather for some communal drinking—either water or diluted wine.[38] Thus some consumption of wine was allowed, but only at the Master of the house's discretion. Silence was an absolute requirement, especially from Compline in the evening until Matins the following morning. Hence the bulk of the day, beginning at 4 A.M. and except for the afternoon meal, was committed to prayer and devotions of one form or another.

When the Templars weren't at prayer or war, they were laboring at simple tasks or out in the fields, as they were never to remain idle. It may be hard for many of us today to imagine such a life of daily sacrifice.

God as "length, width, height, and depth"

Some of the Templar castles in the Holy Land, or their ruins, exhibit designs and structures that impress professional architects even now. In recent decades, Israeli archaeologists excavating around the Temple Mount area have found a tunnel they maintain was built by the medieval Knights Templar (see chapter 6).

The German monk Theoderic, having made a pilgrimage to Jerusalem, commented in 1174: "On the other side of the palace [i.e., the al-Aqsa Mosque], the Templars have built a new house, whose height, length and breadth, and all its cellars and refectories, staircase and roof, are far beyond the custom of this land. Indeed its roof is so high that, if I were to mention how high it is, those who listen would hardly believe me."[39] The building to which Theoderic referred was unfortunately destroyed by the Muslims in the 1950s during renovations of the Temple Mount. Graham Hancock comments:

> The German monk's testimony was, however, valuable in itself—and what I found most valuable about it was its breathless tone. Clearly he had regarded the Templars' architectural skills as almost supernaturally advanced and had been particularly impressed by the soaring roofs and arches that they had built. Reviewing his statements, I thought it far from accidental that soaring roofs and arches had also been the distinguishing features of the Gothic architectural formula

as expressed at Chartres and other French cathedrals in the twelfth century.[40]

This is an interesting point indeed, especially considering that none other than St. Bernard of Clairvaux had defined God as "length, width, height, and depth." Clearly, design, number, and proportion were important to the Templars. Moreover, some experts believe the Templars may have been more influential than previously supposed in introducing Gothic architectural style into twelfth-century France; in fact, they may have helped spearhead this extraordinary change in ecclesiastic architecture. We know the Order had its own mason brothers from Rule number 325: "No brother should wear leather gloves, except the chaplain brother . . . And the mason brothers may wear them sometimes, and it is permitted them because of the great suffering they endure and so that they do not easily injure their hands; but they should not wear them when they are not working."[41] As the Rule shows, these mason brothers, while not full knights, were nevertheless members of the Templar Order who specialized in building skills. They may also have worked with local stonemasons where construction was taking place or may have worked with masons from other Orders or guilds. However, few specifics are now known, as many of the Templar archives were destroyed or have disappeared—if such information was ever recorded at all. More remains to be determined about the meanings of the mason's marks carved on medieval buildings and cathedrals, and scholars from various disciplines are conducting research. Indeed, to understand the many aspects of this complex subject an interdisciplinary approach is required.

St. Bernard was translating material relating to sacred geometry after 1128. Medieval rumors abounded that the Templars had retrieved something from the Ark of the Covenant—perhaps the Tables of Testimony—that would have had formulas or other material relating to the divine law of number, measure, and weight. And historians know the Templars returned from the Holy Land in 1127. Hence, some maintain that the Templars (as well as other Orders of the day) may have learned the same alchemical stained glass technique used by the eleventh-century Persians—yet another example of Europeans applying knowledge gained from the East. To this day, scientists cannot explain the extraordinary luminescence of the special stained glass—especially the formulation of the color blue—that graces such towering edifices as Chartres Cathedral.

Supporters of the theory that Gothic architecture may have had Templar origins—or, at the very least, input—point out that, shortly after the Templars returned from the Holy Land (in late 1127), an extraordinary transformation began to take place in Europe. In addition to the Gothic cathedrals beginning to appear in France, some of the Templars' own buildings had interesting architectural designs. The plan of the Temple Church in London, for instance, is based on the Tau cross; and the Philosophical Cross—the plan of the Third Temple as prophesied by Ezekiel— is illustrated in some of their building schemes. The Templars, in fact, were known to be good builders. In 1139, Pope Innocent II granted the Templar Order the right to build its own churches. In Jerusalem, for example, the Templars built, among other things, three of the magnificent central bays of the porch of the al-Aqsa Mosque during the time when the Order's headquarters were based there—from 1119 until they moved their headquarters to Acre after the Battle of Hattin, in 1187. Their famous fortress of the Crusades, Atlit ("Castle Pilgrim"), was built in 1218 at the direction of the fourteenth Templar Grand Master, William of Chartres. So the Templars probably had learned more than a little about geometry, mathematics, and certain architectural designs in the East.

The Templars are also famous for building some of their churches with circular naves, after the Church of the Holy Sepulchre in Jerusalem. After the Templars' era, however, round churches were considered heretical in certain areas in the West and were discouraged. One can view such a circular nave at the Church of the New Temple, London, and the ruins of such a nave at the Templars' church in Garway, Hertfordshire.

We also know that the Templars were especially interested in the design of the Temple of Solomon. Western researchers have sometimes overlooked the possibility of Templar contacts with Islamic and Jewish scholars and the extent to which they may have had contact with Eastern Christians. Not all Templars were full-fledged knights; in fact, only a minority were. Some affiliated with the Order were what we might now call specialists or outside consultants—perhaps experts in translation and so on. Some of these outside experts were Arabs—for example, Grand Master Jacques de Molay was known to have had a Saracen scribe who accompanied him on important business in the Holy Land. Knowledge of subjects like astronomy, mathematics, the telescope, herbal medicine, and even mouth-to-mouth resuscitation came to western Europe via crusader contacts in the East. No doubt the Templars played a role in the new cultural flowering that brought Europe out of the so-called Dark Ages. One key area of Templar activity in the West that seems underresearched is the importance of the Islamic and Kabbalistic centers in Spain, where the Templars, as well as other Orders, are believed to have had contact with those who were well-versed in geometry, astronomy, alchemical philosophy, Kabbala, and mathematics. Geometric symbols have been found on the walls of the prison tower of Chinon Castle, where sixty Templars—a number of whom held high offices—were incarcerated in 1308, so we know that at least some Templars were familiar with geometry. These carvings remain undeciphered today. Some of the monks of the Cluniac Order were also interested in such knowledge, spearheaded by the able Peter the Venerable, who inspired Robert of Chester to translate the Koran and also consulted with converted Jewish scholars about the Talmud. Even Abbot Suger of St. Denis, who supervised the first Gothic building at St. Denis, admitted that his source of inspiration was the Temple of Solomon and, along with it, the Hagia Sophia in Constantinople. While not all Templars were highly literate, certainly some were. They, like members of other Orders, undoubtedly engaged in important exchanges of ideas with other learned men of their time. Medieval Spain witnessed a unique situation in which Christian, Islamic, and Jewish scholars lived and worked together, often translating major texts, in cultural centers like Toledo. Wolfram von Eschenbach, for instance, claimed that his true source for his Grail romance, *Parzival*, was a learned Jewish astrologer from Toledo who had recorded the story of the Grail in a foreign language under the Moors—very likely Arabic.

Alchemy and Hermeticism

Until recently, most academic historians have been reticent to openly study such esoteric subjects as alchemy and Hermeticism. As a result, such topics with regard to the history of the Templars have often been ignored. However, times seem to be changing, as Roelof van den Broek, emeritus professor in the history of Christianity at the University of Utrecht, recognizes:

> Most literature about the various aspects of "Western esotericism" has traditionally been of an apologetic or polemic nature: a debate, basically, among believers and their opponents. Academic researchers generally tended to avoid an area of cultural expression that was widely regarded as inherently suspect; openly to express interest in these traditions might too easily endanger a scholar's prestige among colleagues. During the last few decades, the realization has been growing that this attitude has little to commend it from a scholarly point of view, and may on the contrary have blinded us to important aspects of our cultural past.[42]

To be sure, certain tracts linking the Templars with alchemy and Hermeticism, especially those written by certain groups in eighteenth-century France, should be dismissed as propaganda. But while we must proceed very cautiously, it is not scientific to merely disregard such subjects altogether—declining, for example, to even view enigmatic carvings relating to geometry at certain medieval French Templar sites. This attitude is reminiscent of the Cardinals who refused to look into Galileo's telescope or the Protestant witch hunters who would not consider all of the evidence. Many Christians are known to have studied alchemy and Hermeticism, including some of the early Church Fathers. In medieval Spain, for example, there were a number of Christian Kabbalists known to have interacted with Jews and Muslims. More careful research may bring the possible cultural contributions of such proponents to light. The Templars were *not* known as practicing alchemists, according to the surviving historical record, though some may have studied its philosophy—as did many eminent churchmen of the time, including St. Thomas Aquinas, the Blessed Ramon Lull, Roger Bacon, and Albertus Magnus. Alchemy was often studied in tandem with studying Aristotle and natural philosophy. Some medieval Christians believed that to know Christ was to experience an inner alchemy of the spirit, a transformation.

The importance of Our Lady

The Templars showed a great reverence for Mary. Rule 306 states that "the hours of Our Lady should always be said first in this house ... because Our Lady was the beginning of our Order, and in her and in her honour, if it please God, will be the end of our lives and the end of our Order, whenever God wishes it to be." Mary was also linked with the Templars in other ways. One tradition said that "the Annunciation had taken place in the Temple of the Lord (the Dome of the Rock) and a stone on which Mary rested was outside the Templar fortress of Castle Pilgrim."[43]

Templar novices, at their reception into the Order, made their solemn pledges to the Blessed Mary as well as to God, even as the preceptor of the province at Cahors instructed Gerard de Vaux to do in 1311: "You should understand fully what we are saying to you; you should swear and promise to God and the Blessed Mary that you will always be obedient to the Master of the Temple."[44]

St. Bernard of Clairvaux had a passion for Mary beyond that of many saints before or since. His extraordinary sermons on the Song of Songs—some 120 of them—and his letters demonstrate his fervent devotion to her. His interest extended to sites important to the Black Madonna; for instance, he preached the Second Crusade from Vezelay, a well-known center of devotion to traditions of the Black Madonna and Mary Magdalene. In fact, Bernard was born at Fontaine, which was said to have its own Black Virgin on the outskirts of Dijon where the ancient Lady of Good Hope already reigned; he grew up in a locale steeped in legends about Mary and the Black Madonna, in particular.

Jungian analyst Ean Begg, in his study of the Black Madonna and Black Virgin sites in France, tells us that accounts say Bernard "received while still a boy three drops of milk from the breast of the Black Virgin of Chatillon."[45] Perhaps this is symbolic of his steadfast devotion to Mary throughout his life. In ancient Celtic myth, receiving "three drops" of a special liquid from a goddess often symbolized a hero's spiritual initiation, resulting in a life-altering experience. In helping to revise the Templar Rule in 1129, St. Bernard commended to the knights "the obedience of Bethany, the Castle of Mary and Martha."[46] Templars imprisoned and awaiting death in the dungeons of the castle of Chinon after their arrests in 1307 composed a prayer dedicated to Our Lady, acknowledging St. Bernard as the founder of the religion of the Blessed Virgin Mary.[47] Perhaps they were honoring, once again, the solemn oath taken at their reception ceremony. Our Lady was the patroness of the Templar Order, and many donations through the years were recorded in her name as well as in God's. Not surprisingly, Mary was also the patroness of the Cistercian Order.

Some popular authors postulate that the "Our Lady" of the Templars could in fact be Mary Magdalene. The reception ceremony oath shows no direct evidence for this idea, so scholars understandably refute this argument. However, though rarely mentioned, a Vatican document does show evidence that the Templars on the island of Mallorca venerated a "Black Maria."[48] Even today, the Black Madonna is the patroness of Mallorca, and the museum in Palma has some works relevant to her tradition on the island. As historians point out, the Templars' great devotion to Our Lady was not at all unusual or "heretical," especially for a Catholic Order in medieval times.

The Black Madonna

While the majority of images of the Madonna are white or light in color, there has always been a tradition of Black Madonnas. In fact—though apparently not widely known today—during the High Middle Ages the shrines to the Black Virgin were the most venerated in Europe. Some modern orthodox Catholic priests attribute the darkness of these figures to exposure through the centuries to candle smoke—hardly a comprehensive explanation! Indeed, a number of them were actually made from black materials, such as jet or ebony. It was common for several "Marys" to be venerated with great devotion at the same site, and many legends have grown around these traditions. The most famous Black Madonna pilgrimage site today is Les Saintes Maries de la Mer, in Provence, where there is a special cult of St. Sara, the patron saint of the gypsies in southern France; this site also has special connections to Mary Magdalene. Black Madonnas may have been revered as far north as Scotland, where according to researcher Niven Sinclair, a Black Virgin may still be hidden, among other objects, in the vaults of Rosslyn Chapel.

Clearly more research is needed beyond what theologians have already discovered concerning the Black Madonna, the Old Testament Sophia wisdom tradition, the Queen of Sheba legends, and possible connections of the European Black Madonnas with Isis and Egypt. Especially in the Languedoc, sites of devotion to both the Black Madonna and Mary Magdalene, which happen to be located in the same areas where there were important Cathar and Templar communities in medieval France, are still visited by many today.

An especially strong Black Madonna tradition existed in the Pyrenees and in parts of Occitania, centering on Montserrat. Many of these sites, especially in southern France, were visited by medieval pilgrims, including kings, saints, and nobles. Dominic Selwood writes:

> Not only did pilgrims pass through on their way to Jerusalem, Rome and Santiago de Compostela, but there were many pilgrimage sites in Occitania itself. A strong tradition existed that Saint Mary Magdalene was buried in the basilica of Saint-Maximin near Aix, and despite the claims of Vezelay, many, including Saint Louis, visited this shrine. Further north . . . was the most famous Marian shrine of the Midi; and the *Miracles of Our Lady of Rocamadour* (c. 1172) testify to its importance to both Occitanians and those from as far afield as Acre.[49]

One of the shrines at Chartres Cathedral, arguably one of the most extraordinary buildings of all Christendom, once held a very ancient statue of Our Lady, famously described as a black Virgin by the celebrated art historian Pintard in 1681:

> The Virgin sits on a chair, her Son sits on her knees and he gives the sign of blessing with his right hand. In his left hand he holds an orb . . . His face, hands and feet are bare and they are of a shining grey-ebony colour. The Virgin is dressed in an antique mantle . . . Her face is oval, of perfect construction, and of the same shining black colour. Her crown is very plain, only the top being decorated with flowers and small leaves. Her chair is one foot wide with four parts hallowed out at the back and carved. The statue is twenty-nine inches tall.[50]

In our modern, high-tech society, it might seem hard to understand the fervent devotion to shrines or relics in medieval times. But appreciating any period in history requires seeing it from our subjects' point of view. For a medieval pilgrim—whether knight, noble, peasant, or king—making a pilgrimage to Jerusalem or to a major shrine of a saint was extremely important—a goal not only for this life but for the afterlife.

The concept of a Black Madonna may be based on the material used to make some of her earliest images—a black meteoric stone. Historians show that the Romans brought early images of the goddess Cybele from Phrygia in 204 B.C. to what is now Vatican Hill in Rome and also to other areas in Europe. Some of these early images of a black stone goddess, whom the Romans called "Magna Mater," were later Christianized and became the Black Madonna. Similarly, the shrine containing the black stone sacred to Islam, the Kaaba in Mecca, is said to have been dedicated in pre-Islamic times to the triple goddess Manat, Al-Lat, and Al-Uzza, and the new religion subsumed the sacred sites of the old one. The statue of Diana at Ephesus is widely believed to have originally been black. Scholars in a number of academic fields have noticed the connection between the earliest images of a goddess and the color black, considered symbolic of wisdom in ancient times.[52]

Certainly, the Black Madonna is an image and theme of very early origins that reached its height in Christendom in the eleventh to thirteenth centuries—contemporaneous with the Templar Order, the rise of Gothic architecture, an alchemical revival, the Cathars, the writing of Grail romances, the troubadours, and the cult of chivalry.

When the Templars were persecuted in the early fourteenth century, their inquisitors never accused them of revering the Black Madonna, as the medieval Catholic Church did not necessarily consider veneration of Our Lady a heresy or view her image as an idol. (Rather, it was an alleged severed head called Baphomet that most interested the inquisitors in this regard.) St. Bernard, who wrote extensively on Song of Songs, was known to occasionally visit sites where the Black Madonna was venerated. Far from being called a heretic, he was canonized.

Of the many sites in medieval Europe venerating the Black Madonna, several are in southern France, in or near Provence, or in the Languedoc—a major heartland of the European Templars and also home to many Cathar nobles. A number of these nobles were known to be Templar patrons; moreover, in certain instances the Templars not only sheltered dispossessed Cathars in this area but also allowed them be buried on their consecrated land, a treatment forbidden for condemned heretics. With the fall of Montsegur in 1244, the Cathars were almost completely exterminated. Oddly, the one thing the Inquisition did *not* later charge the Templars with was their affiliations, however loose, with such outcast groups. We know inquisitors were fully aware of these ties, since they dug up "Cathar bodies buried on Templar land in order to burn them as deterrents to other would-be heretics, even more than thirty years after the end of the crusade [against the Cathars]."[51]

Women in the Templar Order

Although the Rule of the Order forbade the reception of full sisters, scholars verify that in certain localities and situations the Order had women members. Their membership was usually as associates, a status also afforded to men. Such associates would assist the Templars in a number of ways. Many women brought with them money, influence, and other valuable gifts in addition to family connections. Sometimes the women lived on Templar property but in a house that was separate from the brothers.' Helen Nicolson writes:

> The Templars had at least one nunnery. In 1272, Bishop Eberhard of Worms gave the Order of the Temple ownership and responsibility for the administration of the nunnery of Muhlen, and the duty of supporting the women there. After the dissolution of the Order of the Temple the nuns … *quondam ordinis Templi*, "formerly of the Order of the Temple," were transferred to the Order of the Hospital, although the sisters did not want to be transferred.[53]

A Sister Adelheide of Wellnheim is recorded at the Templar house of Mosbrunnen in the diocese of Eichstatt in the early fourteenth century. Nicolson found that "she was the former wife of Templar Rudiger of Wellnheim, and had chosen 'continual habitation' in the house of the Temple of Mosbrunnen for the rest of her life in order to serve God better."[54] She lived on Templar property, although in a separate house, for the remainder of her days. Her case is interesting in that the Rule permitted married couples to become associate members but stated that wives could not become full sisters and could not live in a house of the Order. Yet in this instance "the Brothers stretched the Rule to meet the needs of the Order and its donors."[55]

So the presence of women seems to have depended on the needs of the community in question. As leading scholar Professor Alan Forey puts it, "Despite the prohibition in their early rule, the Templars accepted women who renounced their goods and took the normal monastic vows . . . There was inevitably scope for local initiatives."[56]

Based on records of the donations they gave upon reception, we also know that men and women joined the Order at the same time:

> Gombau and Ermengarda d'Oluja joined the Order as "donats," a type of association with the Order. Gombau was the lord of the castle of Vallfogona . . . the couple gave their property and themselves to the house of the Temple at Barbera, and entered the house as resident donats. Gombau then disappears from the record: presumably he died. We next encounter Ermengarda as commander of the nearby house of Rouell, where there were also other Sisters . . . Her title of *preceptrix*—commander—is beyond doubt.[57]

Many of the women on record as sisters *(soror)* or associates *(donata)* of the Order were in houses in Catalonia, one of the few places where extensive Templar records have survived. Perhaps in the future scholars will discover other records in other locations, unearthing more material on the presence of women in the Order.

CHAPTER

4

The DOWNFALL of the ORDER

In the early morning hours of Friday, 13 October 1307, every known member of the Templar Order in France was suddenly arrested on suspicion of heresy by agents of King Philip IV, in collusion with Pope Clement V. Heresy was a serious charge in medieval times, and many were astonished to hear of this event. People have wondered ever since: How could such a thing have happened to the powerful, wealthy Knights Templar? How could the "white knights" of Christendom have been heretics? Who was behind the arrests, and what was their motive?

This tragic story must be understood in light of the fall of the port city of Acre to the Saracens in 1291. This event was a terrible blow, psychologically and otherwise, to not only the Templars but all of medieval Christendom. Because of it, the Order lost its base in the Holy Land, almost all of its military equipment, many men, and a number of valuable castles and fortresses that had been a major investment for years. The Templars also lost much of their raison d'être, and many of those who survived returned to Europe. Moreover, and crucially, they lost their best military personnel, including the Master, William de Beaujeu, and the Marshal, Peter de Sevrey, who had bravely commanded the final defense of Acre to no avail. Stephen Dafoe, who has studied the fall of Acre in detail, tells the story:

Some five days passed as the Templars held the women and children in the safety of their fort. Annoyed that this one remaining building was obstructing the defeat of the city, Khalil sent an envoy to make a deal with the Templars. If they relinquished the fort, the lives of the women and children would be spared and the Templars could take with them not only their weapons but all they could carry . . . De Sevrey . . . seeing no other possible solution to the stalemate, quickly agreed to the terms. The castle gates were opened and the Moslems entered and hoisted the sultan's banner, but contrary to the deal that had been made, quickly began molesting the women and young boys. This outraged the Templars, who obviously felt duped by the negated arrangement.

The door of the castle were quietly closed, barred and swords silently drew out of sheaths. In true Templar fashion, they slaughtered the attackers to a man. The sultan's flag was hoisted down and the Beauseant replaced. The battle was back on . . . That evening, under the cover of darkness, Tibauld de Gaudin, the Temple's treasurer, was escorted in to the fort. He loaded the Templar treasure and as many women and children as he could back on his ship and set sail for the Templar castle at Sidon.

The following morning, the sultan sent an envoy to the fort and they expressed their deepest regrets for the actions of a few guilty men . . . The envoy said that the sultan wished to meet with the commander . . . to offer his personal apologies . . . [so] de Sevrey . . . selected a few Templars to accompany him on the trip to the sultan's camp. Once the party was outside, they were brought to their knees and beheaded . . . The sultan's miners continued to work on the foundations of the fort and when all was ready they set timbers ablaze. As the walls began to crack, Khalil ordered a party of some 2000 soldiers to storm the fort. The added weight of the attacking forces on the crumbling structure was too great and the entire building collapsed, killing all who were inside and those who were trying to get inside. With the destruction of this last Templar stronghold, Khalil's conquest of Acre was completed.[1]

The few remaining Templars managed to save some precious relics from the treasury as well as other possessions that had been kept out of danger at safe properties such as Castle Pilgrim, but they were apparently so demoralized they didn't even write to their European brethren about what had happened. Nevertheless, the disasters of 1291 did not change the basic aims of the Order, as Malcolm Barber tells us, since de Molay "pursued an active crusading programme from the beginning of his mastership in 1293."[2]

In the years that followed, various ideas were put forth concerning how to recover the Holy Land. Although the Templars had lost some of their former glory and occasionally were blamed for the loss, on the whole they were still highly regarded. There were also discussions about combining the Templar and Hospitaller Orders into one. Helen Nicolson explains:

> In 1306 Pope Clement V called the Masters of the Temple and Hospital to his court at Poitiers in the kingdom of France to submit their own comments on the crusade and on the suggestions that their Orders be unified. James de Molay [Templar Grand Master] objected to the plans for unification. He said that the rivalry between the Orders had led to the Orders vying to do the best for Christendom—so it was beneficial . . . The comments of the Master of the Hospital . . . do not survive, but his crusade proposal assumes that the Military Orders . . . will continue to operate as independent entities. [So] the plans to unify the Military Orders did not proceed as planned. Yet although these plans came to nothing . . . even after 1291, the Military Orders as a whole and the Templars in particular were viewed very positively in the west.[3]

The 1307 arrests: "A bitter thing, a lamentable thing"

King Philip IV's secret orders to his *baillis* and *senechaux*—his law enforcement authorities—instructing them to prepare for sudden dawn raids on every Templar they could find are dated 14 September 1307. The charges were horrific, even by medieval standards, and would result in one of the most notorious trials in the history of Western civilization. Ironically, Philip's order began with these words: "A bitter thing, a lamentable thing, a thing which is horrible to contemplate, terrible to hear of, a detestable crime."[4]

The entire Inquisition and ensuing trial occurred in a series of councils held between the 1307 arrests and the burning of Templar Grand Master Jacques de Molay in March 1314. Thus it was an ongoing process, with several stops and starts. (In fact, the first "Inquisition," which ended in 1244, was against the Cathars in France.)

On 22 September, the Inquisitor-General of France, the Dominican Friar Guillaume de Paris, "wrote to the inquisitors in Toulouse and Carcassone, listing the alleged crimes of the Templars, advising them of the forthcoming arrests, and preparing them for the difficult task ahead of collecting and recording depositions."[5] Barber comments:

> In the early 14th c. no one would have disputed that cases of heresy appertained to the Church or that they fell under the jurisdiction of the ecclesiastical authorities in one form or another. The motivating force in the arrests evidently came from the French government, but in a strict sense, the action preserved the forms of legality for Philip IV had been careful to explain that he was following the just request of Guillaume de Paris, the Inquisitor of France, who held his authority as a deputy of the Pope. However, Guillaume was a French Dominican, so closely involved with the royal power that he held the position of royal confessor . . . the Inquisition was becoming, through its leader in France, another arm of state power.[6]

Though we know the French king and the Pope had discussed the arrests of the French Templars in general, the Pope was apparently not advised about the actual arrests themselves. Barber says the Pope categorically stated in 1308 that "the king did not proceed in the arrests of the Templars 'through letters of the Pope.'"[7] He continues:

> Philip, Nogaret, and Plaisians were never able to assert unambiguously that the Pope had actually authorised their actions on 13 October 1307, although they did try by innuendo to suggest that Clement had been a party to the affair. At Poitiers in May 1308, during prolonged negotiations between Philip IV and Clement V over the affair, Jean Bourgogne reports Plaisians as claiming that the king had acted on the authority of the Pope, an assertion which Clement strongly denied . . . After the arrests . . . late in October, the Pope wrote to the king in tones of great indignation at what he regarded as the king's contemptuous treatment in not consulting him.[8]

Scholar Peter Partner comments on the background of Guillaume de Nogaret, the king's minister mainly responsible for the Templars' arrest and prosecution. Nogaret had played a major role in the downfall of Pope Boniface VIII for alleged heresy, idolatry, witchcraft, and similar crimes. He received the royal seals on 22 September 1307, the very day when the instructions went out for the arrests. His appointment was a slap in the face for the papal court; here was the minister responsible for the outrage committed against [Pope] Boniface VIII at Anagni, still under sentence of excommunication from the Church, and working energetically to obtain the condemnation of Pope Boniface for heresy. To make such a man head of the French royal administration was a direct menace to Pope Clement V.[9]

Evelyn Lord notes:

> Clement was weak and ailing and dominated by Philip, who held over him the threat of a posthumous trial of Boniface that would reveal the corruption in the papacy. The King of France and the papacy were on a collision course with the Templars caught in the middle. They owed allegiance to the Pope and were under his protection, but a large number of the Order were resident in France, where they could be seen as a threat against civil authority should it come to an outright confrontation between the king and the Pope. By devious means, Philip was to marginalise the Templars and pull Clement into the web of prosecution, and this would result in the suppression of the Order.[10]

Notably, on 12 October, 1307, one day before the Templars were imprisoned, the Templar Grand Master, Jacques de Molay, had been honored as one of the pallbearers at the funeral of King Philip's sister-in-law. The next day he, along with every trackable Templar in France, was in prison.[11] Clement V estimated there were about two thousand Templars in France at the time, but this number would have included everyone from full knights to servants. A few weeks after the arrests, "the French government told the University of Paris masters that over five hundred Templars had confessed to the charges; it did not disclose how many at that time still affirmed innocence but were believed guilty."[12]

The day after the arrests, the learned masters of the University of Paris and the cathedral canons met at Notre Dame Cathedral in Paris, where Nogaret and others spoke to them regarding the events. "On Sunday, the 15th, an invitation was extended to the French people to come to the garden of the royal palace, where they were addressed by spokesmen of the king and Dominican inquisitors. Similar town meetings were held throughout France to mold public opinion."[13] These town meetings served much the same purpose as newspapers and television do today. There was much talk about the arrests and horrific charges, and many found it hard to believe that the Templars, known to be heroic in the Crusades, could ever be guilty of such unimaginable crimes.

On Monday, 16 October, Philip sent letters to all the kings and princes of Christendom explaining his actions and trying to enlist their support against the Templars in their own lands. His requests were largely rebuffed. In fact, at first, they did not believe him. Edward II of England and James II of Aragon refused to arrest the Templars and even wrote letters to other kings and to the Pope in the defense of the Order.

Meanwhile, back in France, the interrogations began in earnest. The royal orders clearly indicated that the prisoners were to be terrorized by threats and torture even before their official appearance before the Inquisition. Barber comments, "It is not difficult to imagine the fear and panic of the victims, many of whom had been wrenched from quiet, rural preceptories, and pitched into harsh captivity. Not all the Templars were fighting knights, fresh from battle with the infidel; many were involved in the routine agrarian and domestic tasks to be found on the estates of any medieval landowner in France."[14] In addition, the Templars were used to living in community, so the sudden, stark loneliness of prison must itself have been a terrible shock. James Wasserman states:

> "Due process" for an imprisoned medieval Frenchman opened wide the gateway of judicial abuse to authorities. Torture was the legal and accepted method of conducting interrogations. The Inquisition exerted its brutality convinced of its divine mission. The Templars were doomed.
>
> The French secular officials . . . were instructed to begin interrogation and torture at once. Within days, these tasks were transferred to the . . . Inquisition . . . The excruciating reality of torture demands a descriptive paragraph. The technology of torture during this period included the rack, to which the ankles and wrists of the

victim were tied with ropes attached to a windlass. As the crank turned, the arms and legs would be progressively stretched until they dislocated from their sockets. Another infamous method . . . was the strappado. This involved tying the hand with a rope behind the back and throwing the other end of the rope over a ceiling beam. The victim would be hoisted upward and precipitously dropped— then yanked to a halt inches from the floor, cracking and dislocating arms, shoulders, wrists, and ribs.[15]

If this doesn't seem horrific enough, the officials also used torture by fire, mainly by smearing fat on the soles of the feet and holding them up to flames.

One unforgettable account of this came from a Templar priest whose bones dropped out of his feet several days after the torture. He brought the bones to his hearing before the papal commission. Other forms of torture involved such time-proven techniques as beating, starvation, diets of bread and water, sleep deprivation, restriction in irons or chains, unspeakable sanitary conditions, and verbal and psychological abuse. Many Templars died in prison—some took their own lives in desperation.[16]

One of the worst blows came on 24 October 1307, when imprisoned Templars heard that Grand Master Jacques de Molay had admitted the Order's crimes to a prestigious assembly of legal scholars at the University of Paris. De Molay was probably in his sixties by this time, and throughout the trial he appeared a confused and frightened man, worn down by the pressure of the king's officers. The Templars generally sent younger men to the Holy Land to fight. Many of the French knights were middle-aged, and de Molay was even older. No doubt his age would have made the interrogations and torture even harder to bear. Barber comments:

> He was out of his depth in the circumstances of the trial and never provided any decisive leadership at this time of crisis. Although in the years that followed he was to shop and change, first retracting and then confessing again, he was never able to erase the impact of this first confession, for it was an event cleverly stage-managed by the French government to achieve maximum propaganda effect in the right quarters . . . The effect would be to create scandal on a scale too great to be easily forgotten.[17]

Barber suggests that de Molay later retracted this confession because he "thought he had been tricked, that the proceedings were not to be rapidly concluded as he had been led to believe. If this was so, it must have appeared to him that Philip was determined to destroy him and that his only chance was to revoke his confession in front of the cardinals. [He] must have known that as a relapsed heretic his position would be even more precarious than before. He could . . . have concluded that the risk involved in cooperating with the French authorities was greater than the one he ran as a possible relapsed heretic."[18]

Making matters worse, the day after de Molay confessed, thirty more leaders and other Templars did the same. Then, on 9 November, Hugh de Pairaud, Visitor of the Order and second-in-command to de Molay, also confessed, adding to the demoralization of the remaining imprisoned Templars. Most historians agree that torture was probably used. All in all, 138 depositions "survive from the examinations held in Paris between 18 October and 24 November, 1307. Of that number, only four Templars proclaimed their innocence."[19]

As the interrogation wore on, King Philip needed Pope Clement's power to legitimize his actions. Clement's response is telling:

On October 27, [Clement] wrote an uncharacteristically courageous and angry rebuke to Philip for interfering with Church affairs. The king was a secular ruler who had arrested members of a religious order, responsible to the pope, for crimes of heresy. The proper authority for crimes committed against Christ was the Church . . . For their part, the Templars looked to the pope for protection from the persecution of the king and rescue from their predicament, or at least some guarantee of justice and a fair hearing. De Molay clung to this misplaced hope for years.[20]

However, soon afterwards, on 22 November 1307, Clement issued a bull requiring the kings of England, Ireland, Castile, Aragon, Portugal, Italy, Germany, and Cyprus to arrest the Templars within their borders, *but* to do so in the name of the Pope. He had been affronted by Philip's disregard for papal opinion, and though he could not reverse the king's action, he wanted to emphasize his own higher authority—which he seems to have valued over the fate of the poor Templars. Wasserman continues: "Clement announced that he would investigate charges against the Order, and that he would be especially pleased if they were proved baseless. The Pope had placed himself in the centre of the hurricane that Philip had unleashed. Philip undoubtedly hoped the matter might be over within a couple of weeks after the arrests. Clement's intervention stalled the proceedings for seven years."[21] Indeed, it was seven years from the arrests until Jacques de Molay and his treasurer, Geoffrey de Charney, were burned at the stake in Paris in 1314.

Barber comments on the relations between the French king and the Pope: "The polemics of the Templars' trial demonstrate in microcosm the fundamental problems faced by the secular powers of the early 14th century in their struggle to perceive the proper order of the world around them...Philip IV did not succeed in convincing the world that he had a right to ignore traditional and established procedures or to defy conventional power relationships."[22]

The papal investigations in France began with the arrival of two cardinals Clement sent in December of 1307. After interviewing the inquisitors and the king's ministers, they reported to Clement that matters were being handled appropriately. Clement, however, sent them back, demanding they question the prisoners themselves. The cardinals then reported the shocking news that Grand Master Jacques de Molay, his second-in-command Hugh de Pairaud, and sixty others were retracting their earlier confessions, which had been made under torture. Encouraging as this might sound today, then it did not matter. By the terms of the Inquisition, the accused were already guilty:

> The accusation was a crime. There were no provisions for mounting a defense; no legal counsel was allowed. Witnesses were reluctant to testify on behalf of the accused lest they be branded as accomplices. Witnesses for the prosecution could remain anonymous... Confession was the only practical avenue—if no confession was received, torture would certainly follow. In rare cases where a confession was not obtained by torture, excommunication as a demonically inspired heretic would be followed by burning at the stake. If a confession obtained by torture was retracted, the same punishment awaited the unfortunate soul, for he was perceived as a relapsed heretic.[23]

In other words, the accused in a heresy trial was "framed" from the beginning. As Partner comments:

The examination of the Templars was entirely in the hands of royal officials, and it is not even certain that Church officials were present at some of the interrogations. The torture of the accused was carried out with a barbarity that even medieval men found shocking: it was said that at some examinations the torturers were drunk, and that at others the accused, while under torture, were teased by young boys who had been allowed to be present at the spectacle.[24]

Notably, the charges of heresy only affected the Templar brothers; the sisters, associates, and servants were not asked to testify even though they could have given good, eyewitness accounts of what had gone on in the Order's houses. As Nicolson says, "Clearly the investigators did not want their testimony. Very little third-party evidence was heard during the French trial. On Cyprus, third-party evidence was heard at length and was virtually unanimous: the charges were absolutely false. In England, where the Brothers refused to confess to anything, a good deal of third-party evidence was heard."[25]

The charges

No fewer than 104 articles were brought against the Templars.[26] These were based on testimony from Philip's informers and on confessions made under torture. The intent in medieval heresy trials was more to convict the already guilty than to discover the truth. Lord explains that historians have grouped the articles, or charges, into six categories: (1) reception into the Order, (2) idolatry, (3) heresy, (4) sodomy, (5) charity and the acquisition of property, and (6) secrecy of proceedings.[27] Here is a summary:

Errors of Belief:

The Templars denied Christ when they were received into the Order or soon after. They spat on the Cross and defiled it.

They exchanged obscene kisses at their reception into the Order.

There were other dubious activities at their reception: they were made to swear that they would not leave the Order, receptions were held in secret, and sodomy was encouraged.

They had to swear not to reveal what was said at their reception.

They adored a cat.

They did not believe in the Mass or other sacraments of the Church. Their priests did not speak the words of consecration in the Mass (so donations for Masses to be said for a donor's soul would be wasted).

They were taught that the Master, Visitor, and Commander (who were laity) could absolve them from sin—which only ordained priests could do.

They practised sodomy.

They venerated an idol, a bearded male head, and said that the head had great powers. Each of them wore around their waist a cord which had been wound around the head.

They were only allowed to confess their sins to a Brother of the Order.

They did not correct these errors, which were said to be "of long and general observance," or "ancient custom."

Errors of practice:

The Order did not make charitable gifts as it ought, nor was hospitality practised.

The Brothers did not reckon it a sin to acquire properties belonging to another by legal or illegal means.

They did not reckon it a sin to procure increase and profit for the Order in whatsoever way they could.

Perjury was not reckoned a sin if done to win gain for the Order.

Other suggestive evidence against the Order:

The Brothers held chapters in secret, at night.

Many Brothers left the Order, "because of the filth and errors of their Order."

There was widespread scandal about these things.[28]

One of the most infamous charges against the Templars was that of denying Christ, even spitting on the cross. Yet their behavior had been just the opposite. For example, when eighty Templars were captured after the loss of the castle at Safed, the sultan offered to spare them if they would deny Christ. Every one of them refused and was either flayed alive or beheaded—hardly the stance of men familiar with denying Christ.

The 1889 groundbreaking work of American historian Charles Lea established the Templars' innocence.[29] Lea showed that the charges were carefully crafted and stemmed from popular myths and superstitions about so-called heretics and magicians. Interestingly, before 1307, the Templars had never been accused of heresy—unlike the Hospitallers, whom Pope Gregory IX had accused in 1238. Also in 1307, the Teutonic Knights, who had been founded at the siege of Acre in 1190, were accused of heresy by the archbishop of Riga; their Grand Master was able to save their Order only after great effort. But by far the most vociferous attack was on the Knights Templar.

Many of the charges against the Templars had also been leveled at the Cathars in the first half of the thirteenth century, or were used during the European witchcraft trials of the thirteenth through seventeenth centuries. In *European Witch Trials*, Richard Kieckhefer comments that the practice of such trumped-up charges grew exponentially from 1300 to about 1330 in Europe. He shows how there were a number of trials in Europe during this time, especially in France, citing those of Pope Boniface, the Knights Templar, and Guichard of Troyes as examples. Kieckhefer associates this unsavory trend with the anxieties of a dynasty—the Capetiens, who had held power since the tenth century, facing possible extinction.[30] This era also witnessed much fear, not only of alleged plots by Jews, but also of lepers, Muslims, homosexuals, and gypsies, let alone so-called witches.[31]

Malcolm Lambert, in *Medieval Heresy*, comments on the Templars' charges:

> The Templars, it was said, imposed a denial of Christ and blasphemous rejection of the cross on their novices, required them to kiss their receptor's posterior, told them that homosexuality was lawful, adored an idol, and had the custom of not consecrating the Host when priests in the order celebrated Mass. To this extraordinary

farrago of nonsense were added other variant tales—of eucharistic heresy, worshipping a cat, betraying the cause of Christendom to the Moslems, of laymen in the order hearing confessions and granting absolution, of unlawful gains and sinister secrecy in chapter meetings … it does not seem that anyone outside of France believed them, and no modern historian of repute will accept them as true.[32]

The medieval definition of heresy was rarely specific. One scholar comments that its schematization "took the form of constructing and even inventing individual heresies as well as linking these heresies with one another."[33] Thus there would often be a string of charges, as with the Templars. Sometimes, what constituted heresy under one regime would not be so defined in another.[34]

The series of councils and trials

In May 1308, King Philip called representatives of his kingdom, including the army, to a meeting at Tours. Shortly after, they accompanied Philip to Poitiers to pressure the Pope into continuing with the Templars' trial. In fact, a number of historians believe that the idea of settling the papal court permanently in Avignon came to Clement during the weeks of pressure from this entourage, as he was largely undefended at the time and felt intimidated by Philip's maneuvers.

King Philip and his armed men stayed in the royal palace, literally across the road from the Pope and his advisors in the Franciscan monastery just to the south. Clement, though pressured by Philip and his ministers, at first insisted that a religious Order "could not be judged by a lay authority. Time, he insisted, was necessary in order to ensure a judicious decision."[35] But when Philip and Nogaret, his "right-hand man," responded by bringing several carefully hand-picked Templars before the Pope to repeat their confessions, Clement shifted. On 12 August 1308, he issued three papal bulls supporting Philip's stance, and one of them announced a General Council of the Church to be held at Vienne in October 1310 to judge the guilt of both the individual Templars and the Order as a whole.[36]

At this point, Philip had obtained nearly everything he wanted, including, apparently, the Pope's support. Historians have commented, however, that with Philip's large numbers of armed men stationed outside for a number of weeks, the Pope no doubt felt he did not have much choice. We also know Philip and Nogaret had conducted a clever campaign of slander against the Pope himself through a series of anonymous leaflets implying that he protected heretics out of his own corruption.

Tellingly, the very next day after the Pope had issued the papal bulls, he left Poitiers, which placed the legal procedures against the Templars on hold for some time. Clement also announced that from 1 December 1308, he would set up his new court at Avignon. "There he would be on his own land, inside the territory of the Angevin kings of Naples and separated from the kingdom of France by the famous bridge. In March 1309, Pope Clement finally did take up residence in a wing of the Dominican monastery in Avignon, while the Templars languished in their prisons throughout the kingdom of France."[37]

In late August 1308, the French investigation took yet another strange turn:

> Clement sent three cardinals to question further the five senior Templar leaders. They reversed themselves again, returning to their confessions of nearly a year before. The renewed confessions took place under the watchful eyes of three of Philip's officials—Jean de Jamville, their brutal jailer; Guillaume de Nogaret, whom they knew to be responsible for their travails; and Guillaume de Plaisians, who pleaded with them as a friend to confess their crimes for the salvation of their immortal souls.[38]

Wasserman continues:

> While the provincial councils pursued their nefarious efforts against individual Templars from the summer of 1308 until the convocation of the Council of Vienne in October 1311, the papal commission on the Order opened its first session in Paris on November 12, 1309 to consider the fate of the Order as a whole. The eight church dignitaries appointed as commissioners by Clement had all received Philip's approval. No one came forward to defend the Order, despite the invitation to do so that had been issued in August . . . The strategy of reserving the leaders for separate judgment by the Pope appears to have accomplished its purpose—to separate the heads of the Order from the membership, and perhaps to encourage them . . .

to believe they stood a better chance than the brethren . . . Hugh de Pairaud pleaded for a private audience with the Pope . . . De Molay . . . weakened and confused . . . sought an audience with the Pope . . . His halting and weak attempts to speak well of the Order resulted in nearly irrational and incoherent ramblings.[39]

Obviously, the Templar leaders were near the breaking point. Yet a number of historians believe that many of the other Templars were unwilling to vigorously defend the Order at this time, as they were afraid that their conditions of imprisonment would be made worse, or that they would be bullied in other ways. James de Molay finally agreed to defend the Order, but stated that he needed legal advisors. Then he went back on his undertaking and said that he would only give his testimony before the Pope. It is possible that his jailers had put pressure on him to dissuade him from defending his Order.[40]

De Molay may well have been in a fragile state. At one point he even challenged the commissioners to battle—who, although shocked, convinced him to let his previous confession stand. In the following months he seemed unable to provide strong leadership in the Order's defense.

The second session of the papal commission began on 3 February 1310. Philip, feeling that matters were going his way, told the jailers to bring forth more prisoners who wanted to defend the Order:

A group of 15 Templars came forward to declare the Order's innocence. Suddenly, a stampede followed, eventually growing to 597 brothers . . . On March 28, four brothers were chosen as spokesmen for the groups, two of whom, Pierre de Bologna and Renaud de Provins, were able, educated, and articulate Templar priests. On March 31 and April 7, . . . de Bologna made lengthy statements in which he vehemently denied all the charges. He explained that any confessions made by the brethren had been extracted under torture. He reminded the council that in countries where torture was illegal, virtually nothing was said against the Order. He accused the king and his henchmen of attacking the Order in a shameful vendetta of foul lies. He explained the pernicious effects of torture on the human psyche, stating that torture left its victims devoid of freedom of mind . . . and made a mockery of any semblance of justice . . . By May 1310, the situation had shifted in the Templars' favor.[41]

Alarmed, Philip reopened a provincial Church council near Paris on 11 May, under the powerful, newly appointed Archbishop de Marigny, despite de Bologna's arguments to the papal commission to prevent it. The very next day Philip decreed that fifty-four Templars who had just testified in defense of the Order were guilty as "relapsed heretics." They were taken to a field and burned alive, even as they heroically proclaimed their innocence. This traumatic incident left the remaining Templars terrified. And the burnings continued; 120 men were dead within a few days. Then the archbishops of Reims and Rouen joined in with their own provincial councils: "An uncounted number of Templars went to their deaths, many of whom were chosen from the dwindling ranks of those willing to testify in support of the Order. Archbishop de Marigny had Order spokesman de Provins brought before his provincial council."[42] The papal commission protested, forcing de Marigny to back down, and de Provins was returned to the papal commission. But Pierre de Bologna, the eloquent spokesman for the Order, "disappeared," never to be seen again; most likely he was murdered. The second session of the papal commission adjourned by 30 May.

Unsurprisingly, by the time the third papal commission reconvened in November of 1310, few Templars were left, let alone any willing to testify for the Order. It must have been a pathetic sight to see some two hundred remaining Templar brothers, broken from imprisonment, trembling, some even weeping on their knees, confessing to trumped-up charges. "On June 5, 1311, the papal commission rendered its findings to King Philip. A complete record of the hearings was prepared for the Pope. The commission concluded that the case against the Order was unproved."[43] That is, *the Order itself had not been found guilty.* But the question of the guilt or innocence *of individuals* was a different matter.

At the Council of Vienne in October 1311, a number of the Church fathers supported the idea that the Templars should be allowed to make a defense of the Order as a whole. This infuriated both King Philip and Pope Clement, who wanted to wrap up the proceedings. Notably, none of the invited European royalty came, and one-third of the invited clergy did not attend. Clement's main concern seems to have been how to divide up the extensive Templar property, rather than how to defend the Order. His own papal authority was also on the line, and King Philip was exerting pressure. The implicit threat of the Boniface matter hovered in the background as well. In March 1312, Philip again demanded that the Order be suppressed, and he arrived on 20 March with a military force. As Wasserman states,

> The matter was to be closed forever. On 22 March, a secret consistory of the Council of Vienne was convened. Clement presented his bull *Vox in excelso* to the assembled cardinals and prelates. In it he stated that while the evidence against the Order did not justify its definitive condemnation, the proceedings had so scandalized the Order that no honorable man would consider membership. This state of affairs would so weaken the efforts of Christendom in the Holy Land that he was bound to abolish the Order. The consistory voted by a four-fifths majority to suppress the Order.[44]

Once again, the Order itself was not declared guilty. Rather, Clement had argued that by then it had been so badly defamed that it could no longer properly defend Christendom. On 3 April, Clement read out the bull in public, and the dissolution of the Order was complete—something for which, ironically, many a Saracen army had long wished!

In May 1312, another bull, the *Ad providam Christi Vicarii*, was issued, turning over the Templar properties to the Hospitallers. Regarding the Templars themselves,

> The end eventually came with the decree of abolition in March 1312, although this was clearly less than the king had wanted, for the Order was not condemned as such . . . The bull *Ad providam* (2 May 1312) transferred the Order's property not to the French crown but to the Hospitallers . . . As for the Templars themselves, a distinction was made between those who had been reconciled to the Church or against whom nothing had been found, and those claimed to have relapsed or to have remained impenitent. Most of those in the first category received pensions and some even continued to live in former Templar houses; others were sent to the houses of other orders like those of the Cistercians or Augustinians . . . The relapsed and impenitent received various terms and degrees of imprisonment . . . while the leaders were reserved for papal judgment, a decision which was to lead to the Grand Master's dramatic death by burning in 1314.[45]

Four officials of the Order (along with other Templars) had been imprisoned from the time of the suppression in 1312. On 8 March 1314, as Partner tells us: "The four main officials of the Order were brought for final judgment before a small commission of French cardinals and ecclesiastics, which included the Archbishop of Sens who had in so timely a manner burned 54 Templars in May 1310. The Church Council . . . proceeded to condemn the four men to perpetual imprisonment, assuming that this would be the end of the whole matter."[46]

But they were wrong. In an extraordinary moment, Grand Master Jacques de Molay, and Geoffrey de Charny, his treasurer, bravely denied all confessions of guilt and defended the innocence and holiness of the Order. Surprised and disturbed by this unexpected drama, the churchmen turned the two men over to the French authorities. King Philip immediately had them both burned at the stake. The event took place on a small island in the middle of the Seine opposite the royal gardens on 18 March 1314.

But as history has shown, the influence of the Templars did not end there. To the contrary—and no doubt to Philip's dismay, if he could know—the Templar "mythos" gained new life. Legend has it that as he was dying, engulfed by flames, de Molay uttered what has become famous as his "curse:"

> According to tradition, he called his persecutors—Pope Clement and King Philippe—to join him and account for themselves before God within the year. Within a month Pope Clement was dead, supposedly from a sudden onslaught of dysentery. By the end of the year Philippe was dead as well, from causes that remain obscure to this day . . . The apparent fulfillment of the Grand Master's curse lent credence to belief in the Order's occult powers. Nor did the curse end there. According to legend, it was to cast a pall over the French royal line far into the future. And thus echoes of the Templars' supposed mystic powers reverberated down the centuries.[47]

A "lost document" from the Vatican archives?

On 30 March 2002, an article in the *London Times* claimed that a lost document from the Vatican archives may show the Pope had pardoned the Templars. This article naturally attracted much interest and spawned some controversy. To quote from its first part:

> *L'Avvenire*, the Catholic daily, said that the record of the Pope's investigation was thought to have been lost when Napoleon looted the Vatican during his invasion of Italy in the 18th century, and that its rediscovery was an exceptional event. The Templar Grand Master, Jacques de Molay, was burnt at the stake on the orders of Philip IV of France . . . who coveted the Templar order's land and treasure and began a campaign of dawn arrests and torture in 1307. At least 2,000 Knights were killed in an attempt to obliterate the order altogether . . . Barbara Frale, a researcher at the Vatican School of Paleontology, said that the consensus among historians was that Clement V . . . had been pliant and weak, and had colluded in Philip the Fair's scheme to wipe out the Templars and seize their fortune.[48]

This account broadly reflects what we know from the historical record. However, the only Templars executed were in France, and the total number of full knights was about *one* thousand (there were about two thousand members in all). When the French occupied Rome in 1808, many of the Vatican archives were moved to Paris, in part because, as is well known, Napoleon had great interest in the Knights Templar. After his exile, the archives were returned to Rome. The article goes on to say:

> But documents found in the Vatican archives, including a long-lost parchment, proved that the Pope had in fact maneovered "with skill and determination" to ensure that his own emissaries questioned de Molay and other leading Templars in the dungeons of Chinon castle in the Loire in 1308 . . . [49]
>
> Noting that de Molay and the [five] [*sic*] knights had asked his pardon, the Pope wrote: "We hereby decree that they are absolved by the church and may again receive Christian sacraments."[50]

More specifically, as we know from the historical record, the Pope had sent three of his cardinals to question the imprisoned senior Templar leaders in 1308, especially the top five officers—Grand Master de Molay, Hugh de Pairaud (financial head of the Order), and the preceptors of Normandy, Cyprus, and Aquitaine and Poitou. He felt the Templars' arrest was not under the king's jurisdiction but was a *papal* issue, and he wanted to get the story straight from the Templars themselves. But this is when these Templar leaders did the seemingly inexplicable thing in retracting their earlier retractions—perhaps by then they had lost faith in the Pope's ability to protect them, so they returned to their original confessions and then asked to be reconciled to the Church. As we know, the Pope did absolve these five from their sins—in his capacity as a priest, forgiving them as individuals. This is not the same as a papal verdict, and conferring individual absolution is not the same thing as exonerating the entire Order. However, as we saw earlier, the charges against the Order itself were judged "not proven," as historians know from the 5 June 1311 findings of the papal commission.

The article in the *Times* also discusses the charges:

> The Pope had accepted the Knights' explanation that the charges against them of sodomy and blasphemy were due to a misunderstanding of arcane rituals behind closed doors which had their origins in the Crusaders' bitter struggle against the Muslims, or Saracens . . . These included "denying Christ and spitting on the Cross three times" . . . [etc.] . . . these were intended to simulate the kind of humiliation and torture that a Crusader might be subjected to by the Saracens if captured.[51]

That is, like a modern-day intelligence agency or elite military group, the Templars may have learned various survival techniques to use in case they were captured by the enemy, as nineteenth-century scholars such as Jules Michelet have postulated. In her book *L'ultima battaglia dei Templari* (*The Last Battle of the Templars*), Barbara Frale concludes that the Templars had a form of a humiliation ceremony, akin to those conducted by some modern military organizations, and that such "hazing" practices may have been part of admission to the Order. Frale says the papal commissioners carefully investigated this hazing ceremony, and although they declared it not heretical per se, demanded that it cease immediately. However, until historians can see the actual dated document in its original Latin, nothing definitive can be said.

Moreover, unanswered questions remain: If there was a hazing ceremony, why didn't the imprisoned Templars simply say so, explain what it was about, and receive absolution? Furthermore, if the Pope had in fact already absolved de Molay in 1308, why didn't he object when the Grand Master was executed as a relapsed heretic? Perhaps it was because of the Pope's own political troubles and fear of a schism in the Church. Frale is currently working on another book that will discuss this "lost document" and her interesting theory about it, so further insights into these issues may be forthcoming.

Did the Templars
have the Ark?

Extraordinary courage and perseverance being Templar characteristics, many have wondered why Grand Master Jacques de Molay did not more vigorously defend the Order. Some conjecture he may have "lost his mind" due to torture and prolonged imprisonment while in his sixties. Yet at the end of his long ordeal, he did make an impassioned defending speech that was coherent by all accounts. Some wonder if he was "stalling for time," perhaps hoping to see the Pope himself, as he had requested. Perhaps he thought further negotiations could be worked out.

Others speculate he might have been stalling for a different reason: Perhaps he wanted a private audience with the Pope because there was something so secret and important that it could only be discussed with Clement himself; although he certainly would have sought absolution, could something else have been at stake here, too?

Proponents of this theory also ask: Since King Philip was married to the daughter of the Count of Champagne, could he possibly have heard through her that the Knights Templar had found something of immense value and importance in the Holy Land that was guarded in great secrecy—like the Ark of the Covenant?

The Ark of the Covenant, constructed during the Israelites' wanderings in the desert and used until the destruction of the First Temple, was the primary symbol of the Jewish faith in ancient times. Described in the Old Testament as a chest made of acacia wood and gold-plated inside and out, it was considered the single physical manifestation of Yahweh on earth. Scholars have debated its precise contents and generally conclude that it may have held the first tablets of the Law and the second tablets of the Law, known as the Ten Commandments, remained unbroken. Some authorities believe the Ark also contained a golden vessel of manna and the rod of Aaron.

Obsessed with his own divine right to rule and eager to have his grandfather Louis IX canonized, the ambitious Philip would certainly have coveted an object like the Ark, prompting him to go after the Templars with a vengeance. "There was, after all, the palatine Chapel of Saint Chapelle in Paris waiting to receive it," as Patrick Byrne, an English Masonic researcher, points out.[52]

If, as Byrne further speculates,

> de Molay had been subjected to special torture in order to wrest the whereabouts of the Ark from him, that would help explain his collapse under torture. Assuming for a moment that this supposition is correct, we can speculate whether the Ark was still in Cyprus at that time or whether it had been removed from the Paris temple . . . In either eventuality, King Philip would have been unable to gain possession because, if it were still in France, then it is unlikely that any of those arrested would have known the location.[53]

So, the story goes, Philip would have desperately wanted to learn the precise location of such a priceless holy object. The rank-and-file Templars would not have been in on such a secret, according to Byrne. There are apparently no primary sources giving direct evidence of the physical torture of de Molay, as some historians point out, but this of course does not mean that it did not happen. Byrne implies, moreover, that de Molay's torture would have been not only physical—emotionally, it would have been very painful for him to appear to his brothers as though he was not defending the Order, when in fact he was trying to protect their greatest secret, according to Byrne.

Perhaps de Molay was hoping his brothers in distant Cyprus (or wherever the Ark may have been) could move the Ark in time to save it from Philip's greedy hands. There are persistent accounts, however legendary, that the Ark was in Ethiopia during this time. Historians know a rather large contingent of Ethiopian diplomatic envoys visited the Pope at Avignon in 1306—the year before the Templars' arrest. They do not know, however, exactly what was discussed. Byrne asks: Did the Ethiopians inform the Pope that the Templars had the Ark in their country, and could they have warned him of a possible power threat? Could they have also asked for his help in eliminating the Templars—something that would have been in the interests of both parties, as well as the French king? We will learn more about this theory in chapter 6. Byrne believes de Molay may have even feigned insanity to deter the inquisitors from submitting him to excruciating torture and to gain a bit more time to see what unfolded. If de Molay did know that the Order had the Ark, yet did not know its exact location, perhaps he felt that by "confessing" soon after imprisonment—as he did—he could somehow eventually negotiate something with the Pope.

Byrne comments about King Philip's behavior throughout this entire affair:

> For someone who is purported to have been very short of funds, he was remarkably generous with his key helpers, Nogaret, Plaissans and now Presles, all of whom finished up incredibly wealthy . . . De Presles became very wealthy indeed. A number of royal rents were made over to him together with a house and revenues at Courdemaine and a manor near Filan. His wealth continued to multiply and within only a few years he was the largest landowner in the lower valley of Aisne.[54]

What did Raoul de Presles do to earn such favor from the king? According to Byrne, de Presles was not a Templar but a lawyer, a royal advocate, who had spent several years advising the bailiffs of Laon in Champagne, where he had befriended the local Templar Master. Then:

> Sometime around 1305, Presles moved to Paris where he became an advocate of the *parlement*. It was during his time in Laon that as a Royal official he became "very friendly" with the Master of the local preceptory, one Gervais de Beauvais. Presles was to open a window onto the reasons behind the secrecy of the Chapters' secret meetings. He told how Beauvais had spoken to him about a certain "point":

"So extraordinary and so well concealed that the same Gervais would rather have his head cut off than see the point revealed."[55]

Byrne informs us that the term "point" refers to a long-lost secret of a Master Mason. Apparently, according to Byrne's research, there was a second such "point" that Beauvais had told de Presles; he also said that Beauvais had acquainted him with his book containing the Rule and that there was *another* secret book which he "would not be able to show him for all the world."[56] Many believe de Presles simply fabricated this testimony for his own personal gain, and this may be so. However, Byrne believes otherwise:

> The substance of the story is so supportive of the suggestion that the Knights Templar had possession of the Ark of the Covenant as to warrant further consideration. The reference to the secret as being a "point" must draw us to the Masonic ritual where the "long lost secret of a Master Mason" is called a "point." The reference to another "book" also bears a remarkable similarity to my interpretation of later Masonic ritual that the "word" is used as a metaphor for the Ark. The big, unanswerable question is—did Presles get this information from Beauvais, or someone in the Court of Champagne? One thing is for sure, however, and this is that Presles reported the matter to either the king or someone very close to the king.[57]

So, the reasoning goes, was King Philip especially grateful to de Presles for such intelligence about the Templars? Did the king then come to believe they possessed the Ark? Of course, the medieval Templars were certainly not the Freemasons, but, as some have attempted to claim, they may have been the predecessors for Freemasonry. John Robinson, in his recent book, *Born in Blood*, examines this theory further, and it is still studied and hotly debated by Masonic researchers today.

Byrne believes the Royal Arch Masonic ritual may refer to the discovery of the Ark of the Covenant by the Knights Templar. The ritual of the Royal Arch ceremony is constructed around the building of the second, or perhaps the third, temple on Mount Moriah, in Jerusalem. The purpose of the second temple on Mount Moriah, according to Byrne, was the same as the Tabernacle and King

Solomon's temple—it was specifically built to house the Ark of the Covenant.[58] Byrne believes that the Ark ultimately ended up in France, near Rennes-le-Chateau, and that it is still in the hands of a secret group today—a highly speculative theory we will examine further in chapter 6.

Some theorists conjecture that if Ethiopian envoys visited the Pope at Avignon in 1306 to inform him that the Templars had the Ark, and if de Presles provided King Philip with the same information—and was handsomely rewarded for doing so—then perhaps both of them knew this secret. Moreover, Philip may have had an infiltrator in Clement's camp as well. As Byrne implies, could *both* the king and the Pope have found out, each through his own channels, that the Templars supposedly had the Ark? Obviously, neither the Pope nor the king would have ever revealed how he had learned about something so sensitive, and that is why the historical record does not show it—or so the story goes. And again, if de Molay also knew the Templars had the Ark, yet could not reveal it, could this be why he seems to have stalled for time or acted inexplicably on occasion? Of course, we have no definitive proof either way. Historians believe King Philip probably wanted to start another crusade and coveted the Templars' wealth either to create his own military Order or to make one of his sons the Grand Master of the Templars. While this remains a good possibility, it, too, ultimately leaves some questions unanswered.

What happened to the Templar archives?

Malcolm Barber says of the incalculable loss of the central Templar archive:

> At some point after the suppression (1312), the central archive of the Order, containing charters which would have been so important for the reconstruction of its activities in the east, disappeared altogether . . . The loss for the serious historian is incalculable . . . The Templar archives must have been kept in the Temple of Solomon until 1187, but there is no evidence about their fate between the capture of Jerusalem by Saladin in October of that year and the

re-establishment of the Christians in Acre in 1191 ... Yet, today, this archive has completely vanished; only two documents survive which appear to be transcripts from originals in the Templar collection from the east ... The most obvious inference, therefore, is that the archive survived the disasters of 1291 and was taken over by the Hospital in 1312.[59]

The most likely development is that the central Templar archive was taken to Cyprus after the evacuation of Acre in 1291 and remained there. Legends say that if the Templars did have the Ark, then Kolossi Castle on Cyprus would have been a logical resting place for it. After the Order was suppressed, the archive probably remained there along with the Hospitaller documents relating to Cyprus. Then in 1571, the Turks conquered the island and both sets of documents were destroyed. That the Hospitallers' Cypriot documents have also never been found strongly supports this scenario.

The woeful lack of records that survived such turmoil means we have little documentation about the Templars in the Holy Land. Thus speculation is rife. Historians are trying to piece together what happened from other extant Templar records, like cartularies and charters, though these mostly pertain to the European Templars. They have unraveled much of the story, but many questions remain. Fortunately, records and sources are being found all the time. Perhaps one day a key document will be discovered that will shed more light on the events of the downfall of the Templar Order.

The aftermath

What happened to the Templars after the suppression in 1312? Where did they go? Did they manage to escape, supposedly taking their treasures and documents with them?

The papal bull *Ad providam,* issued on 2 May 1312, declared that since property owned by the Knights Templar had originally been donated for sustaining the crusading effort in the Holy Land, it should continue to be used for that purpose. So all property and lands were to be transferred to the Order of the Hospital of St. John. The only exceptions were the Templar properties in Portugal, Castille, and

Majorca, which were to be transferred to local crusading Orders. This sounds simple enough, but in some cases these arrangements took quite some time to carry out.

Templar knights who were still in custody would be allowed to live on what had been Templar properties, and those who had been absolved and reconciled to the Church were to be treated fairly and even given pensions. Many ended up joining other monastic communities, such as the Cistercians.

As we know, the worst treatment of the Templars had occurred in France under King Philip's control. But contrary to popular belief, not all Templars were tortured in prison or burned at the stake. In fact, thousands survived. As historian Edward Burman points out in *Supremely Abominable Crimes*, the majority of Templars were freed after 1312:

> But how many of the 14 or 15,000 Templars of all ranks . . . were given their freedom after Pope Clement's 1312 constitution? How many had survived Philip the Fair's onslaught? The answer must be most of them. Thousands. Retellings of the legend often give the impression that *all* members of the Order of the Temple died between 1307 and 1312, or were at least imprisoned for life. The truth was quite different . . . Ironically, there is no need to fabricate stories of dramatic escapes or local survivals in order to sustain continuation myths. There really were a lot of ex-Templars around: some repentant, some camouflaged, and some still proud of their own and the Order's past—like many old soldiers.[60]

Outside of France, the situation for the Templars after the 1307 arrests and the 1312 suppression of the Order was often quite different. Not surprisingly, where torture was used, the prisoners often confessed to the charges; in locales where no torture was allowed, they would be found innocent. This pattern appeared in nearly every country. Although unanswered questions remain about if, when, where, or how the medieval Templars may have survived, historians know a fair amount. Many theories exist about where the Templars may have fled to or what may have happened to their treasure, and of course this book cannot begin to cover all of them. But we will start with what historians say took place in each country, particularly after the arrest orders in 1307.

Aragon, Majorca, Castile, and Portugal

Considering the gravity of the situation in France, the treatment of the Templars on the Iberian peninsula was less severe. In Aragon, after 1307, they took refuge in their castles and appealed to the Aragonese king and the Pope, declaring their innocence. At first, after receiving the arrest orders, James II of Aragon strongly defended the Templars. He even wrote to the Pope himself, as well as to the kings of neighboring Castille and Portugal, saying that as his predecessors had believed the Order was without error and had always labored for the exaltation of the faith, he wanted more information before he took any action. He held out against King Philip's pressuring until late November 1307, but then finally ordered the Templars' arrest. It seems he was trying to appear to cooperate with Philip. He besieged the Templar castles—though not without a fight, as the last Templar castle did not surrender until 1309. The Templars were imprisoned, but as little torture was used due to Aragonese law, none of the brothers confessed to any charges, much to the Pope and King Philip's displeasure. The papal inquiry in Aragon did not even start until January of 1310; and although some torture was used in 1311 on eight Templars in Barcelona, on orders from the Pope, still none confessed. The Templars were found innocent in Aragon, and in 1312 the Church council at Tarragona released them all and gave them pensions.

Majorca was closely associated with the Aragonese crown. However, its lands were more scattered and included not only the Balearic Islands but also the mainland French counties of Roussillon and Cerdagne, as well as the Lordship of Montpellier. Apparently King James I of Majorca did not resist papal authority to the extent that James II of Aragon did, as the arrests of the Templars occurred fairly soon after the 22 November 1307 orders. Barber describes the ensuing events:

> Most of the documentation for this kingdom comes from Roussillon, which was in the diocese of the Bishop of Elne, and relates to the Templars of the important Preceptory of Mas Deu, of which Ramon Sa Guardia was the commander. Mas Deu had command of seven subsidiary preceptories, and the personnel were scattered, mostly in

ones and twos, in these dependencies. At the time of the arrest, twenty-six members were taken into custody, to which number was added Ramon Sa Guardia in August 1309 after he had been extradited from Aragon. Probably these men were little different from those arrested in the Kingdom of France, mostly following peaceful agricultural pursuits. Despite the reasonably efficient arrests, no hearings began before 1310. Ramon Costa, Bishop of Elne, was the suffragan of Gilles Aicelin, Archbishop of Narbonne, from whom Ramon received the relevant documents ... The Archbishop ordered that the papal commands be carried out in a letter dated 5 May 1309, but the Bishop of Elne did not begin his inquiry until Wednesday 14 January 1310, explaining that the delay had been caused by his illness and that even now he was not fully recovered ... During the second half of January, the commission heard the depositions of twenty-five Templars ... All these men unambiguously asserted their innocence.[61]

Guy Patton and Robin Mackness, in *Web of Gold*, examine the importance of the Languedoc-Roussillon area, and the commandery of Mas Deu in particular, in relation to the fate of the "lost treasures" of the Temple of Jerusalem. They believe that the Templars of Mas Deu, situated in the remote valleys of the Corbieres, may have been the custodians of the Templar wealth—and perhaps something far more valuable. Some have asked: Could the bishop of Elne's prolonged illness and the apparent attempt to drag out the proceedings have something to do with Patton's theory?

In the kingdom of Castile-Leon, the Templars were arrested sometime during 1308, as we know that two commissions were set up in August of that year. At Medina del Campo, the archbishop of Compostela questioned thirty Templars and three witnesses but found nothing incriminating, as no confessions were made. Wasserman tells us that "after their acquittal, many surviving Castilian Templars went off to live as anchorites in the mountains. It is said that after death their bodies remained incorruptible in eloquent testimony to their innocence and martyrdom."[62]

In Portugal, the bishop of Lisbon conducted an inquiry at Orense, before which twenty-eight Templars and six other witnesses appeared. Again, nothing incriminating was found. The provincial councils, too, found nothing, so no confessions were obtained in Portugal.

The Templar properties on the Iberian peninsula, especially in Portugal and Valencia—which was part of Aragon—largely stayed in Templar hands. In 1317—ten years after the arrests—the Pope approved the founding of two new military Orders. The new Order in Portugal, set up by King Diniz in 1319, with its central house at Tomar, was called the Order of Christ. It received the Templar lands directly. The Knights of the Order of Christ were deeply involved in the exploratory and missionary activities of the Portuguese. Prince Henry the Navigator became Grand Master of the Order in 1420, and Vasco da Gama was also a Knight of Christ.

The Order of Montesa, headquartered in Valencia, began in July 1319 when James II of Aragon gave it the castle of Montesa. The Order received both the Templars' and the Hospitallers' lands in Valencia—in compensation for which the Hospitallers received the former Templar lands in the remainder of Aragon.[63]

Other Spanish Orders, such as the Knights of Santiago (founded in 1158) and the Orders of Calatrava and Alcantara, were said to have taken refugee Templars into their ranks as well.

Italy

Compared with the numbers of Templars arrested in other parts of Europe, the number in Italy seems small. Only seven papal and epis-copal commissions were set up. Little documentation has survived, but historians have pieced together a picture of what happened. Hardly any witnesses were found for the inquiries, so it seems many Templars were able to flee.

Local rulers responded variously. The only unified monarchy was that of Charles II, King of Naples. Being an uncle of Philip IV in France, he no doubt toed the French line and used torture, as some forty-eight Templars were rounded up and killed. In the papal states, no record exists of the initial seizures, but, as Barber informs us, "a commission . . . did perambulate the region, visiting Rome, Viterbo, Spoleto, Aquila, Penne, Chieti, Albano, Segni, Castle Fajole, Tivoli and Palombara between October 1309 and July 1310."[64] But nothing came of it, as no Templars confessed and witnesses were scarce. In Lombardy, the authorities refused to use torture, even against the orders of the Pope, and the Templars were found innocent.

In Venice, the state ran the investigation and the Templars were not even arrested! In Ravenna, only seven Templars were brought before the inquiry, and they were found innocent. In Tuscany, the archbishop of Pisa and the bishop of Florence held inquiries in Florence in September of 1311. Here the use of torture was legal. Not surprisingly, some Templars were found guilty; out of the thirteen brothers interrogated, six confessed.

In 1318, Pope John XXII, the successor to Clement V, completely contradicted Clement's earlier rulings about the Templars in Naples. He commanded that the religious Orders there support the surviving Knights Templar and said their vows remained in force; for instance, they could not marry. He obviously did not believe they had been heretics.

Germany

In Germany, matters concerning the arrests sometimes became heated, as, by and large, the Templars were quite popular. Much depended on the local rulers and their political inclinations. For example, at Trier a number of witnesses were heard, and the Order was acquitted.

The archbishop of Magdeburg was not at all favorable toward the Templars; he stormed one of their castles and imprisoned a number of them, including the Preceptor of Germany. This angered the bishop of Halberstadt, a Templar ally, who, believing his rights had been infringed upon (as the castle was in his territory), excommunicated the archbishop! The Templars escaped. Pope Clement V was thus forced to intervene, and he revoked the excommunication in September 1310.

One of the most dramatic incidents connected with the Templar trials occurred in Mainz, where the archbishop was conducting an inquiry. On 14 May 1310, while the council was in session, the archbishop was "suddenly confronted by Hugh of Salm, Templar Preceptor at Grumbach, who burst in accompanied by twenty fully armed knights. The archbishop, clearly frightened, asked the Preceptor to be seated and if he had anything that he wished to put to them."[65] Hugh of Salm said he and the other knights understood that this council was assembled on the Pope's orders for the express purpose of destroying the Order and that the Templars had been charged with heinous crimes. This was harsh and unfair, as they had been condemned without a proper hearing or conviction—and so they had now come to appeal to a future Pope and all his clergy for justice. Hugh also declared that the Templars who had constantly denied these enormities "had been delivered up to the fire, but that God had shown their innocence by a miracle, for the red cross and white mantle which they wore would not burn. The archbishop, frightened that there would be a riot, admitted their protest and replied that he would take the matter up with the Pope."[66]

The council adjourned after this incident until the first of July. Then, in another moment of high drama, Frederick of Salm, Hugh's brother and Preceptor of the Rhine, offered to prove the Order's innocence by submission to the red-hot-iron ordeal. He told the council that he had been twelve years in the Order and had had extensive experience in Outremer, where he knew Jacques de Molay well. The Grand Master he "held and still held to be a good Christian, as good as any Christian could be." In all, thirty-seven Templars deposed and asserted their innocence. Twelve outside witnesses, three of whom were Counts, also spoke in favor of the Order.[67]

Ultimately, the archbishop of Mainz declared the Order innocent—a decision that Pope Clement angrily annulled.

Many Templars in Germany were not even initially arrested, and their later fate is unknown.[68] Some German Templar lands were turned over to the Hospitallers, but many were returned to the families who had originally donated them to the Order. In 1317, German Templars were allowed to join the Hospitallers, but others either fled or possibly joined other Orders.

Switzerland and Austria

Alan Butler and Stephen Dafoe, in *The Warriors and the Bankers*, theorize about a possible Templar survival in what is now Switzerland. They point out that Templar symbolism appears on the flags of certain Swiss cantons, that the Red Cross originated in Switzerland, and that Switzerland is a world banking center as well as a center for Protestantism. They believe it no coincidence that the Swiss national flag, a white cross on a red field, is a simple reversal of the most famous

Templar symbol. There are also a number of folk tales about "white-clad knights" fighting bloody battles for the fledgling confederation.[69]

Regarding Austria, Rayelan Allan, author of *Diana, Queen of Heaven*, offers an unusual but intriguing theory. She suggests that surviving Templars created the Austro-Hungarian empire and that it was largely built and financed by Templar wealth and information. Much of this wealth, Allan says, was actually the Templar gold obtained from the Temple of Solomon; it has essentially been fought over ever since by competing vested interests. She believes Hitler knew this, which explains why he looted the Austrian treasury in 1939. Controversial as this theory may be, one thing seems certain—at the time of the arrests in 1307, the bulk of the Templar gold was definitely not in the Paris Templar headquarters' treasury, much to the chagrin of King Philip IV and his men. Theories, including this one, concerning the fate of that treasure have lingered ever since.

England

King Edward II of England did not believe the charges against the Templars were true, so he did not immediately act against them, even though Philip IV of France was his father-in-law. There is no evidence that Edward had any personal or political animosity against the Order; in fact, the Templars had long served his family loyally. Remarkably, Edward wrote to the Pope himself, saying the charges were the work of the evil-minded. However, "when he received the papal bull *Pastoralis praeemienitiae* and instructions to arrest the Templars, his own soul was put in jeopardy and he acted."[70] At this point, he basically "turned against the Templars."[71] Lord describes the events surrounding the Templars' arrest: On 15 December 1307, "an order was sent to all county sheriffs telling them to choose 24 men to attend them early in the morning on the next Sunday to hear what was contained in a sealed mandate . . . from the king." On 26 December, "Edward wrote to the Pope telling him he had done what was required, although the arrests did not take place until 9–10 January 1308." On 30 December, "the sealed mandates were prepared and given to royal clerks to deliver to the sheriffs."[72] Clearly, the King had done as much as he thought necessary at that point. "He did it legally through a royal writ, he assured that an inventory was taken of the

Templars' possessions that was witnessed by one of the Order, and he made sure they were not to be kept in close confinement. He . . . made sure they were treated honourably."[73]

The Templars were arrested and taken by county sheriffs to the nearest royal castles: at Newcastle upon Tyne, York, Lincoln, Cambridge, Oxford, Warwick, and Canterbury. "It was to the latter that William de la More, Master of the Templars in England, and other officers of the Order were taken, having been arrested at Temple Ewell."[74] Their estates were placed in the hands of keepers. The remaining Templars were apparently put on open arrest, since "shortly before the papal inquisitors arrived, Edward sent a hurried notice to his sheriffs telling them to re-arrest all Templars still at large."[75] The sheriffs, however, were seemingly unenthusiastic, especially in York. In Kent, too, Templars were believed to have remained roaming "at large," supposedly in disguise. As Lord points out, "This laxity must have been shocking to the papal inquisitors fresh from the harsh regime meted out to the Templars in France. A second shock was in store for them, as English law did not permit torture, so no confessions had been arranged for them in advance, and they could not extract these by physical means."[76]

Clearly irritated, the papal inquisitors kept pressuring Edward II to allow the use of torture. Finally, in December 1309, he succumbed. However, no one was prepared to torture the brothers. In a letter of 16 June 1310 to the archbishop of Canterbury, the inquisitors "complained that they could find no one to carry out tortures properly and that the procedure ought to be by ecclesiastical law as in France."[77] In other words, they wanted to use torture, as the French had done, but were prevented by English law. The inquisitors went on to recommend eight ways to speed up the proceedings, the most extraordinary of which was to send all of the English Templars to the county of Ponthieu, just across the Channel. (Although Ponthieu was one of Edward II's lands, it was not under English law per se.) Fortunately, this did not happen, as all of the English Templars were tried in England.

"It now seems that a more concerted effort was made by the king to enforce the demands for torture; on 26 August and the 6 and 23 October he ordered procedure 'according to ecclesiastical law.'"[78] So some torture was applied in England. But it was apparently still not enough to satisfy the Pope. Clement by this time had presumably become rather desperate about the situation in England. In his letter to Edward II dated 23 December 1310, he "offered the king remission of sins and the eternal mercy of God if the trial could be transferred to Ponthieu."[79]

Since events were not preceding smoothly for the inquisitors in England, they used a high proportion of witnesses from outside the Order. In France, where brutal torture resulted in many confessions, hardly any outside witnesses were called—only 6 out of the 231 extant depositions. But in the British Isles there were 60 outside witnesses in England alone, plus 41 in Ireland and 49 in Scotland. Of the outside witnesses in England, only 6 were *not* ecclesiastics! All in all, 144 English Templars were questioned.

At last, in London, three Templars confessed. But in the diocese of York no torture was used, and so no brothers confessed. The three who made the standard confessions to the charges were absolved and reconciled with the Church. In order to please the Pope, a compromise was achieved in 1311. All of the English Templars declared that the whole Order was now so defamed that the members were unable to purge themselves. So, in Lord's words: "All but two of those remaining in prison confessed publicly that they abjured all heresies, they asked for penances, forgiveness and absolutions and for reconciliation with the Church. Those who were able did this on the steps of St. Paul's Cathedral, and the elderly and infirm in the chapel of St. Mary, Barking. They were given a pension . . . and sent to monasteries across the country."[80]

Grand Master William de la More, as well as Himbert Blanke, Preceptor of the Auvergne, who was in England at the time, both adamantly refused to ask for absolution for something they had not done. De la More died in the Tower of London in February 1311; Blanke also died in prison. But compared to the fate of de Molay and the Templars in France, their deaths were peaceful.

In England, problems arose concerning the transfer of Templar estates to the Hospitallers. Edward II had not only placed keepers in the manors but had given some manors away and allocated the revenues of others, and the descendants of those who had made the grants in the first place now wanted the properties back. "Even when the Hospitallers did at last acquire some of the Templar properties, they found heavy outgoings on these . . . Many of the estates were derelict with mills no longer working and buildings in disrepair . . . [Edward] did nothing when he received the bull . . . referring the matter to Parliament and refusing the Prior of the Hospitallers permission to take over the lands until Parliament agreed to this. Once more it was only the threat of excommunication that eventually made him concede the estates to the Hospitallers."[81]

Put another way, Edward II had been using Templar lands to reward his friends and finance his Scottish campaigns, so he was reluctant to let them go. It was 1324 before the title deeds were given to the Hospitallers. The Hospitallers had to go to the English Parliament as late as 1334 to confirm their right to the Templar lands, but even with this confirmation, they didn't get the title to the London Temple until 1340. Lengthy litigation continued with the families who had originally given the lands to the Temple, and some lands were never transferred, as evidenced by a 1338 inquest of holdings, which revealed that at least thirteen estates had still not been turned over by that date.[82]

Scotland

According to Lord, only two Templars were arrested in Scotland, and both were English:

> Walter Clifton had been in the Order ten years and was Preceptor of Balantradoch, and William Middleton had been at Balantradoch but was then the Preceptor of Culter. They were called to answer the articles against them on 17 November 1309 in front of the Bishop of St. Andrews and the papal nuncio, John de Solerio. Both said that their receptions had been according to the Rule . . . Fifty hostile witnesses were called, including a number of heads of religious houses, friars and rectors. Hugh, the Abbot of Dunfermline, said he had heard of the clandestine reception of brothers. Patrick, the Prior of Holyrood, said that he had heard this as well. Servants from Balantradoch said they knew of secret meetings at night. A number of the Scottish nobility, including Henry and William St. Clair, said they heard things against the brothers' secret receptions, and that their fathers said that the Templars had lost the Holy Land.[83]

The situation in Scotland in 1307 was unique in all of Europe, as the Pope had recently excommunicated King Robert the Bruce for murdering a rival to the throne. As Baigent and Leigh, in *The Temple and the Lodge*, explain:

> In 1306, a year before the persecution of the Temple began, Bruce himself had been ex-communicated, and was to remain at odds with the Papacy for another twelve years. Because he had ceased to be recognised by the Pope, it was impossible for Rome to treat with him or impose her will in his domains. In effect, the papal writ no longer ran in Scotland—or, at least, those parts of Scotland which Bruce controlled, and which lay, therefore, "beyond the pale." And thus, in those parts of Scotland, the decree which abolished the Temple elsewhere in Europe was not, in accordance with the strict letter of the law, applicable. If knights of the Order, fleeing persecution on the Continent, hoped to find a refuge anywhere, it would have been under Bruce's protection. A spate of archaic legends and traditions has for centuries linked Bruce with the Templars.[84]

One such legend is that refugee Templars may have helped Bruce win his stunning victory at the Battle of Bannockburn in 1314. During this battle, which decided the issue of Scottish nationhood, the Scots had a sudden, unexpected advent of fresh forces at a critical moment, causing Edward II and five hundred of his best knights to flee the field. Panic spread through the English ranks but not, apparently, among the Scots. Baigent and Leigh pose the question: Was this mysterious contingent a group of Templars—who, once recognized, would have understandably invoked such fear? Scottish historians still debate precisely how the Battle of Bannockburn was won. And some Scottish researchers now believe, however controversially, that Templars may have fought on *both* sides of the battle, which would have occurred about two years after the 1312 suppression of the Order. The theory goes that some Templars may have fled to Scotland, where the papal edict had little or no effect and they could help Bruce, while others were loyal to Edward and England.

Another persistent legend is that a network of families, many of the Scottish nobility who served in the Scots Guard, may have provided a conduit for a Scottish Templar tradition after the 1312 suppression.

Proponents of a Scottish Templar perpetuation also like to point out that Bruce, a descendant of David I, married the daughter of the Earl of Ulster, so he would have had access to support and manpower from Ireland to aid his cause against the English. Historians know so because by January 1310, Edward II was angered by reports of Bruce receiving shipments of weapons, equipment, and materials from Ireland and officially proclaimed: "The king commands the Chancellor and Treasurer of Ireland to proclaim all towns, ports . . . prohibiting under the highest penalties all the exportation of provisions, horses, armour and other supplies . . . to the insurgent Scots, which he hears is carried on by merchants in Ireland."[85]

Historians believe that whatever weapons and armor may have been in Ireland probably got there from the Continent. Baigent and Leigh suggest that contingents of the Scottish forces were already being trained by refugee Templars, who were, after all, the most disciplined and professional soldiery in Europe at the time, and who could have brought with them from the Holy Land the kind of Saracen tactics that Bruce had now adopted. As for arms from the Continent finding their way to Ireland and thence to Scotland, "it is hard to imagine a more likely conduit for such traffic than the Temple—whose installations in Ireland, when raided by royal authorities, proved . . . to be virtually denuded of weaponry."[86]

Was there possibly a "Celtic alliance" to aid Bruce in trying to establish a Celtic kingdom of Scotland? Of course, Baigent and Leigh are purely speculating, but the circumstantial evidence does look interesting. Moreover, the Battle of Bannockburn occurred on St. John's Day, 24 June 1314, a day of special significance for the Templars.

What happened to the Templar lands in Scotland after the Order was suppressed? The situation, from what little we know about it, seems to have been complex, with roots in the early history of Scottish Templarism.

David I, King of Scotland in the twelfth century, made the new warrior-monks welcome and formed a Scottish headquarters for the Order. Lands were granted by David I at Balantradoch, now called "Temple," a village about four miles from Roslin and six miles south of Edinburgh. The Balantradoch/Temple lands would have come under the jurisdiction of the Sheriff of Lothian, Sir William St. Clair, the Fourth Baron of Rosslyn. Unfortunately, none of the surnames of

Templars in Scotland at that time are recorded. A medieval Scottish version of the Templar Rule, written in Latin, still survives in the National Library of Scotland.[87] This Rule bears the title *Regula Pauperum Commilitonum Christi Templique Salommonci*, and was written by Johannes Michaelensis, who describes himself as a resident of Albanensis. "Alba," of course, was the earlier name for what is now called Scotland.

The first documented trace of the Templars in Scotland appears in a charter in the town of St. Andrews dated 1160. Two of the witnesses are "Richard of the Hospital of Jerusalem" and "Robert, *Brother of the Temple*" (emphasis mine). The Hospitallers, or the Order of St. John, was also introduced into Scotland under the reign of David I. It seems that wherever the Hospitallers gained property in most major Scottish towns, the growth of the Templar Order was also dramatic. By 1300, over six hundred properties of different types, large and small, were accounted for in the Order's holdings in Scotland, and building and maintaining them obviously required a considerable workforce. By 1312, when the Templar Order had been suppressed internationally, and although no Order of Suppression was legally issued in Scotland, the Order was essentially disbanded for all but administrative purposes.

It is rarely acknowledged that other Continental chivalric Orders also had branches in Scotland. The Order of St. Lazarus claims to have been the earliest chivalric Order in Scotland. The Teutonic Knights, who had been founded largely by German merchants from the Bremen and Lubeck Guilds, were later concerned mainly with Baltic area shipping, and they maintained a small but influential diplomatic outpost at Leith, on the Firth of Forth, adjacent to Edinburgh. This suggests a possible connection with the St. Clair family, pending further research. Other national Orders, such as the Spanish Knights of Santiago— of which the founder of Rosslyn Chapel, Sir William Sinclair, was a member—and the Portuguese Order of Christ (founded July 1319) also had small representations in Scotland. These Orders transported currency, goods, equipment, and pilgrims back and forth by sea. So obviously, medieval Scotland did not exist in a vacuum—as some have implicitly assumed, probably because they are unaware of the scale and significance of medieval maritime travel.

In Scotland, as in France, the Cistercians were known to have connections with the Knights Templar. The Rule of the Templars also had connections with the Benedictine Rule, as we know, and many Benedictines joined the Cistercians in England.

After the official dissolution of the Templars in 1312, all the lands, preceptories, and other properties owned by the Templars in Scotland were granted to the Scottish Hospitallers. In England, as we saw, the same process was a litigious, drawn-out affair; in Scotland the process, although largely amicable, seems to have been more complex and taken even longer to resolve. Strangely, with only one exception, there seems to be no evidence of the Hospitallers—or anyone else—attempting to obtain Templar property in Scotland, quite unlike the situation in England and other countries. It appears that the Hospitallers worked together in some way with the Templars in Scot-land, and probably with the full knowledge of King Robert the Bruce. For some two hundred years or so the Scottish Templar lands, legally called *Terrae Templariae*, were maintained and administered by the Scottish Order of St. John (the Hospitallers), or, in some cases according to legal documents, by a *combined* Order called "the Order of St. John and the Temple." Properties were leased and a designated official acted as an overseer and collected the rents. This person, usually re-ferred to as the "Temple bailie," reported back to the Prior of St. John at Torphichen. For example, in one legal document, an Alexander Spens is named as Temple bailie for Fife in 1490. A "bailie of the Temple lands" is named in other legal documents, pertaining to Lennox, Angus, Berwick, and Ayr.[88] A charter granted by King James IV of Scotland, dated 1488, has the interesting title *Fratribus Hospitalis Hierosolimitani, Militibus Templi Solomonis*. In this charter, the king *reaffirmed* all the ancient rights and privileges of not only the Order of St. John but also the Templars. This may indicate that as late as the fifteenth century the Scottish Templars had some kind of legal existence.[89]

However, vexing questions remain. Did the Order of St. John take into its ranks fugitive Templars? Did they foresee a revival of the Templar Order and so agreed to hold Templar lands in trust until then? Baigent and Leigh summarize:

> After 1338, the Hospitallers began to acquire Templar holdings in Scotland . . . Prior to 1338, no Templar property was passed on . . . The Templar lands, when the Hospitallers did receive them, were kept separate. They were not parcelled out, [or] integrated . . .

On the contrary, they enjoyed a special status and were administered as a self-contained unit in themselves. They were handled, in fact, not as if St. John actually owned them, but were simply, in the capacity of agents or managers, holding them in trust. As late as the end of the 16th c., no fewer than 519 sites in Scotland were listed by the Hospitallers as 'Terrae Templariae'—part, that is, of the self-contained and separ-ately administered Templar patrimony . . . For more than two centur-ies in Scotland—from the beginning of the 14th to the middle of the 16th—the Templars, it would appear, actually *merged* with the Hospitallers . . . During the period in question, there are frequent references to a *single joint Order*—the 'Order of the Knights of St. John and the Temple.'[90]

Clearly, there is a need for more research. But whatever did occur in Scotland after 1307, there seems to have been some kind of legal acknowledgment of the Templars up to the mid-sixteenth century. The two Templars who had been arrested and questioned before the inquiry were absolved and sent to Cistercian monasteries in the Borders. Many speculate that other Templars in Scotland in 1307 must have faded into the background as well, perhaps protected by this kind of legal maneuvering. Much, however, still remains unresolved today.

Ireland

The Templars came to Ireland in the second half of the twelfth century, along with the other Anglo-Norman, Welsh, Scottish, and French colonists and invaders. They were given donations of land and founded many commanderies. The earliest reference to Templars in the English royal administrative records for Ireland dates to September 1220, when Henry III's government instructed the Irish authorities to deposit proceeds with the Templars and Hospitallers, a function both Orders often performed in England. During the 1230s, the Templars were very much aligned with Henry III and his officials, and their role continued to expand in Ireland. In 1301, for example, the Templars were involved in the collection of a new custom duty in Waterford and in auditing accounts and performing other financial functions.

The Templars arrested in Ireland were sent to Dublin Castle, and it appears that most of their surnames were English.

The inquisitors arrived in Ireland in September 1309, but the trial did not start until January 1310. By this time one renegade Irish Templar, Henry Tanet, had been sent to England to give evidence that the Templars had made treaties with the Saracens. Fourteen brothers gave evidence in Ireland. Most of them had been in the Order for over 30 years, and all denied the articles against them . . . None of the witnesses could give concrete evidence, and . . . evidence against the Templars in Ireland was hearsay and lacking in proof. The Templars in Ireland did penance, were absolved and sent to Irish monasteries to repent.[91]

The Baltic island of Bornholm

One of the most interesting theories to emerge recently is that of Erling Haagensen and Henry Lincoln, who have researched little-known or rarely acknowledged links between Jerusalem, the Rennes-le-Chateau area of France, and medieval Scandinavia. In their groundbreaking book, *The Templars' Secret Island*, they show how men of influence like Bernard of Clairvaux, the Templar Grand Master Bertrand de Blanchefort, and a Danish bishop worked together in the twelfth century to preserve the secret of sacred geometry. The churches on Bornholm, a tiny Danish island in the Baltic Sea, show extraordinary mathematical skill in land surveying, geometry, and design. Moreover, they use various geometric patterns known to be of great interest to the medieval Templars. The blurb on the book's jacket says that "the trail has spanned Europe and has led as far as ancient Palestine. A further twist came when the authors found that in 1911 a forgotten Swedish-led expedition had burrowed beneath the City of David, echoing the activities of the . . . Knights Templar, almost eight hundred years earlier. What that expedition unearthed forms a bridge to the island two thousand miles away."[92]

Haagensen and Lincoln also reveal the basis for a theory of a possible medieval Templar survival within the Swedish system of Freemasonry. In the system of Freemasonry of Charles XIII, King of Sweden (1748–1818), when a member is initiated into the eighth degree, he is admitted as a Knight Templar. "The Scandinavian System insists that this is the real, but covert, continuation of the original, medieval Order and demonstrates what purports to be a most important link with the first Templars."[93]

Cyprus

After the loss of the Holy Land in 1291, Cyprus became the head-quarters for the Templar Order in the Latin East. But the situation in Cyprus was highly political for the Templars, which seems to have had direct impact on their fate. Wasserman summarizes what happened on Cyprus after the arrest order went out in 1307:

> In May 1308, the Cypriot Master of the Order and two other leaders presented themselves before the governor, proclaiming their inno-cence and that of the 118 Templars on the island. On June 1, 1308, Amaury laid siege to the Templar castle at Limassol. The Templars surrendered and were placed under limited arrest. Hearings were not held until May 1310. All those questioned proclaimed their inno-cence. Amaury de Lusignan, however was assassinated on June 5, which allowed Clement to institute new trials and make extensive use of torture to reach a more satisfactory verdict.[94]

According to Helen Nicolson, the Order could have survived if they had handled matters differently: "By assisting in the overthrow of King Henry II of Cyprus in 1306, the Order had also got a ruler in Cyprus (Amaury de Lusignan) who would support it . . . The Order could have survived and continued its military activity in the East, as the Hospital of St. John did . . . [But] in Cyprus, the murder of Amaury de Lusignan left the Order without a protector and open to the wrath of the returning King Henry II."[95]

After Henry II came back into power in 1310, he destroyed the central Templar convent on Cyprus in retaliation for the Order's support for Amaury. Nicolson comments: "The Order could not con-tinue to operate. Trial or no trial, once Henry II of Cyprus had destroyed its center of operations, the Order would have ceased to exist in the East, whatever was happening in Europe. In a sense, the trial of the Templars was irrelevant. It was their involvement in the political affairs of Cyprus . . . that directly brought about the destruc-tion of the Order."[96]

Barber recounts an incident of a very different nature on Cyprus. A knight who was sent to guard the Templars, and who did not view them favorably at all, ended up fraternizing with them:

Raymond de Bentho had seen the Templars fight against the Saracens . . . but had been sent by Amaury . . . to guard the Templars at the castle of Khirokitia, and because of what he had heard in the papal letters, his mind had been very much turned against them. He did not wish to hear mass with the Templars, nor to participate in anything with them; on the contrary he avoided their company as much as he was able. But he lacked a priest with whom he could conveniently hear mass and so one day he joined with the Templars to hear divine offices. But when the priest lifted the body of Christ to the altar, the host appeared to him as great as an *oblea* and white as snow. He told no one, but afterwards went to the priest and asked him to show him the hosts that had been used, and he saw that they were smaller . . . He believed therefore that there had been a divine miracle which had occurred because of his wrong presumptions against the Templars. Thereafter, he began to join the Templars at meals and divine services.[97]

Many theories abound about what happened to the Templars after their suppression in 1312. Much research is still being done in this area, and perhaps one day, much more light will be shed on the specific fates of the Templars and their purported treasures worldwide. One of these treasures, legend says, is the Holy Grail—an equally powerful and enduring "mystery of history." Its legacy, like that of the Knights Templars, is still potent in Western consciousness today.

PART

II

The Templars and the Grail Quest

CHAPTER

5

LEGENDS of the GRAIL: The CHIVALRIC VISION

The Grail and the quest for it have gripped the Western imagination possibly more than any other legendary tradition. It "is the embodiment of a dream, an idea of such universal application that it appears in a hundred different places . . . Yet, although its history, both inner and outer, can for the most part be traced, it remains elusive, a spark of light glimpsed at the end of a tunnel, or a reflection half-seen in a swiftly-passed mirror."[1] Though usually thought of as a medieval theme, it is very much alive today—like the memory of the Knights Templar, which also continues to hold our fascination. Both the Grail legends and the Templar mythos have resonated through the centuries. And despite the lack of concrete historical evidence, people have tried to link the two in various ways—even believing that the Templars had the Grail.

Like the Ark of the Covenant, the Grail is presented as profoundly mysterious. It can be dangerous, even deadly, to certain people—with good reason, tradition says. Some people see the Grail, but others don't. To those who do, it often appears surrounded by brilliant light, sometimes carried by a beautiful maiden, in other accounts moving by itself in midair. In the end, it may be not an object at all but a spiritual treasure—the truth and love of God.

The era of the Grail romances

Despite the enormous antiquity of the Grail material, it did not appear in literary form by and large until the Grail romances of the twelfth and thirteenth centuries. Given the complexities of medieval dating, scholars cannot always determine the precise date for a manuscript; they can say, however, that many Grail romances were written between 1190 and 1240—within the Templar Order's era. Many were authored by monks, in particular, Cistercians and Benedictines. These two Orders, though associated in some ways, were distinct from each other as well as from the Templar Order. There is no historical evidence that a Templar wrote a Grail romance, although some romances have Templar-related themes and details.

The years 1190–1240 fall during the High Middle Ages, one of the great experimental and creative epochs in European history. This period saw not only the writing of the Grail romances and the rise and fall of the Templar Order but also—among other things—construction of the High Gothic cathedrals, the peak of the cult of chivalry, a tremendous upsurge in pilgrimage, the great popularity of the Black Madonna shrines, the troubadours and the Courts of Love, and the rise of certain Hermetic and alchemical themes after a period of dormancy in the West. This cluster of cultural phenomena, expressing the spirit of the times, was contemporaneous with such political and social developments as the Crusades, the signing of the Magna Carta, the time of the Cathars, and the growth of the famed universities of Paris, Oxford, and Bologna—and the lives of such figures as Henry II, Eleanor of Aquitaine, Richard the Lionheart, and St. Francis. Historians note that the quest for knowledge and the arts during this time was nothing short of phenomenal. It was an era of extraordinary flowering.

The notion of a single Grail story is a common present-day misconception. There is no such thing. The Grail romances are many and varied and often do not agree with each other. One could say there is a general, prototypical Grail story, but even that must be an amalgamation of themes, people, and places from different manuscripts. Another popular misconception is that the Knights Templar are the same as the Arthurian knights of the Round Table. This is not the case.

Remarkably, however, the first Grail romance, like many of the first Templar knights, came from the area around Troyes, Champagne.

With both subjects—the Templars and the Grail legends—Troyes seems to figure prominently.

Chrétien de Troyes and Robert de Boron

One of the earliest known instances of the Grail motif in writing is *Le Conte du Graal*, written by Chrétien de Troyes in 1190, just a few decades after the Templar Order's founding. Chrétien's main character, Perceval, is a guileless knight, the archetypal Fool, whose primary trait is innocence. He sees the Grail during a feast at "a mysterious castle presided over by a lame man called the Fisher King . . . Chrétien calls the object simply 'un graal,' and its appearance is just one of the unusual events which take place during the feast . . . at this time, Perceval is also shown a broken sword which must be mended. The two objects together, sword and grail, are symbols of Perceval's development as a true knight."[2]

Unfortunately, Chrétien died before he could finish his story, so other writers attempted to complete it. These versions, called the *Continuations*, embellish the tale and bring in other Grail themes, such as the Grail floating on a platter in midair, the bleeding lance, the broken sword, and the curious theme of the Chapel of the Black Hand, where a mysterious hand continuously snuffs out the candles. As more *Continuations* were written, other details—such as the magic chess board, the spear, the cup, and the Precious Blood—were added, and Perceval has even more challenging adventures. In one *Continuation*, a lady at the Chapel of the Black Hand offers Perceval a white stag's head and a dog, which he loses and must find again before he can return to the Grail castle. Once a certain broken sword is mended, Perceval "as grail ruler heals the land. After seven years he retires to a hermitage, and when he dies, the grail, lance and dish go with him."[3]

Burgundian poet Robert de Boron wrote two Grail romances, *Joseph d'Arimathie* and *Merlin*—his most famous works—sometime between 1191 and 1200. Walter of Montbeliard, his patron—who, like Chrétien's patron, was a crusader—commissioned de Boron to write both. De Boron gives a definitively Christian tenor to his Grail story, presenting the knights' quest as a spiritual search rather than the usual courtly adventure undertaken for a lady's love or the king's honor. In *Joseph d'Arimathie*, which scholars now believe may have been written in Cyprus, Pilate gives the cup used at both the Last Supper and the Crucifixion to Joseph of Arimathea. Joseph is later put in prison, where he has a vision:

> Christ brings the grail to Joseph in prison where it sustains him and teaches him its secrets. Joseph is freed by the emperor Vespasian who has been cured by Veronica's veil (another mysterious relic associated with Christ's passion) . . . Joseph establishes a second table of the grail, and Bron catches a fish which is placed on the table and separates the just from the unjust. The object is called the Holy Grail . . . Alain, the leader of Bron's twelve sons, goes to Britain to await the "third man" (Perceval?) who will be the permanent keeper of the grail.[4]

Bron then becomes the Fisher King, and Joseph returns to Arimathea. Bron himself eventually goes to Britain, taking the Grail with him.

Early-thirteenth-century prose versions of Robert de Boron's works link the Grail story more closely with Arthurian legend. *Diu Krone*, by Heinrich von dem Turlim, presents Sir Gawain as the hero, while the Cistercian *Queste del Saint Graal* features Galahad. In the latter, the quest for the Grail becomes a search for mystical union with God. Only Galahad can look directly into the Grail and behold the divine mysteries. The *Queste* presents Galahad as the son of Lancelot, thus contrasting chivalry inspired by divine love, as with Galahad, against that inspired by human love, as between Lancelot and Guinevere. This is the best-known version of the Grail story in the English-speaking world. It was the basis for Sir Thomas Malory's famous late-fifteenth-century prose work *Le Morte d'Arthur*—in turn, the story-line source for much of the film *Excalibur* and the musical *Camelot*.

Wolfram von Eschenbach

Wolfram von Eschenbach, a gifted Bavarian poet, authored "several unfinished works and one complete poem, *Parzival*, composed between 1197 and 1210, in which he undertook the tale of the quest of the hero brought to light by Chrétien de Troyes."[5] In Wolfram's work, the Grail is a stone—a luminous stone fallen from Heaven—not a cup, as is common in other versions, and it is guarded by knights whom Wolfram calls *Templeisen*.

The young hero of Wolfram's story, Parzival, heads for the Grail Castle on Munsalvaesche, the Mount of Salvation, and encounters adventures on the way. At the Fountain of Salvation he meets a wise old hermit, Trevrizent, who turns out to be his uncle. Scholar Harald Haferland believes "Trevrizent" may be a bastardized version of the French *treble escient*, meaning thrice-knowing—a reference to Hermes Trismegistus, the Thrice-Great-Hermes, a classical god with Egyptian roots who by late Roman times was credited with many learned works on medicine, philosophy, alchemy, and astrology. His works were also read by some of the early Church Fathers.

For fifteen days Parzival stays with the wise old hermit to hear the teachings concerning the Grail. Trevrizent tells him the Grail story came through one Kyot of Provence, a knowledgeable man. Most scholars suppose Kyot was a troubadour from Provence—or from Provins, in Champagne. According to historical record, one Guiot de Provins, a troubadour, was present at the knighting of Frederick Barbarossa's sons, including the future emperor Henry VI, at Mainz on Whitsun in 1184—before the writing of *Parzival*.[6] However, this Guiot did not write a Grail romance. According to another theory, Kyot was from Provence on Lake Neuchâtel, in present-day Switzerland— an interesting idea since some consider the nearby town of Sion to be Parzival's home. This would also give the story a Merovingian twist. The Merovingians were important early kings of France and are associated with Jerusalem (that is, Sion) and several Grail legends. Trevrizent says Kyot had found the Grail story in a book "in a heathen language"—most likely Arabic—in Toledo, Spain, and that it was originally written in the wisdom "of the stars." Another key character in Wolfram's *Parzival*—the learned Cundrie, the Grail messenger and "loathly damsel"—speaks to Parzival about the planets, even using their Arabic names. Scholars believe these references to astronomy may be allusions to the sophisticated astronomical tradition of medieval Islamic Spain, which was centered in cities like Toledo.

The Toledan book, Trevrizent tells Parzival, was written by Flegetanis, a man born of a Jewish mother of Solomon's lineage and a heathen father who compared human destinies to the courses of the stars. "Flegetanis first read the name 'Grail' in the constellations; angels brought it down to earth. It has since their departure remained on the Mount of Salvation guarded by a race of royal Grail kings, each

one of whom was called, as Parzival was being called, to its service."[7]
Esoteric historian Walter Johannes Stein believes "Flegetanis" is a
Persian word meaning "a person familiar with the stars," that is, an
astrologer.[8] Flegetanis, "a heathen, able to obtain astronomical knowledge through visions, had acquired this power not through training but
through his special heredity. He was the first who put into writing what
was revealed in these visions, the Message of the Grail. The book in
question is . . . an astronomical book . . . We see that the visions were
starry wisdom."[9] Stein comments:

> Flegetanis points to the Old Testament and particularly to Jewish
> sources. In them still lived something of the old star-wisdom.
> Kyot, the authority used by Wolfram . . . had learnt to know this
> star-wisdom from old oriental sources. This star-wisdom flowed into
> the Hebrew writings in the form of genealogical books, in which
> Israel as a nation organised itself according to the laws of the stars.
> What is reflected in an earthly form in the twelve tribes, has its
> origin in the starry script.[10]

The twelve tribes of Israel are the most famous Western expression
of a social philosophy found among peoples all over the world. John
Michell and Christine Rhone note: "The foundation plan of these
12-tribe societies was a symbolic chart of the heavens, divided into 12
sectors which were named after 12 constellations and governed by 12
principal gods. It is impossible to say when or where this idea arose,
for it occurs in the earliest traditions and histories of virtually every
nation."[11] In the context of the Grail legends, the knights of King
Arthur's court, who search for the Holy Grail, number twelve. And
Joseph of Arimathea, "who brought Christianity and the Grail vessel
to England soon after the Crucifixion, was one of 12 hermits."[12]
The Knights Templar used an electoral college of twelve, plus a chaplain—mirroring the twelve disciples plus Jesus—to choose a new
Grand Master.

Trevrizent explains to Parzival that God gives a young person, like
himself, freedom to choose between wisdom and foolishness, good and
evil ways, purity and corruptness. Only God can judge whether someone is fit to achieve the Grail. Parzival complains that as much as he
has tried to attain it, he has only suffered and failed. He longs for the

Grail—and for his wife and child, whom he greatly misses.[13] Trevrizent chastises him for believing his success is guaranteed, as no one achieves the Grail alone. One must be known by name in Heaven; God calls a person to the Grail's service. In other words, you don't seek the Grail; it summons you.

Parzival leaves Trevrizent and eventually returns to the Grail Castle for the second time, where he at last asks the Fisher King the right question. The king is thus healed, and Parzival himself becomes the Grail King.

Parzival has a Muslim half-brother, Feirefiz, who becomes a Christian. When Feirefiz emerges from the baptismal waters, he has a luminous vision of the Grail. Words miraculously appear inscribed on the Grail, saying the name, race, or origins of a Grail guardian should never be queried. That is, family background is unimportant; the Grail itself, as determined by God, knows a person's deepest intentions and calls a person to the Grail family. After this extraordinary experience Feirefiz becomes a Grail guardian. He marries the Grail Queen, Repanse de Schoye, at the Grail castle and, with her, fathers the famed Eastern Christian emperor Prester John. Wolfram's *Parzival* was thus a remarkable work for its time. Among other things, it gives an ecumenical dimension to the group that serves the Grail; that is, the Grail calls those it deems worthy—Muslims included.

The many forms of the Grail

Various Grail romances present the Grail as different objects: a cup or chalice, a relic of the Precious Blood of Christ, a cauldron of plenty, a silver platter, a stone from Heaven, a dish, a sword, a spear, a fish, a dove with a communion Host in its beak, a bleeding white lance, a secret Book or Gospel, manna from Heaven, a blinding light, a severed head, a table, and more. Indeed, a truth about the Grail is that it takes different forms. In Chrétien's *Le Conte du Graal*, the Grail is a platter bearing a single Eucharist wafer. Robert de Boron's account introduces the Grail as the chalice Jesus used at the Last Supper. In the *Queste del Saint Graal* it is the dish from which Jesus ate the Passover lamb, which now holds the Eucharist wafers. Wolfram presents it as a luminous pure stone. The anonymously written *Perlesvaus* describes it as five different things. There is no single Grail story, and no single Grail—this point cannot be emphasized enough.

The Grail can manifest differently to each seeker. It can be an earthly object, which may or may not be endowed with sacrality; it may be the goal of a spiritual search. Ultimately, it remains a mystery. "So the pointers to the Grail may only suggest a path to a beatific vision of its manifestations. Each finder discovers a unique insight into the divine... Through the control of the body and the refining of the spirit, an understanding of self might be followed by a revelation of the divine. To attain the ever-changing Grail is to search deep within and so reach out to a personal path to God."[14]

The cup or dish

A common Christian interpretation of the Grail is as the cup Christ used at the Last Supper. A close variant is the cup or vial with which Joseph of Arimathea collected Christ's blood while preparing his body for burial. Legends dating as early as the third century say Joseph eventually brought the Grail to Britain via Gaul.

The earliest portrayals of the Grail as a cup, or chalice, simply call it the *Graal* and say little about it. The Celtic cauldron of plenty was a Grail prototype, later Christianized as the cup associated with Christ. The best-known recent portrayal of the Grail as a cup is in the movie *Indiana Jones and the Last Crusade*. The Grail cup has special powers and is often surrounded by a blindingly brilliant light. It can summon to its presence those who are worthy; it can bestow on certain individuals immortality, invisibility to evil, healing and restorative abilities, or direct communication with God. As a cauldron of plenty, it can feed everyone and never run out.

According to Vatican declaration, the authentic Grail is a chalice at the cathedral in Valencia, Spain. Other prominent contenders—and there are many—are a wooden bowl found in Wales, a vessel said to be hidden in the Apprentice Pillar at Rosslyn Chapel in Scotland, and a glass chalice associated with Genoa, Italy. Members of the powerful Embriaci family of Genoa were prominent in the eleventh- and twelfth-century Crusades. In 1102, Guglielmo Embriaci brought back to Genoa a green glass chalice captured from Caesarea and gave it to Genoa's Cathedral of San Lorenzo. Napoleon later took it to Paris, where it unfortunately broke into eleven pieces while being examined scientifically. Ten pieces were returned to Genoa in 1816; the Louvre retained the eleventh.

The Grail is sometimes a dish or a platter. In early Welsh accounts, for instance, the "dish of Rhydderch" is one of Wales's royal treasures. As we have seen, in some Christian Grail romances it is the dish from which Jesus and his disciples ate the Passover lamb at the Last Supper. According to another Christian interpretation, the Grail is a reliquary for the consecrated communion Hosts. Yet another theory proposes that the Grail is crystal or glass balls, filled with water and set on a tripod, that can kindle fire from sunlight, akin to the Jewish Urim and Thummim—objects associated with the Ark of the Covenant.

The Precious Blood

Relics of the Precious Blood come from several possible sources. One is the blood collected at the Crucifixion by Joseph of Arimathea—or by Nicodemus, Mary Magdalene, or Longinus, depending on the account you read. Legends associated with Joseph or Mary Magdalene, in particular, connect the Precious Blood directly with the Grail. Another idea, which has persisted for centuries, especially in France, is that the Precious Blood represents the bloodline of Jesus Christ, continued through his children with Mary Magdalene, his wife. In this context the Grail is "the vine," linking Jesus' bloodline to the Merovingian kings of France. This idea was popularized in the 1980s in the bestselling, though controversial, book *The Holy Blood and the Holy Grail*. At some pilgrimage centers, such as Bois-Seigneur-Isaac in Belgium and Bolsena in Italy, the bread and wine of the Eucharist were said to have spontaneously turned into the literal body and blood of Christ—another source of the Precious Blood. In other cases, the Precious Blood was reputedly particles "of blood of unknown provenance," like those found in St. Philomena's tomb in Rome. And several miracles concerned drops of blood suddenly appearing on certain statues of saints, the most famous being the statue of St. Januarius at Naples. Another source for such bodily relics was said to be Jesus' circumcision.

The Precious Blood cult was very popular in the early Middle Ages, and the many cathedrals and chapels claiming to have a vial of the Precious Blood were popular places of pilgrimage. By late medieval times it shared popularity with the cults of the Sacred Heart of Jesus and the Immaculate Heart of Mary.[15]

The King of Jerusalem, Baldwin III, with the consent of the Patriarch of Jerusalem, gave a vial of the Precious Blood, reputedly that collected by Joseph of Arimathea, to Dietrich of Alsace. When Dietrich returned from the Holy Land in 1149, he gave this relic to the town of Bruges. Dietrich's son and successor, Philip, was also a crusader knight—and was Chrétien de Troyes's patron. Walter Johannes Stein elaborates:

> Chrétien dedicates his work to Philip and very likely wrote it at his court . . . Philip's niece was Elizabeth of Hennegau who in 1181 married the young French king Philip II . . . Philip of Alsace was his trustee and guardian. Through him . . . whether in Bruges or Paris, at any rate in connection with a tradition bound up with the possession of the relic, arose the poem of Chrétien de Troyes.[16]

The differences between Wolfram's *Parzival* and Chrétien's *Le Conte du Graal* in part reflect their sources. Chrétien identifies as his source a book belonging to his crusader patron, Philip. Wolfram's "informant is not the owner of a blood relic, but Kyot, through Flegetanis, the possessor of the wisdom of the stars."[17]

The Holy Lance

In some Grail romances, a mysterious blood-tipped spear or bleeding white lance accompanies the Grail. It "was said to be the weapon that pierced the hips of the Fisher King. It was identified with the Biblical spear of Longinus," the Roman centurion who pierced the side of Jesus on the cross.[18] It was made by "Phineas, grandson of Aaron, according to a legend, admittedly transmitted by the Gnostic Ephrem the Syrian. Saul, in his madness, hurled it at David, and it was later used by Longinus to pierce the side of Christ and release blood and water into the Grail."[19]

The cult of the spear took hold during the High Middle Ages. Later it became suspect in the Church's eyes, especially in areas where it had possible connections with a pagan symbol—the spear of the Celtic sun god, Lugh, or the Teutonic god Wotan's spear of death and victory.

Many relics attached to the Grail stories are credited with special powers and can be used for either light or dark purposes.[20] Few are aware of Hitler's interest in the Imperial spear, which he saw as a young boy in Vienna's Hofburg museum. According to legend, this is the very spear that pierced the side of Christ, and whoever possesses it will rule the world. "Some of the German Emperors of the Middle Ages had associated the legend with this very Spear . . . Napoleon . . . demanded it after the Battle of Austerlitz, before which it had been secretly smuggled out of Nuremberg and hidden in Vienna to keep it out of his tyrannical hands."[21] Strangely enough, the Imperial spear has indeed passed through the hands of several major world leaders—Herod the Great, Otto the Great, Charles Martel, Charlemagne, Rudolph II, and Hitler. Hitler obviously wanted the spear for himself, and we know Himmler kept an exact replica in his office.

Trevor Ravenscroft, in *The Spear of Destiny*, tells how at the end of World War II, American soldiers found the spear and other Imperial regalia in an underground bunker in one of the many tunnels under Nuremberg Castle. General Patton was one of the few who saw the spear at the time and realized its significance. On 4 January 1946, General Eisenhower ordered that the spear and other items should be returned to Austria. At the Nuremberg Trials, most of the occult-related materials, entered as factual evidence, were left out of the public domain at the request of Sir Winston Churchill and others. Though surprising to some, esoteric matters may have influenced Nazi German policies more strongly than previously thought. Churchill knew of this and during the war had consulted esoteric historian Stein to better understand this aspect of the Germans' thinking. In other wars throughout history, those wishing to dominate have believed that certain relics' perceived powers could help them, so this idea is not new. What *is* new is that professional historians are now recognizing the significance of such beliefs.

Vienna and Nuremberg have long remained pilgrimage centers— Vienna because of the Imperial spear, Nuremberg because of its reputation as the center of Germany's Grail cult. Rudolf Steiner and Stein, his student, however, thought Externsteine was actually the center. This ancient group of large stones, situated in the Teutoburger Wald, was associated with the winter solstice. The Saxons' sacred tree, the Irminsul—destroyed by Charlemagne's Christian armies—once stood nearby. An unusual twelfth-century sculpture of the Descent from the Cross at the site, carved in living stone, shows the sun and moon in mourning on either side of the crucified Jesus. Outside the main group of stones is a twelfth-century replica of the Holy Sepulchre in Jerusalem. Also at the site are a grotto chapel and a hermit's cell containing runic carvings. Externsteine was clearly sacred to both pagans and Christians.

Another weapon identified as the spear of Longinus was discovered at Antioch during the First Crusade. A monk named Bartholomew had had a vision in 1098 as to its whereabouts. Thereafter, it passed for a time into the hands of the Count of Toulouse. This was presumably the relic discovered by St. Helena, mother of the Emperor Constantine, along with the True Cross and other instruments of the Passion. The Lance was for a time in the possession of the Emperor of the East in Constantinople, who pawned the head, later redeemed it, and sent it to St. Louis IX of France. The rest of the Lance remained in Constantinople until the fall of the city in 1453, when it passed to Sultan Mohammed II. His son, Bajazet, gave it to the Grand Master of the Knights of St. John of Jerusalem in exchange for certain favors. The Grand Master, in turn, gave it to the Pope. It was received with rejoicing in Rome, in 1492 and placed in St. Peter's.[22]

Yet another "spear of destiny" is the one that had belonged to St. Maurice. Maurice had been leader of the Theban legion, primarily Egyptian Gnostic Christians, that in the late third century was stationed in what is now Switzerland. When they refused to follow Roman emperor Maximian's dictates—which included orders to kill all Celtic Christians in the area—they were ruthlessly slain to a man. Emperor Maximian himself is said to have taken the spear from the dying Maurice.[23] In the late fourth century, St. Theodore the Just of Valais built a sanctuary to house these martyrs' relics, and in the early sixth century King Sigismund of Burgundy founded the Abbey of St. Maurice at the same site. The spear is presently housed in the abbey. The stone on which St. Maurice knelt and was decapitated by the Romans—described as a "stone from Heaven"—is in the chapel at nearby Beriolez.

The theme of a sword—rather than a spear—associated with the Grail is exemplified in the mystical sword given to Parzival, which had a ruby hilt; Tristan's sacred sword; and of course, Arthur's legendary Excalibur.

The Grail as a stone

Wolfram clearly identifies the Grail in his account as a stone: "A stone of the purest kind . . . called *lapsit exillas* . . . There never was human so ill that if he one day sees the stone, he cannot die within the week that follows . . . and though he should see the stone for two hundred years [his appearance] will never change, save that perhaps his hair might turn grey."[24] The term *lapsit exillas* can be translated as either "stone from Heaven" or "stone from exile"—which some scholars believe could mean a meteorite. Later in the story Wolfram says the Grail stone is an emerald that fell from Lucifer's crown during the war in Heaven; angels who took neither side in that war brought it to earth, where it remains.

The hermit Trevrizent tells Parzival that the Grail guardians, the *Templeisen*, living at the Grail castle exist by virtue of this stone alone. Some analysts believe this relates to the idea of manna, the special food from Heaven that sustained the ancient Israelites as they wandered in the desert. So also, the Grail knights receive their only nourishment from a divine source. They exist on its luminosity and holiness, and it sustains them physically, rewarding them, as Wolfram points out, with perpetual youth. It can also heal the sick.

When Parzival arrives at Trevrizent's hermitage, he seems unfamiliar with Christian customs. Trevrizent shows him the chapel and stresses that it happens to be Good Friday, so the altar has been stripped bare and no consecrated Host is left there. (The centuries-old custom in the Catholic Church was to "banish the Host" on Good Friday. Since the Vatican II Council, the Host is no longer banished but is removed to a darkened "altar of repose" until Easter morning.) Trevrizent says that on Good Friday at the Grail castle, a dove descends from Heaven and deposits a wafer on the *lapsit exillas*. This empowers the stone to provide continual nourishment for the *Templeisen*.

Various writers through the centuries have suggested that the Grail as a stone refers to the famed philosopher's stone, *lapis elixir*, mentioned in alchemical writings. French Celtic scholar Jean Markale comments:

> There is first of all an alchemical allusion, *lapis exillis* being quite close to *lapis elixir*, which is the term used by the Arabs to designate

the Philosopher's Stone. Next the stone of the Grail guarded by angels irresistibly summons thoughts of the Ka'aba stone in Mecca . . . One is reminded in particular of the tradition that states that the Grail was carved into the form of a vessel from the gigantic emerald that fell from Lucifer's forehead . . . In addition, Wolfram's Grail/Stone bears a great resemblance to the Manichaean jewel, the Buddhist *padma mani*, the jewel found in the heart of the lotus that is the solar symbol of the Great Liberation and which can also be found in the Indian traditions concerning the Tree of Life.[25]

Wolfram's stone could also derive from the legendary *lapis exilii*, the Stone of Death. Wolfram tells us that a phoenix sits on the luminous stone and is burned to ashes and reborn there—an echo of the alchemical theme of death and rebirth.

Templar-related elements in the Grail romances

What kinds of connections exist among the Templars, the Grail, and the Grail romances? The historical record provides no evidence that a Templar wrote a Grail romance—or that the Templar Order ever possessed the Grail, though people through the centuries have been certain they *did* have it. We do know, however, that some of the romance authors' patrons were crusaders, though not necessarily Templars, and that these writers certainly knew of the Templars' achievements in the Holy Land. And a number of Templar-related themes and details appear in some Grail romances, ranging from symbolism to the portrayal of the perfect knight to important concepts of chivalry and chivalric behavior.

The Grail and Templar themes mingle the most closely in Wolfram's *Parzival*. Wolfram is the only Grail romance writer to intimate that his Grail guardians were Templar knights. The medieval German word for "Templars" was *Tempelherren*, but scholars generally acknowledge Wolfram intended his *Templeisen* to be viewed as Templars. *Parzival*'s unique focus on the Templars may be partly because both Wolfram and his patron, Hermann I of Thuringia, were drawn to the East. In an earlier work, *Willeham*, Wolfram shows sympathetic interest in Muslim culture. Hermann I, a promoter of the knightly ideal, himself took up the cross and went on the German crusade of 1197–98. He was also fascinated by astrology, which was gaining popularity in twelfth-century European courts following the influx from Spain of Arabic texts in Latin translation.[26] Scholars believe Wolfram's Mount of Salvation—on which the Grail castle sits and where the *Templeisen* live—is a veiled allusion to Mount Sion in Jerusalem, since the original nine Templars lived on the Temple Mount. However, unlike the Templars, his *Templeisen's* shields bear a turtle dove—a symbol of peace, not holy war.

Wolfram portrays Parzival as related to the Arthurian line through his father and to the Grail family through his mother. Wolfram's Grail family is not the courtly society of Arthurian legend but a divinely chosen vehicle in world affairs, comprising the *Templeisen* and others whom the Grail silently selects to carry on its tradition. Women are included in the Grail family. Although Wolfram mentions a Grail succession, he also says the Grail lineage derived from it is a secret only the angels know. Certain people are assigned, by God through the Grail, to guard the Grail for posterity, thereby reuniting humanity with God, that is, "restoring the wasteland."

The early-thirteenth-century Old French Arthurian romance *Perlesvaus*, known also as *The High Book of the Grail*, was authored by a cleric with Benedictine connections.[27] In this tale, the Grail castle sits in both the earthly and the heavenly Jerusalem—an idea with obvious Templar connotations. Perlesvaus (Perceval), is a knight of Christ, though not explicitly a Templar. He travels overseas to an island where he visits the Castle of the Four Horns. Here he encounters thirty-three men in white robes with red crosses on their chests, like the medieval Templars' dress. His own shield displays a red cross with a gold border around it, similar but not identical to the historical Templars' shield. *Perlesvaus* stresses throughout the idea of holy war against the infidel—clearly mirroring the Crusades, in which the Templars played a starring role. It relates Arthur and his knights' efforts to impose by force the New Law of Christianity in place of the Old Law. Atypically for a Grail romance, Arthur's knights are portrayed collectively as a kingdom, not as individuals on their own quests. This resembles the Templar Order's underlying ethos, where the group's intention is more important than an individual's personal quest.

The *Queste del Saint Graal*, written by a Cistercian monk in 1215 for another crusader patron, Jean de Nesle, makes numerous allusions to the Templars. The star of this romance is Galahad—here a descendant of King Solomon—who is devout, chaste, and destined from birth to achieve the Grail. Galahad isn't called a Templar; he is a secular knight. However, at a monastery of white brothers he receives a white shield with a red cross on it that once belonged to Joseph of Arimathea—perhaps because he is portrayed as a direct descendant of Joseph through his mother. The medieval Cistercians were called the White Monks, and the Templars' white mantle was marked with a red cross.

While in *Perlesvaus* the Grail castle is Jerusalem, in the *Queste* the Grail knights go to Jerusalem with the Grail, but only *after* they complete their quest. When Galahad, Perceval, and Bors reach the Grail castle, they encounter nine more knights who have achieved the Grail. One has to wonder if this is a veiled reference to the original nine Templars. All twelve knights then celebrate communion, and Christ himself is the priest—a reenactment of the Last Supper. Galahad, after eating the consecrated host administered by Christ, has a vision of himself as Christ crucified and dies in ecstasy before the altar. Grail scholar R. S. Loomis comments: "In this celestial liturgy Christ is the officiant as well as the victim . . . Presumably it is [the] well-established belief in the presence of angelic visitants at the celebration of the Eucharist and in the assumption of the priestly office by Christ Himself which has led to the introduction of these two features . . . [in the *Queste*'s] re-enactment of the Last Supper."[28]

The great Cistercian abbot St. Bernard in mystical states sometimes experienced himself as Christ crucified. In his famous *Sermons on the Song of Songs* he discusses extraordinary mystical experiences, some involving the mysteries of the consecrated Host, or Eucharist "bread." He refers to "Solomon's bread," an Israelite forerunner of the Christian Eucharist that often induced mystical experiences.[29] Seeing oneself as Christ crucified, especially after ingesting the consecrated Host, was central to the Syriac Mystery of the Cross. Theologian Dan Merkur writes:

> It is significant that Bernard began the very first of his *Sermons* with a series of allusions to the Eucharist. Among them was a discussion of Solomon's bread . . . Bernard was privy to the mystery of manna.

He knew of a bread that had had use as a mystical sacrament in the temple of Solomon. How did Bernard come by his knowledge of manna? A passage in the fifty-second Sermon tends to indicate that Bernard was familiar with internal controversies in the Syriac mystical tradition. By the late seventh century, Syrian mystics had developed alternative techniques for the performance of the Mystery of the Cross.[30]

That Bernard knew of mystical experiences concerning the consecrated Host with roots going back to the time of Solomon's temple is amazing enough. Note too that the *Queste*'s author was also a Cistercian; the Templars and Cistercians were closely connected, especially in France; and Bernard was active in both Orders. Clearly these links formed a web of associations. We know some Templars spent time in Syria; they may have learned about the Syriac Mystery of the Cross from fellow Christians there.

The figure of Galahad in the *Queste* underscores the secular ideal of Christian knighthood and chivalrous behavior. It is the nonmonastic Galahad—*not* a Templar—who is the successful Grail knight. He embodies the perfect Christian knight, perhaps even as the Templars conceived this. Yet he dies not in glory on a battlefield but in the Grail castle. Perhaps the *Queste*'s Cistercian author is saying one can reach Christian chivalrous impeccability without joining a military religious Order. Or perhaps he is suggesting that a knight must seek salvation on his own, not as part of an enclosed community. Rather than fighting the enemies of Christ on the battlefield, the task is to slay one's own demons within and perfect one's character.

Bernard's teachings describe a person's progress toward spiritual perfection as a series of states of grace. The *Queste*, heavily influenced by Bernard's views, presents Galahad's quest for the Grail in similar terms. He is portrayed, as the Templars are portrayed, as striving for knightly perfection in word and deed. However, the mystery of the Grail is in fact found at another level of experience, as an ineffable inner knowing. Nearly all the romances agree on this. It is this aspect of the Grail that beckons many to their own spiritual journeys today.

CHAPTER

6

A MYTHOS in the MAKING

Were the Templars searching for something in the Holy Land—the Ark of the Covenant, ancient scrolls, or what some might call the Grail? And if they found such an object, where did it end up? Did some knights escape with treasures or manuscripts after the Order's suppression in 1312? Or, as others argue, is there simply no evidence that the Templars ever searched for something, so the case is closed?

The idea of a quest is so universal, and so deeply embedded in Western cultural consciousness, that its presence often goes unacknowledged. Classic quest legends include King Arthur and the Grail, Odysseus's long voyage home, and Jason's search for the Golden Fleece. The central characters of children's stories are often on a quest. Even Indiana Jones searched for the Ark of the Covenant. So also, a prominent geneticist once described the human genome project as the quest for the Holy Grail of science.

A powerful mythos surrounds the Templars—to the understandable frustration of many academics and skeptics, who decry sensationalism. Try as they might to rein in discussion about the Templars, limiting it to hard evidence, the Templar mythos won't go away. Its durability through time is a phenomenon worth examining, alongside the tenacity of beliefs about the Templars' quest in the Holy Land. The Templar mythos plus the archetypal Western quest seems to be a formula guaranteed to capture the imagination.

For a strictly historical account of the medieval Templar Order, the reader should consult *The New Knighthood: A History of the Order of the Temple* by Malcolm Barber or *The Knights Templar: A New History* by his colleague Helen Nicolson. Up to this point in the book, I have drawn on these and similar academic sources. The purpose of the present chapter is entirely different. It explores alternative views of Templar history and the Order's mythos. It takes a look at the views of a variety of researchers ranging from archaeologists and historians to Templar archivists and popular authors. Recent books on the Templars advocate various theories about what treasures the first nine knights may have found under the Temple Mount and what may have happened to the knights and to the Order's wealth after the suppression. Before examining specific alternative historical views, legends, and myths, however, we need to consider the debate that currently frames discussion of these theories.

Academic and alternative research

The dearth of both archaeological evidence and medieval documentation has allowed many hypotheses—some substantial, some downright sensational—to proliferate over the years about what the Templars may have found in Jerusalem. Academics tend to avoid the subject, maintaining there is little or nothing to discuss, as no concrete evidence that the early Templars were looking for treasure is available. Alternative researchers say there is equally little proof that the first nine Templar knights were doing nothing but assisting pilgrims full time. Both arguments are reasonable, given that we have no material verification of the knights' specific activities during their first nine years in Jerusalem.

The absence of conclusive documented evidence only adds fuel to the lively debate, which, as many note, seems to be getting fiercer, not going away. Scholars report frustration with "the acute problem of increasing sensationalism" concerning Templar history and accuse popular authors of taking wild leaps of speculation. Critics in the alternative camp say academics merely want to "scoff on the sidelines" and not bother to ask the difficult, unresolved questions. They claim the experts start with a preconceived viewpoint and discount whatever doesn't fit this view. They point out as well that ignoring the sensationalism only makes it worse.

The drawing of lines hopefully means this contentious situation is ready to be resolved. In recent years, some academics and popular authors have met and exchanged ideas at conferences and public events. People say it is good to see the two sides coming together more often and more debate taking place. This is likely to increase in the future, and not just in history and religious studies—archaeology, for instance, is grappling with similar issues.

Honest inquiry and a genuine search for truth—which both sides say they represent—inevitably mean encountering ideas that conflict with one's own views. The scientific method dictates that a hypothesis remains a possible truth until proved false beyond reasonable doubt. Moreover, something may be true and have influence even if it doesn't fit one's present worldview; this especially applies to study of the Templars, since, like it or not, their mythos undeniably exists and has powerful influence. That something was not written down does not mean it did not happen, since history is usually written, or destroyed, by the victors. History can come down to us by both written and non-written methods. Visual symbolism, architectural designs, oral traditions, and so on are part of the history of those who preceded us. These should be considered alongside the manuscripts and books that, according to those in the alternative camp, comprise the limited view of history of most academics. At the same time, not all alternative researchers are averse to written sources or "hard evidence," nor are all academics averse to considering well-thought-out alternative theories. It is the earnest search for truth that unites—rather than divides—researchers in both camps.

One thing is certain—interest in the Knights Templar is flourishing, and the public wants more information.

Were the Templars excavating?

Were the Templars excavating during their first nine years? I was highly skeptical, like many academics, yet I was also deeply curious about the sheer staying power of this question. After years of detailed study I am convinced of the need for further research concerning possible crusader—including Templar—activities under the Temple Mount, drawing on not only history but also other fields, such as archaeology.

Whatever the early Templars were doing, both the Patriarch of Jerusalem and King Baldwin II would have known of it. To excavate, the knights would have needed permission from the Patriarch, to whom they had pledged allegiance. And it is King Baldwin who gave the fledgling Order its prestigious accommodations at the Temple Mount platform's southern end. Joshua Prawer says the medieval military Orders in the Holy Land had exclusive jurisdiction in their own quarters and suggests that "only members of the Order or the closely affiliated lived or were allowed to live in these quarters."[1]

On the one hand, there is little reason to doubt the early Templars' expressed intention, which was to help pilgrims. Given their reputation as especially devout Christians, they very likely did assist pilgrims early on. We do know the earliest Templars cooperated with the Hospitaller Order to some degree. Barber says: "In December 1120, Hugh of Payns was a witness to Baldwin II's confirmation of the privileges of the Hospital, while Robert, 'knight of the Temple' is among the witnesses to a charter of Bernard, Bishop of Nazareth, dated October 1125, exempting the Hospital from payment of tithe in his diocese."[2] Historians know the Hospitallers were already protecting pilgrims in Jerusalem when the Templars first arrived. However, there are no concrete records of how, when, or where the Templars did the same.

On the other hand, the first nine Templars were quite plausibly not protecting pilgrims full time. As some academics and researchers point out, they apparently made no effort to recruit new members during their first nine years. Yet if their full-time work was protecting distressed pilgrims, who historians know were arriving in the Temple Mount area in increasing numbers, recruitment would presumably have been a high priority. Nine older men, even with extraordinary martial skills, could hardly have seemed enough to police pilgrims' routes into Jerusalem or hold off groups of robbers.

As historians note, Fulk de Chartres, King Baldwin's royal historian, says absolutely nothing about the Order or its founding knights, even though they were present in Jerusalem when he was. Some wonder if he was ordered to remain silent about them and their activities.

For it may be that medieval Western crusaders were doing something in the tunnels under the Mount. The remnants of a lance, a spur, a sword, and a Templar cross, found in the tunnel system beneath the Mount during a British archaeological dig, were given to the grandfather of Robert Brydon, a Scottish Templar historian, in 1912. These artifacts are included in the Brydon family's private collection, but are not available for public display. Other items are on display as part of the Rosslyn Chapel museum exhibition (see appendix).

The Warren expedition (1867)

Beginning in February of 1867, Captain Charles Wilson of the British Royal Engineers and his chief excavator, Colonel Charles Warren, undertook on behalf of the London-based Palestine Exploration Fund one of the most extensive and detailed excavations of the Temple Mount ever done. Warren's most important discoveries were water wells connected to the Spring of Gihone; he published his findings in two books, *Discovering Jerusalem* (1871) and *Documenting Jerusalem* (1884). Colonel Wilson conducted a subsequent excavation in 1894.

Warren excavated many tunnels and passageways under the Mount and in his books describes vividly the difficulties he and his team encountered. Graham Hancock, referring to Warren's account, describes how on one occasion, when they had finally cut through to a certain tunnel, "the noise from the sledgehammers and other tools used by his team had disturbed the prayers of the faithful going on above them in the al-Aqsa Mosque. The result had been a hail of stones, a riot, and an order from Izzet Pasha, the governor of the city, that the dig should be suspended forthwith."[3] Yet Warren remained undaunted and finally persuaded the Ottoman Turks to let his team resume.

Dame Kathleen Kenyon, director of the British School of Archaeology in Jerusalem from 1951 to 1966, discusses the Warren expedition in her landmark book, *Digging Up Jerusalem*: "The excavators encountered...problems [such as] vaults, drains, aqueducts, cisterns, sewage. The underground of the Old City is a warren, that has gradually levelled up several separate hills into a near plateau. The process has been gradual, but the constituent elements in vaults and terracing walls are quite considerable. Into all of these, Warren penetrated and mined."[4] Warren found and explored a "complicated series of vaults and passages that apparently constitute a causeway crossing the central valley, following the line of the earliest wall that joined the western ridge to the original city on the eastern ridge . . . Warren penetrated what he describes as a 'secret passage' along the line of this causeway, for a distance of 250 feet."[5]

Though Warren could not accomplish all he had originally planned, due to time and money constraints among others, he and his team did an extraordinary amount of key work, and his findings remain of lasting value to scholarship.[6]

The Parker expedition (1911)

Undoubtedly one of the most unusual archaeological expeditions undertaken in Jerusalem was the ill-fated Parker expedition of 1911. Neil Asher Silberman describes its beginnings:

> Parker's expedition . . . was the brainchild of a Finnish mystic named Valter H. Juvelius, who in 1906 had presented a paper at a Swedish university on the subject of the destruction of King Solomon's Temple by the Babylonians. Juvelius claimed to have acquired reliable information about the hiding place—inside the Temple precincts—of the "gold-encrusted Ark of the Covenant" . . . After poring over the reports of Charles Warren's excavations, he had convinced himself that this secret passage would be found to the south of the Al-Aqsa Mosque, in the area that Warren had already dug. Proffering the lure of the US $200 million that he believed the Ark would be worth if it could be recovered, Juvelius therefore sought investors to finance an expedition which would locate and clear that passage in order to gain access to the treasure.[7]

Dr. Juvelius claimed to have discovered an Old Testament cipher, mainly from chapter 1 of Ezekiel, that showed where the Ark of the Covenant was hidden beneath the City of David. Erling Haagensen and Henry Lincoln clarify:

> The codes found by Dr. Juvelius are of a . . . more concrete kind. They are more akin to the unquestionable Atbash Cipher, described

by Dr. Hugh Schonfield . . . in his later book, *The Essene Odyssey* (1984). Dr. Schonfield convincingly demonstrates the use made of this code by the Knights Templar . . . The Old Testament cipher unravelled by Juvelius proved to be a detailed description of how the Ark of the Covenant was secreted in a hidden cavity beneath the City of David and deep inside the mountain. The cipher was supposedly encoded within the biblical texts during the sixth century BC, when the Tribe of Judah was enduring its "Babylonian Captivity." The Ark, it seems, had been concealed at the time of the plundering of Jerusalem by . . . Nebuchadnezzar, when the Temple was destroyed. The priests then ensured that the secret of its hiding place would be preserved for future generations, by the ingenious device of encrypting precise directions for its recovery in the otherwise opaque Book of Ezekiel. Valter Juvelius' painstaking uncovering of the coded messages in the original texts had provided what was, in effect, a detailed treasure-map . . . The coded text describes an extremely complex system of underground passages . . . one of which eventually leads to the cave containing the Ark of the Covenant.[8]

During his fund-raising efforts, Juvelius met thirty-year-old Montague Parker, son of the Earl of Morley, in London and won his support. Using his extensive contacts among the British aristocracy and abroad, including members of Chicago's wealthy Armour family, Parker managed to raise a large sum of money quickly. The Parker expedition began in August of 1909, establishing its headquarters on the Mount of Olives, which directly overlooks the Temple Mount.[9]

Henry Lincoln writes that from 1909 to 1911 a Swedish engineer named Johan Millen, the Parker expedition's head excavator, labored beneath Jerusalem to clear the tunnel that conveys water from the Spring of Gihone to the Pool of Siloam. Warren had discovered an access route to the Spring of Gihone in 1867, but Parker's expedition, led by Millen, was the first to identify the Spring of Gihone—called the Virgin's Fountain on Christian maps—from biblical descriptions. Lincoln comments:

They were thus able to establish, beyond doubt, that the City of David, the veritable Mount Zion of the Jebusites, was the hill to the south of the Temple Mount. Millen and his expedition then spent some two years digging their way through the heart of the mountain and clearing Hezekiah's tunnel. Curiously, the undertaking seems to have been cloaked in a veil of security—if not absolute secrecy . . . Fanciful speculations grew about Millen's true purpose, but nothing came close to the eventual revelation which he made in a small, privately-printed and limited edition book published in Stockholm in 1917.[10]

Millen admitted in this book, *Pa Ratta Vagar* (*On the Right Roads*), that his real purpose had been to locate the Ark of the Covenant, and that he had based his quest largely on the work of Juvelius, whom he had known ten years or so before joining the Parker expedition.

Unbelievable as it sounds, Juvelius's decoded text was so detailed that, using it, the team could immediately identify the Spring of Gihone and the connected tunnel. Lincoln comments: "From then on, Millen assures, us, the excavations were guided entirely by the detailed instructions derived from the text encoded in the Bible."[11] So, digging began on Warren's site, with Parker, Juvelius, and Millen brimming with enthusiasm. As winter approached, however, the faithful of all religious persuasions protested the excavation—and mud flooded the site. Graham Hancock describes the situation:

> Understandably, Parker was discouraged. He called a temporary halt and did not resume the dig again until the summer of 1910. Several months of frenetic activity then followed. The secret tunnel, however, still obstinately refused to reveal itself, and in the meantime, opposition to the whole project had grown decidedly more pronounced. By the spring of 1911, Baron Edmond de Rothschild, a Zionist and a member of the famous international banking family, had made it his personal mission to prevent the potential desecration of the holiest site of Judaism, and to this end his purchased a plot of land adjoining the excavations from which he could directly threaten Parker. The young British aristocrat was rattled by this development. In April of 1911, therefore, he abandoned the search for the tunnel and resorted to more desperate means.[12]

To cut a long story short, Parker and his team decided to disguise themselves as Arabs and excavate the southern part of the Temple Mount, where Juvelius believed the Ark had been buried. These efforts proved fruitless. Thus,

... in the small hours of the morning of 18 April 1911, Parker switched his attentions to the Dome of the Rock, and to the legendary caverns supposed to lie far below ... They began to hack away ... Though Sheikh Khalil, the hereditary guardian, had been bought off, another mosque attendant unexpectedly appeared ... Hearing the sound of digging from the Dome of the Rock, he burst in, peered down into the Well of Souls, and, to his horror, saw a number of wild-eyed foreigners attacking the holy ground with picks and shovels ... The reaction of both sides was dramatic. The shocked mosque attendant uttered a piercing howl and fled screaming into the night to rally the faithful. The Englishmen, realizing that the game was up, also beat a hasty retreat. Not even bothering to return to their base camp, they left Jerusalem at once and made for the port of Jaffa—where, conveniently, a motor yacht that they had chartered lay moored in the harbor.[13]

They did manage to escape the furious mob that understandably chased them, but by morning there were full-scale riots in Jerusalem. The authorities—both Muslim and Jewish—were adamant that the Ark or any other sacred relics must not leave the country. The Jaffa police and customs authorities arrested the Englishmen, impounded their belongings, and searched them thoroughly, but they found nothing. Parker and his colleagues arrived in England a few weeks later. They had failed to find the lost Ark, and Parker had also lost the entire $125,000 that American and British investors had entrusted him with—a fortune in those days.[14] Dame Kathleen Kenyon carefully describes the Parker expedition as "exceptional by any standards."[15] Indeed, there has been none like it before or since.

Eminent archaeologist Pere Vincent, who was given special access to the Parker expedition sites by both Parker and Millen, later wrote his own thorough, scholarly report on the excavations. The Institute of Archaeology at the Hebrew University published this as a monograph. Regarding the Parker expedition's specific activities, however, he wrote, "I am committed to revealing nothing to outsiders until such time as shall be decided by the leaders of the expedition. I hope that those who feel frustrated by my silence will consider that a like discretion will be at their disposal, should I be asked to engage in a similar project at some future time."[16] Lincoln comments: "These statements certainly provide grounds for reflection—not least of which is: are they reliable? . . . The monograph of the Hebrew University of Jerusalem . . . refers to him as 'one of the pre-eminent explorers of ancient Jerusalem, whose meticulous and conscientious survey of the subterranean waterworks of the City of David between 1909 and 1911 still stands out as the most comprehensive composition on the subject."[17]

Clearly, a number of eccentric individuals were associated with the Parker expedition. They asked an eminent archaeologist to say nothing about their true objectives. As Kenyon comments, their findings remain mysterious partly *because* they were never published officially.[18] Thus speculation is rife, as many still wonder what, if anything, Parker and his team might have found.

Later twentieth-century excavations

In 1968, Israeli archaeologist Meir Ben-Dov and his team investigated more thoroughly some of the areas Warren had excavated a hundred years earlier. They found a tunnel with an entrance outside the Temple Mount that passes underneath Solomon's Stables and the temple complex. Some researchers have dubbed this "the Templar tunnel."

> The tunnel leads inward for a distance of about thirty metres from the southern wall before being blocked by pieces of stone debris. We know that it continues further, but we had made it a hard-and-fast rule not to excavate within the bounds of the Temple Mount, which is currently under Moslem jurisdiction, without first acquiring the permission of the appropriate Moslem authorities. In this case they permitted us only to measure and photograph the exposed section of the tunnel, not to conduct an excavation . . . Upon concluding this work . . . we sealed up the tunnel's exit with stones . . . The tunnel was indeed built by the Crusaders . . . [as] the Temple Mount served as a military headquarters for the Templars.[19]

This reputable Israeli archaeologist says the medieval crusaders built this tunnel, which implies that these crusaders—very possibly Templars—had good civil engineering and perhaps archaeological skills, or could access others who did. We know that many Templar-built castles in the Holy Land—some of which are still standing today—were very sophisticated for their time, and that the Templar Order had mason brothers. But because the Ben-Dov excavation could not continue, we know nothing more about the tunnel at present. One researcher has commented, however, that if this tunnel extends further inward from the southern wall, it might well penetrate into the heart of the sacred precincts, possibly passing directly beneath the Dome of the Rock.

On 21 August 1981, the Israeli authorities reopened a major tunnel discovered by Warren in 1867. However, Muslims barricaded themselves inside the tunnel and prevented the Israelis from continuing, as they were sure the Israeli authorities intended to use this tunnel to access directly underneath the Dome of the Rock, one of the most sacred places of Islam. The Muslim Awqaf in Jerusalem had the tunnel entrance closed with reinforced concrete on 29 August 1981, and it remains sealed today.[20] So posterity may never know where this tunnel leads.

In a 1996 article, Tel Aviv architect Tuvia Sagiv discusses recent excavations at the Temple Mount's fortification-like southern wall—"which wall was itself the most prodigious work that was ever heard of by man," as Josephus describes in his *Antiquities* (15:11). The work was carried out by Benjamin Mazar of the Archaeological Institute of Hebrew University and Meir Ben-Dov, field director of the 1968 excavation. Their work revealed what appear to be five different periods of construction for the southern wall itself:

> The lower courses are Herodian, with the characteristic fine dressing, double margin, and slightly prominent smooth boss. Next are the large blocks, smoothly dressed, apparently dating to Aelia Capitolina. These are surmounted by smaller, smooth stories, alternating with discs (cross-sections of columns inserted in the wall) which are probably Mameluke. This section is interspersed with small blocks having very prominent bosses and margins, apparently Crusader. The final courses are of small stones of later periods.[21]

The mosques of Omar and al-Aqsa stand at the southern end of the Temple Mount platform, and the ancient Temple of Solomon is believed to have stood nearby. Underneath the Mount's southeastern corner lies the area known as Solomon's Stables:

> Located in this area are long underground halls, the most famous
> among them being Solomon's Stables and the Double and Triple
> gates . . . Herod carried out extensive works in the Temple Mount
> therefore doubling its surface area . . . Onto this levelled area were
> built vaults and pillars which supported the southeastern court of
> the Temple Mount platform. The building of pillars in turn created
> underground halls, some of which in time came to be known as
> 'Solomon's Stables.' The length of these stables is approximately 30
> meters from east to west and 60 meters from south to north . . . The
> underground halls are made of 12-pillared avenues which differ
> from one another in length . . . Here and there can be seen tradition-
> ally decorated stones, which are typical of the Crusaders . . . In the
> Crusader period, the underground chambers were mostly used as
> stables for the Crusader knights. They most probably opened a spe-
> cial gate in the northern wall to let the horses enter in. The holes and
> notches in the arches used for tying up the horses . . . found here,
> prove that this location was used as stables.[22]

Sagiv refers to a description of the area—which includes mention of
the Knights Templar—by Johann von Wurzburg, a priest who traveled
to Jerusalem in the 1160s: "According to Johann . . . 'at the descent
from the road there is a large gate, through it one can enter to the
Temple's court. On the right, to the south is a temple which, from what
has been told, was built by Solomon. There are large stables which can
hold more than 2000 horses or 1500 camels.'"[23]

Historians know the early Templars cleared out the extensive
stables of Solomon and kept their horses there. But were the Templars
aware of any tunnels? Sagiv continues:

> The pillars [in Solomon's Stables] consisted of large, square blocks
> . . . At the bases of the pillars were rings for tethering horses. The
> Single Gate, now walled up, can be seen at the southern end of
> the sixth row of pillars, from the east, and the Triple Gate is at
> the south end of the twelfth row . . . Tunnels and aqueducts were
> found underneath the Double and Triple Gates, and a drain ran
> under the halls . . . When the Crusaders took Jerusalem, they iden-
> tified the halls of pillars as the Stables of King Solomon, as did

Nasir i-Khosrau and other Moslems. The Crusaders used the halls to stable the horses of the Knights Templar, whose headquarters were in the El Aqsa Mosque. The Crusaders entered their stables through the Triple and Single Gates (both now walled up), which they rebuilt . . . The Triple Gate received its present form during the Crusader period.[24]

Since the Templars rebuilt the Triple Gate, it seems likely they would have known about the tunnels and aqueducts underneath it. That they accomplished this task again tells us they had some degree of higher architectural knowledge.

What were the Templars searching for?

The examples that follow are a sampling of the wide range of theories concerning the Templars and their quest. These and other currently popular theories demonstrate the breadth and power of alternative Templar history and the mythos of the Order today. One of these speculates that the Templars may have been the custodians of a wisdom tradition, dating to ancient times, that incorporates elements of Gnosticism, Hermeticism, and alchemy. Another proposes that the medieval Knights Templar were the predecessors to modern-day Freemasonry and is hotly debated in Masonic as well as Templar circles. John Robinson's *Born in Blood* is one recent book on this theory.

Did the Templars find the Ark?

According to one theory, the Templars had access to the Ark of the Covenant not in Jerusalem but in Ethiopia. This is the topic of Graham Hancock's *The Sign and the Seal: The Quest for the Lost Ark of the Covenant*. Hancock's thesis, unusual as it may initially sound, dovetails nicely with certain unresolved issues about the Templar Order, the 1307 arrests, and the ensuing trials.

According to Hancock, Templar knights accompanied the exiled Prince Lalibela from Jerusalem back to Ethiopia in 1185 and helped install him on the throne. At this time, it is said, the Ark was in Ethiopia. A number of Ethiopian tales describe men with "red and white complexions" who are said to have helped build the Lalibela churches in Ethiopia during his reign (1181–1221). These eleven rock-hewn churches are dated no later than the mid-thirteenth century, and are a UNESCO world heritage site today. The crosses in several of these churches appear remarkably similar to the medieval Templar Order's cross. Some accounts say these foreign "white men" were bearers of the Ark in the early 1200s. The implication, Hancock relates, is that the Templars had gained a position of power and influence with King Lalibela and succeeding rulers of the Zagwe dynasty:

> It would be reasonable to assume that the last two Zagwe monarchs (Imrahana Christos and Naakuto Laab) would also have had a good relationship with the Templars—[to] whom they might have continued to grant privileged access to the Ark . . . This state of affairs would have changed dramatically in 1270, however, when (for whatever reasons) Naakuto Laab was persuaded to abdicate his throne and was replaced by Yekuno Amlak—a monarch claiming Solomonic descent. Unlike the Zagwes, the very identity of the Solomonids was irrevocably bound up with the Ark of the Covenant and with the notion that Menelik I—the founder of their dynasty—had brought it from Jerusalem during the reign of King Solomon himself.[25]

Hancock notes that Yekano Amlak, the new Solomonid ruler of Ethiopia, ordered the first written version of the *Kebra Negast*. This legend describes how Menelik I, believed to have descended from King Solomon and the Queen of Sheba, brought the Ark to Ethiopia. Hancock suggests Yekano would have disapproved of the Templars' presence in Ethiopia:

> Although the legend was by then already very old in oral form, Yekuno Amlak wanted it formalised. Why? Because it served to legitimize and glorify his title to the throne. From this it follows that Yekuno Amlak would have been horrified by the presence in his country of a body of armed, militant (and technologically advanced) foreigners like the Templars: foreigners . . . who clearly had a special interest in the Ark and who were possibly plotting to steal away with it. Assume, however, that Yekuno Amlak (new to the throne and still insecure) initially tried to placate these powerful and dangerous white men, perhaps by giving them the false impression that he was

willing to co-operate with them in much the same way as the Zagwes had done... [This] would explain why nothing spectacular happened during his reign.[26]

Yekuno Amlak apparently left the problem of getting rid of the Templars to his successors. His son, a weak ruler, was succeeded by the more powerful Wedem Ara'ad, who reigned until 1314. Hancock comments: "Significantly, it was Wedem Ara'ad who sent a large embassy to Pope Clement V at Avignon in 1306"[27]—the year before the Templar arrests.

Is it possible that the purpose of that embassy was to create trouble for the Templars—and perhaps to give the Pope and the French king (Philip IV) an urgent motive to destroy the order? Such a motive could have been provided by the suggestion that the knights were planning to bring the Ark of the Covenant to France. After all, this was a period when deep superstitions ruled the population. With so sacred and so powerful a relic in their hands, the Templars would have been in a unique position to challenge both the secular and religious authorities of the land—and those authorities would certainly have taken any steps they could to prevent such an eventuality.[28]

To be faced with competitors for power who had the Ark of the Covenant itself in hand would indeed have been a remarkable prospect for Philip to contemplate. Moreover, the Templars were his bankers, and he owed them money.

This theory begins to look particularly interesting when set against the backdrop of the arrests of the Templars in France and elsewhere. All these arrests took place in 1307—that is, about a year after the departure of the Ethiopian mission from Avignon. This fits perfectly with what is known about the behavior of King Philip IV: there is evidence that he began to plan his operation against the Templars about a year in advance of its implementation (i.e., in 1306) and there is also evidence that on several occasions during that year he discussed his plans with Pope Clement, according to Hancock.

"It would of course be folly to imagine that the destruction of the Templars was occasioned *only* by the lobbying of the Ethiopian envoys. Malice and greed on the part of Philip IV also played a role . . . By the same token, however, it would be folly to imagine that the Ethiopian mission to Avignon in 1306 had *nothing* to do with the events of 1307.

On the contrary, it is more than probable that there was a link—and that link, I am convinced, was the Ark of the Covenant."[29]

An interesting scenario, indeed. Although the *Kebra Nagast*, relating the Ark's arrival in Ethiopia—is apocryphal, many have wondered if it contains a kernel of truth. Charles Beckingham, Professor Emeritus of Islamic Studies at the School of Oriental and African Studies, University of London, wrote that in 1306, "ambassadors from Ethiopia came to Clement V at Avignon."[30] What is not known is the precise purpose of their visit.

Notably, the "white men" who went to Ethiopia in 1185 may have been mainly Portuguese. As we have seen, in 1319, seven years after the Templar Order's official suppression, many Templars joined the newly created Order of Christ in Portugal, and all Templar properties and funds in Portugal were transferred to that Order. Scholars acknowledge the greatest ambition of the famous Portuguese, Prince Henry the Navigator, was to seek the mysterious Eastern Christian emperor Prester John and his lands, which many at the time believed were in Ethiopia. Prince Henry was Grand Master of the Order of Christ. Was he perhaps privy to earlier Templar knowledge? He did establish a link with Ethiopia in the last years of his life.

Henry died in 1460, shortly after making his will, and it was not until the early years of the twentieth century that certain secret archives pertaining to the last decade of his life came to light. Amongst these archives (details of which were published by Dr. Jaime Cortezao in 1924 in the review *Lusitania*) a brief note was found to the effect that an ambassador of Prester John visited Lisbon eight years before Henry's death. It is not known what the purpose of this mission was, or what the prince and the Ethiopian envoy discussed. Nevertheless, two years after their meeting "it can hardly have been accidental that King Alfonso V of Portugal granted spiritual jurisdiction over Ethiopia to the Order of Christ."[31]

Web of Gold: The treasures of Jerusalem

In *Web of Gold: The Secret Power of a Sacred Treasure* Guy Patton and Robin Mackness present an intriguing account of what may have happened to the Jerusalem Temple's legendary treasures after the Roman sack of the city in 70 A.D. According to some legends, whatever treasure the Visigoths seized—which may have included the Jerusalem treasure—when they sacked Rome in 410 A.D. ended up in the Languedoc-Roussillon region of southern France. Patton and Mackness say the medieval Templars' power base was in this region and included part of Aragon. They propose that the Templars hid their wealth in the Languedoc-Roussillon area, adding it to an already present stash of considerable wealth:

> The commandery of Mas Dieu, in the centre of this region, had been founded in 1132, only four years after the Order's official endorsement at the Council of Troyes. But with the original sponsor and initiators of the Order from or connected with Champagne, why would it be the Languedoc that was chosen as its principal focus for activities? . . . The Knights Templar could hardly have been unaware of the tradition, if not the actual detail, of the presence and value of the Jewish-Visigoth treasure in the Corbieres. Throughout the nearly 200 years of their existence they were to maintain total military control over this region, exercising virtual sovereignty over its local nobility. They had received donations of a large number of lands and properties . . . By the end of the 13th c. the Templars of Mas Dieu were at the heart of a grand plan that aimed at nothing less than the creation of a fully independent state.[32]

As the Templars' power in the region grew, the Preceptor of Mas Dieu acquired nearly the same authority as the king of Aragon and the sovereign count of Roussillon:

> The Spanish orientated Templars had developed as an independent power and had always exerted a strong influence over the rest of the Order. An opportunity arose to advance their ambition still further when, through a will made at Barcelona in 1162, Jacques I of Aragon divided his kingdom. His second son was to become king of Majorca. The new kingdom of Majorca included the Roussillon and its neighbouring regions, in which could be found the great power base of the Templars . . . The Templars of Mas Dieu were effectively able to establish a sovereign independent state under the titular head of the king of Majorca. Besides the Balearic Islands, this extended from Montpellier in the north to Barcelona in the south.[33]

Local rumor also suggested the Templars had significant treasure:

The prevailing and enduring tradition amongst the locals was that the Templars had discovered and wanted either to exploit a hidden treasure, or to bury one of their own. Certainly, the Templars were to ensure that neither their own nor any treasure of the Temple of Jerusalem would be found by anybody else, including the new king of France. Furthermore, what better place to hide the enormous Templar treasure away from the clutches of King Philippe than in the heart of the Templars' own intended kingdom?[34]

Patton and Mackness believe the Templars in this area were warned of King Philip's intentions and so outwitted the French king's men. After the 1307 arrests, without delay, [King] Philip entered the Paris Temple expecting to seize the Templar treasure: since the Templars had been his personal banker, he assumed they held the royal treasure along with their own. Yet with disbelief he found no trace of it—and very little in commanderies elsewhere.

Not only were their treasuries bare after the Templars' arrest; their fleet had disappeared along with the majority of knights. Sure indications that they must have had prior warning . . . An organization as powerful as the Templars with such an extensive network would doubtless have had an intelligence wing. It is most improbable that they would not have been aware of the factor leading to their demise . . . Mas Dieu was of course not within the realm of the king of France. It is thus quite logical that the isolated valleys of the Corbieres, already containing the legendary treasure of the Temple of Jerusalem, was [sic] also to be chosen as the last hiding place of the treasure of the Knights Templar.[35]

Where is the treasure now? Patton and Mackness believe it is still in the region, vied over with much political intrigue by various groups—clandestine and not—through the years:

The evidence collected from all the various sources . . . indicates that the treasure is probably still deposited in the region of the village of Rennes-le-Chateau . . . The exact locations of these rich deposits are now probably unknown . . . Buried deep in ancient mines, subterranean galleries and extensive cave networks, the Jewish treasure has almost certainly also been supplemented by that of others, including . . . the Knights Templar . . . But the bulk of the treasure, including that of the Temple, appears never to have been found . . . This ancient treasure has ramifications that extend far beyond the borders of France. The ancient treasure pillaged from the Temple of Jerusalem has a value far in excess of its material worth. The seven-branched candlestick, the menorah, and its other religious items have enormous value for all Jews, especially the Orthodox, their value exceeded only by that of the Ark of the Covenant itself. Should any of these items be found and made public, the effect . . . would be dramatic.[36]

Indeed it would. However, some historians—sixth-century Byzantine historian Procopius, for example—believe the Romans later returned the treasure to Jerusalem, so the Knights Templar may not have found anything after all. But, again, no one can say for sure.

Scrolls under the Temple Mount?

According to one popular theory, ancient scrolls or manuscripts had been kept under the Temple Mount, and the early Templars found some of them. There is no concrete evidence to date of the Templars' finding such manuscripts. Exactly, some argue—since relatively little excavation has been allowed underneath and inside the Temple Mount, the remaining manuscripts may still be there; thus, much may remain to be discovered.

Christopher Knight and Robert Lomas, Masonic authors of *The Hiram Key*, write: "We had recently discovered that a duplicate of the Qumranian copper scroll had been deposited in the 'Shith,' or cave, directly beneath the altar of the Temple—the cave that was capped with the marble block with a ring at its centre. Had this been the stone that the Templars lifted and descended to the vault below?"[37] Part of the Dead Sea Scrolls, the Copper Scroll they refer to was found at Qumran, in cave 3 on 20 March 1952, and consists of two fragments on a single scroll of rolled copper. Baigent and Leigh, in *The Dead Sea Scrolls Deception*, comment:

The scroll proved to be an inventory of treasure—a compilation or listing of gold, silver, ritual vessels and other scrolls. Apparently, at the commencement of the Roman invasion this treasure had been divided into a number of secret caches; and the "Copper Scroll," as it came to be known, detailed the contents and whereabouts of each such cache . . . To this day, there is some argument as to whether the treasure ever in fact existed. Most scholars, however, are prepared to accept that it did and that the scroll comprises an accurate inventory of the Temple of Jerusalem.[38]

Scholars attest, however, that the Copper Scroll simply lists, in a rather dry inventory, sixty-four specific sites where gold, silver, and precious religious artifacts were hidden. Many of these sites are in Jerusalem, some under or adjacent to the Temple—information that has fueled much speculation.

Knight and Lomas conjecture that the first nine Templars opened a vault beneath the rubble in the Temple Mount area and found secret scrolls of the Qumran community written in Greek or Aramaic, or both. Recognizing the scrolls as immensely significant and holy, the knights wanted them translated. They chose Geoffrey de St. Omer—the second-in-charge to Hugh de Payns, the leader of the first nine knights—as both capable and trustworthy enough to get this done:

> Geoffrey knew an elderly canon by the name of Lambert, who was a retired school-master of the Chapter of Our Virgin in St. Omer, who was the wisest and most knowledgeable man . . . and who had spent many years compiling an encyclopedia . . . De St. Omer set out with a selection of the scrolls on the long journey back to his home town . . . The old man must have been overcome with joy to see such fabulous documents in the closing years of his life . . . Today, one of the most famous of all of Lambert of St. Omer's works is his hasty copy of a drawing that depicts the Heavenly Jerusalem. It shows that the two main pillars of the heavenly Jerusalem are both named "Jacob" and apparently shows the founder to be John the Baptist . . . It is no ordinary image and we believe it can have come from only one place, the vaults of Herod's Temple.[39]

Knight and Lomas comment that Lambert's drawing appears to have been produced in a great hurry. Perhaps Lambert had permission to copy the scroll in return for translating it, though Geoffrey was in a hurry to return to the Holy Land, so Lambert had to work in haste?

They also point out that the document "dates from over 500 years before the Masonic square and compasses symbol was first used and yet the most dominant feature of the building images are composed of this device."[40] They believe the scrolls found by the Templars eventually ended up under Rosslyn Chapel in Scotland, via the Sinclair family. As the vaults under Rosslyn Chapel have not been excavated, this theory cannot be verified or disproved.

A medieval charter of human rights?

Some time ago, I received an unusual booklet in the mail from an anonymous member of the public who had noticed it on a website and thought I might be interested. Quickly flipping through, I found it unlike anything else I had seen. Titled *Diana, Queen of Heaven* and authored by Rayelan Allan, it mentioned the Templars quite often, among other subjects ranging from Princess Diana to World War II to exiled royal families of Europe to secret gold. The text also presented an alternative history concerning the early Knights Templar I had never heard of before. Increasingly curious, I read on a bit more and stopped at this passage:

> The Knights Templar came to the holy land and to King Solomon's Temple for three things. They came to find the records of births and marriages. They came for the gold that was stored in secret underground chambers, and they came for the ancient manuscripts which were preserved in hermetically sealed chambers deep below the original temple. With these three things in hand, the Knights Templar went back to Europe and became the undisputed rulers of Europe. They ruled until King Philip the Fair of France conspired with the Catholic Pope Clement V to destroy the Templars. But even their destruction was part of their hidden agenda.[41]

The last sentence intrigued me, as it hinted at yet another view of the Templars—as a type of religious military intelligence agency.

Allan writes that the Templars' initial mission was to protect the Holy Blood from which they were all descended and to seek records of births and marriages. "They did this not just to prove they were descended from Jesus and Mary Magdalene, but to find the records of all of the bloodlines from the House of David."[42] She says that some Templars did survive as a clandestine group after the Order's suppression, and that this bloodline continues today. She says, however, that her theory differs markedly from other theories published in recent years about the bloodline.

Allan also suggests that years before the Order's official emergence, the earliest Templars gathered to formalize their group and, after a powerful visionary experience involving Mary and the infant Christ child, drafted a charter of human rights for ordinary people:

> On a rain swept, desolate day . . . a group of dedicated monks and their worldly brothers gathered . . . to form a new Order to keep alive the words which God had granted Solomon, by dream . . . They began to work on the plans to form a new charter, granting that each living being had diverse basic rights . . .
>
> Although the drenching rains continued, a large beam of light filtered down to the statue of the Christ child, securely carried in the hands of his Godly Mother, Mary. The fright and silence were awesome as those gathered beheld the sight. All present began to speak at the same time, each in the language of his birth. Within minutes, the babble ceased and they began to work.[43]

The essence of this charter is: "Each living being possesses basic divine rights. The most basic right is the right of self determination. Each and every being upon Earth is divinely given the right to control his own life. Other inalienable ('in-a-lien-able,' meaning incapable of having a 'lien' placed on them) divinely granted rights include food, shelter, clothing and fair compensation for work well done."[44]

Allan adds that it is unfortunate, even dangerous, when questionable Templar Orders, like the now-disbanded Order of the Solar Temple, are established, as they give true chivalry and Templarism a bad name.

Certainly the Templars greatly revered Mary; she was patroness of the Order. And indeed, several modern-day chivalric Templar Orders give top priority to human rights and humanitarian work. As Christians, Templars—medieval or modern—would naturally be interested in such issues. However, that a document like a human rights charter would even have been conceived of, much less drafted, in the cultural climate of the Middle Ages seems extraordinary, even downright impossible, to us today. As Allan does not cite a specific source for that information, no further analysis is possible, at least not at present. Perhaps her future writings will shed more light on this fascinating issue.

Templars and Templar Treasures in the New World

The theories considered thus far concern the medieval Templars and Templar treasures in the Holy Land, Europe, or North Africa. However, a number of theories focus their attention on the New World.

Is the Ark in America?

One recent—and controversial—theory is put forth by English Freemason Patrick Byrne in *Templar Gold: Discovering the Ark of the Covenant*. Byrne begins with his discovery that the location of Pech Cardou, a mountain on the northeastern slopes of the Pyrenees in the Roussillon region of southern France, is encoded in Masonic ritual. He believes the medieval Templars possessed the Ark of the Covenant and proposes that after 1307 they took it to Limassol Castle on Cyprus and then to France, where they placed it for safekeeping in one of Pech Cardou's caves. According to Byrne, the Ark remained protected there until the outbreak of World War I in 1914. Then the Ark had to be moved elsewhere:

> For the first time since 1307, the guardians of the Ark of the Covenant became fearful about their treasure, for some German intellectuals knew where it was stored. It was not difficult to arrange for the Ark to be transported to safety. Freemasonry has always had a strong representation from the various branches of the armed forces . . . Trusted Freemasons from within the armed forces were dispatched to the Roussillon and the Ark of the Covenant was taken to safety across the sea and out of reach of the German forces.[45]

Byrne adds that "there has long been a rumor that the Ark now resides in the United States," where it would have remained through

World War II: "Only twenty-one years later, Europe was again immersed in war and it was deemed wholly appropriate to leave the Ark in its more secure location. However, in the course of time, peace returned to Europe."[46] According to Byrne, the new custodians of the Ark were reluctant to give it back:

> The more recent representatives of the original French guardians of the Ark seem to be the Priory of Sion, and they let it be known that the time had come when the Ark should be returned to Jerusalem—not to the Jerusalem in Israel, for that was seen as far too unstable a location for arguably the most valuable artifact in the world, but to the New Jerusalem in the Roussillon...Unfortunately for the Priory of Sion, the current holders have become quite attached to their treasure.[47]

Byrne points out that none of the basic questions about the Ark can be answered "until the current guardians put their cards, or rather the Ark, on the table. There must then follow a period of scientific research to authenticate the Ark, to establish whether...it is real or fake."[48] He calls for the elusive "present guardians" to "declare their ownership and proffer proof of its authenticity, or put in hand such scientific examination as is necessary."[49]

Until we have tangible proof that the Ark of the Covenant still exists, let alone was transported somewhere, Byrne's theory must remain speculative. Even so, his book prompts questions: What may have happened to the Ark? Who were his sources? He does not really say. Perhaps he feels he cannot reveal them, for whatever reasons.

Another theory strongly supports the idea that the Ark ended up in the United States. Marie Hall, wife of Manly P. Hall, Masonic scholar of the Western mystery traditions who founded the Philosophical Research Society in Los Angeles in 1934, researched this subject extensively. A fascinating and controversial author, she wrote several books on her research, which centered on the early Bruton Parish Church of Williamsburg, Virginia; the history of Jamestown; and the controversial theory that Francis Bacon or members of his family came to the Virginia colonies.

Henrietta Bernstein, a student of Manly and Marie Hall, summarizes Marie's theory in *Ark of the Covenant, Holy Grail*. Hall proposes that the New World, in particular Virginia, the first permanent English colony in North America, might have seemed a good hiding place for the Ark. She believes Henry Blount, a descendant of Sir Francis Bacon who, she recounts, adopted the name Nathaniel Bacon after arriving in America, may have brought a copy of the Ark, with accompanying records, to Jamestown. (Hall reports rumors of copies of the Ark being made in early times.) Later it was moved to Williamsburg:

> In 1676, the Ark and its treasure were secretly moved from the Jamestown Church and laid to rest in a ten-foot-square chamber, or vault, buried twenty feet deep in the earth directly beneath the tower center of the first and original brick church in Bruton Parish. This was in the first Virginia capital, Middletown Plantation, eventually to be known as Williamsburg... In 1938, Marie Bauer Hall decided to dig up the vault... Before setting out on her Williamsburg quest, Marie Hall discovered in the Philosophical Research Society's Library the *George Wither Book of Emblems*... George Wither was known to be one of the inner group of Rosicrucians, and this book is a collection of emblems, both ancient and, at the time of publication, modern.
>
> Although the George Wither book was written in England in 1635, over a hundred years before most of the original buildings were ever erected in Williamsburg, there are pictures of these very same buildings in the Wither book. Marie Hall said that the capitol building depicted in the Wither book was recognized by a Rockefeller Restoration official when she showed it to him before she recognized it herself! She was also able to discover from Wither's book many verifications of the Bruton Vault, including its existence, the location, size and depth of the vault, as well as its contents, and the circumstances attending its burial.[50]

Marie decoded this same information regarding the Bruton vault from tombstone inscriptions in the Bruton Churchyard with the help of Wither's book:

> She was able to determine—from anagrams, cryptograms and codes deciphered from the tombstones in the churchyard—the exact location of the original brick church... She found that the first tombstone near the entrance gate had a stone engraving with the very

same coat of arms, showing the three crescents of the moon and a shield, that she had seen in the George Wither book...Mrs. Hall soon realized that her goal of uncovering the vault could be accomplished only with the information from the tombstones...From a Masonic record she found in Williamsburg, Marie Hall was further encouraged...These Masonic records stated: "Under the first brick church in Bruton Parish, Williamsburg, Virginia, lies Francis Bacon's Vault [i.e., the Bruton Vault]"...The present structure of Bruton Church does not stand on the same site as the earlier church. The original brick Old Bruton Church, built about the time of Bacon's Rebellion of 1676, was demolished and all the records are missing. Misleading maps were originated and signed by men whose names were recognized by Marie as connected with the original undertaking of burying the vault, presumably another level of secrecy, simply for better protection of the vault and its contents. Annals of the Williamsburg Masonic Lodge are also as completely and mysteriously missing for the identical time period as are the Vestry records of Bruton Parish and its first brick church ...While she was digging in Willamsburg, two Masons came to talk to her...They were carefully watching her work.[51]

Hall's theory is of course controversial and will no doubt remain so as long as the early records are missing. Yet many are intrigued that a book written in England some one hundred years earlier could have pictures identical to the early buildings of Williamsburg, Virginia.

The Oak Island mystery: Nova Scotia

A two-hundred-year-old mystery on uninhabited Oak Island, Nova Scotia, is the object of several researchers' investigations, including U.K.-based Reverend Lionel and Patricia Fanthorpe. The story is summarized on their book's back cover:

> It began innocently enough—in 1795, three boys discovered the top of an ancient shaft on uninhabited Oak Island in Mahone Bay, Nova Scotia. The boys began to dig, and what they uncovered started the world's greatest and strangest treasure hunt. Two hundred years of courage, back-breaking effort, ingenuity and engineering skills have so far failed to retrieve what is concealed there. The Oak Island curse prophesies that the treasure will not be found until seven men

are dead and the last oak has fallen. That last oak has already gone—
and over the years, six treasure hunters have been killed. What can
the treasure be?[52]

The "ancient shaft" apparently leads to what is known as the Oak
Island money pit, via an elaborate engineering system with numerous
"traps." The treasure it contains is believed to be any one of several
famous missing treasures: Sir Francis Drake's jewels, Captain Kidd's
pirate gold, priceless scrolls or manuscripts, Francis Bacon's original
Shakespeare works, or the Templars' riches.

Several wealthy entrepreneurs, past and present, have tried to figure out the mysterious, sophisticated engineering system, but even
using modern technology, none have yet succeeded. In 1909, one
Captain Harry Bowdoin founded the Old Gold Salvage and Wrecking
Company and organized a treasure-hunting expedition to Oak Island.
An owner of a few company shares was a young New York lawyer
named Franklin D. Roosevelt, future president of the United States.

> As a child, F. D. R. had spent many summer vacations on Campo-
> bello, an island between Maine and New Brunswick. Already a com-
> petent sailor by the time he was six years old, F. D. R. met and talked
> to many seafarers in the area about the Oak Island mystery. When he
> was only sixteen, the young Roosevelt sailed with a friend to Grand
> Manan Island in search of Captain Kidd's treasure, which legend
> said lay buried there . . . Small wonder, then, that F. D. R. was inter-
> ested in supporting Bowdoin's treasure hunting syndicate in 1909. It
> was an interest that never died. Even as President, with the New
> Deal and World War II to occupy his attention, Roosevelt was always
> glad to receive reports about the latest events on Oak Island.[53]

To this day, the Oak Island mystery is unresolved and so remains
the focal point for a cluster of theories, some suggesting the Knights
Templar were connected with the money pit's construction, the treasure reputedly stored in it, or both.

Navigating across the Atlantic

An exciting yet controversial body of current research is centered
on early sea explorations by Europeans across the Atlantic to the New

World. Did Europeans make pre-Columbian voyages to the Americas? Did Columbus really discover America in 1492, or did he rediscover it? One theory even suggests that Templars were present in the New World before Columbus's famous voyage. Another line of research examines possible Templar influence on the European explorers. What, after all, was the source of Columbus's maps?

Canadian author Michael Bradley discusses the importance of maps for the early European explorers and navigators who sailed to the New World. He considers the idea of the *mappamundi*, a late-medieval world map showing land west of the Atlantic:

> Was there ever such a world map? Did Templars get possession of it? Did they bring copies to Portugal and to Scotland which served as guides for Atlantic voyages in search of a religious haven in the New World, and not in Asia? . . . Templars did possess such a map of the world. The reason for stating this so strongly is simply that modern scholars have found precisely this kind of mappamundi in Middle Eastern archives. Specifically, two very intriguing maps of the world have been found: the Hadji Ahmed Map was discovered in 1860 in what is now Lebanon; then, in 1929 the Piri Re'is Map was discovered in the old Imperial Palace in Constantinople.[54]

Bradley also considers *portolans*, the fourteenth- and fifteenth-century mariner's charts, based on practical navigational experience, that indicated coastlines, harbors, rivers, and manmade features visible from the sea. Columbus used *portolans* on his journeys. Bradley proposes that these maps came to Europe, particularly to Portugal, possibly through Templar hands after the suppression of the Order at the beginning of the fourteenth century. Portuguese chartmakers added the meridian line, a point useful for latitude sailing and for navigating solely by compass. During the fifteenth century especially, Portugal led the European world in sea exploration:

> Within a generation after Philippe le Bel pressured Pope Clement V into disbanding the Templars, maps called "portolans" began to be distributed throughout Europe. One of the earliest portolans is called the Dulcert Portolan of 1339, which appeared just 27 years after the Knights Templar were disbanded. Scholars of navigation have consistently tried to ignore the portolans because of the

problems they present. It is accepted that they did exist, but the problems they represent have been swept under the carpet . . . Stated simply, the mystery of the portolans is not so much that they appeared so suddenly in 14th-century Europe, but that they are inexplicably accurate . . . The barrier to medieval navigation was that longitude, the position east or west of any given point, could not be determined with any accuracy. The key to finding longitude by celestial observation was some method of keeping time with extreme accuracy. Clocks of such sophistication simply did not exist in the medieval world, and navigators had to wait until 18th-century technology supplied them.[55]

When the *portolans* showed up in the early fourteenth century, "all of Europe was suddenly flooded with sea-charts of inexplicable accuracy. These charts are really the most important result of the Templar dispersal because they accomplished two things: they greatly facilitated purely European trade and commerce by sea, and thus contributed to the further decline of feudalism; [and they also] . . . really made the European 'Age of Discovery' possible because they showed the whole world, and also showed new land across the Atlantic."[56]

We know the Templars had a fleet and, like the Hospitallers, were skilled navigators. Did they pass these skills on, along with the maps? Did they know how to measure longitude? Were Columbus and other explorers influenced directly, or indirectly, by the Templars and what they knew? Bradley asks: "Is it just coincidence that Prince Henry the Navigator was also a Grand Master of the Knights of Christ?"[57] We know the Portuguese Order of Christ was created shortly after the Templar Order's suppression and many former Templar knights joined its ranks.

Bradley points out that Christopher Columbus, John Cabot, Samuel de Champlain, and other explorers to the New World may have been interested in certain esoteric matters. He suggests that some may have been Templars or had Templar affiliations and believes a number of them were part of a secret group interested in the Holy Grail. He even proposes that some explorers' names may have been pseudonyms, which some historians do not dispute.

Indeed, the precise identity of Christopher Columbus remains an enigma, since little is actually known about his early years or lineage; nor are historians certain where he got all his maps from. Given the limited documented evidence, some historians even question whether he was really a Genoese merchant sailor. Others speculate he may have belonged to the Order of Christ and, if that Order had Templar maps, might have obtained the necessary maps that way. No one contests that the Portuguese were extraordinary navigators. He points out that the flags on Columbus's ships bore an insignia nearly identical to the Templar cross—a white background with a red cross on it. This does not mean Columbus himself was a Templar or a Knight of Christ, but he may have known men in those circles. The historical record shows he was close to the Portuguese royals, who we know had a history of Templar affiliations.

Similar uncertainty surrounds the identity of Samuel de Champlain, whose early years and family background are completely unknown; some believe he was actually the pirate Guy Eder de la Fontanelle.

Manly P. Hall, in *America's Assignment with Destiny*, comments that Columbus was a man of great faith and sometimes dressed in a plain Franciscan-style robe:

> It was reported by his son that Columbus died wearing a Franciscan frock. It is not known, however, that he was directly associated with this Order, even as a lay Brother. Several religious groups of the times, including fraternities known to be connected with the esoteric tradition, favored this kind of habit . . . Columbus may have been a disciple of the illuminated Raymond Lully. There is a persistent rumor to this effect. He was also involved with the group perpetuating the political convictions of Dante . . . Columbus made use of ciphers and cryptic allegorical expressions and figures of speech. While such ciphers are known to exist in his manuscripts, no systematic effort to decode them has come to public attention.[58]

Hall speculates that Columbus belonged to the Albigensian church, often associated with the Cathars. One theory suggests Dante was a Templar, though there is no direct proof. The Blessed Raymond Lully (Ramon Lull) did have known connections with Templars, as well as with Sufis, and was one of those who suggested in the early fourteenth century that the Templar and Hospitaller Orders be combined into one.

A pre-Columbian Templar presence?

Another controversial theory, not new but recently featured in more detail, proposes that the Templars were mining silver and gold in Mexico in the thirteenth century. Quebec-based Paul Falaradeau, in *Societes Secretes en Nouvelle-France*, builds on the theories of French authors Jean de la Varende *(Les Gentilhommes)* and Louis Charpentier *(Les Mysteres Templiers; The Mysteries of Chartres Cathedral)*. De la Varende states flatly that the Templars had traveled to America, though he does not specify where. Charpentier asks where the Templars got the money to build Chartres Cathedral and concludes they may have funded it with gold from mines they had established in Mexico.

Falaradeau also refers to a Mexican chronicle, *Relaciones Originales de Chalco Amaquemacan* by San Anton Muñon, that appears to describe the arrival of Templar knights in Mexico:

> San Anton Muñon wrote the history of his people at the beginning of the 17th c., being of the dynasty of the Princes of Chalco. In his chronicle, San Anton Muñon stated that a first contingency of Templars arrived in Mexico around the middle of the 13th c. In 1299, they reached the area of Chalco where they settled permanently, taking control over the whole area and where they became known as the Tecpantlaques . . . The author/researcher Eugene Beauvais took a serious look at San Anton Muñon's writings, and came up with a convincing interpretation of the Tecpantlaques. According to Beauvais, this word is made up of "tecpan," which means "temple" or "palace," and which takes its origin from "tecuhtil," "Lord," and "pantli" meaning, "Building/wall" . . . Translated into our language, this means "People of the House of the Lord, or Temple." It is also interesting to note that another Mexican chronicler, Muñoz Camargo, called the "Templarios" (Templars), Mexican priests. It did not take long for Beauvais to conclude that the Tecpantlaques were none other than members of the . . . Knights Templar.[59]

San Anton Muñon records what appears to be a second influx of Templars, this one after the arrests:

> In 1307, there was an important arrival of Tecpantlaques in Mexico. It is easy to conjecture that this arrival followed the destruction of

the Order in Europe . . . There are some clues that seem to indicate that [some of] this group also may have sailed down the St. Lawrence river and reached the island of Montreal. My colleague Dr. Gerard Leduc and myself have uncovered clues that indicate that some buildings that were erected on the island in the 17th c. were built over ruins of ancient building of unknown origin.[60]

Falaradeau suggests the "Tecpantlaques" also sailed as far north as Nova Scotia and other parts of Canada, perhaps burying some treasure at Oak Island. He also says that behind the founding of the city of Montreal one will find the Company of Saint-Sacrement de l'Autel, a secret society who arose in France at the same time that the Rosicrucian Manifestos appeared in Europe. The Company's goal was to create New Jerusalem in the New World.

Most of the leader's origins were from the Languedoc . . . Cathar country . . . although they seem to have hidden themselves behind the Catholic priesthood in order to avoid the suspicions of the church . . . all prominent members were close to the French Crown . . . For half a century, they did tremendous humanitarian work in France, while supporting the foundation of Montreal . . . This Company of Saint-Sacrement was behind the foundation of the Sulpicians. Today, in the Sulpicians' building in Montreal, it is easy for the trained eye to see plenty of Masonic symbols . . . In the church of Notre Dame de Bonsecours in old Montreal, which was built in the 1670s, Templar symbols are abundant, especially Templar crosses.[61]

Niven Sinclair, patron of Rosslyn Chapel in Scotland and re-searcher of its history, has been in correspondence with Falaradeau. After visiting North America in 2001, Sinclair felt that signs of pre-Columbian industry in North America may point to the Templars:

History needs to be rewritten. The North American Continent is awash with evidence of pre-Columbian settlers who left their imprint on the landscape and their writing on stones . . . Historians have been slow in finding an answer . . . Sufficient be it to say that over 1,000,000 tons of copper had been extracted from the Lake Memphremagog area before the advent of the Knights Templar who came on the scene in the 13th century, i.e., before the suppression of the Order, because we discovered their presence as far afield as Montreal (built by Villeneuve on an old Templar site) . . . What did I discover? Well, I discovered very little but I was shown a great deal which pointed to prolonged European occupation . . .

The Templars had been in the New World some 150 years before Henry Sinclair arrived on the scene. Many of the early French settlers were from Cathar stock from the Languedoc area of France, who arrived incognito, or, as with Champlain, with a name which wasn't theirs. One wonders why? . . .

In particular the hallmark of the Templars could be seen in the dams and mills which they had erected on their many sites. The stonework was perfect. Their expertise in the control of water could be seen in the holding dams; in the "leads" which led to the mill itself, and in the diversionary channels to take any overflow caused through possible flooding.[62]

Sinclair has since consulted with various native North American tribes to seek further clarification on these issues and especially the Micmacs, with their legends that may relate to the Sinclair family, which their tribal elders have acknowledged. But yet again, many questions remain unresolved about a possible Templar presence in the New World.

As we have seen in this brief survey, there are varieties of theories about both the Templars' history and the mythos that has grown around them—largely because of loss of the central Templar archive. Historian Barber comments: "The Templar myths have . . . proved extremely durable and their contribution to the modern image of the real Templars arguably as powerful as that of their documented history between 1119 and 1314."[63] New World Templar theories are gaining ground, to the chagrin of skeptics, who point out the scarcity of concrete evidence or documentation. The lack of material proof may be deliberate, some argue. And so the debate continues. The circumstantial evidence and related questions about the Templars assure the resilient Templar mythos will never die. There is an old Cathar saying: "Every seven hundred years, the laurel will grow green again." The dawn arrests of the Templars were in October, 1307. Perhaps one reason for the current burgeoning of interest in all things Templar, a colleague once told me, is because we are nearly at the seven-hundredth year—2007. Or perhaps it is because "what is remembered, lives."

CHAPTER

7

ROSSLYN CHAPEL: WISDOM in STONE

Not far from Edinburgh stands Rosslyn Chapel, an exquisitely carved medieval stone chapel, unique in all of Europe. Rosslyn's official name is the Collegiate Chapel of St. Matthew, as the foundation stone was laid on St. Matthew's Day, 21 September 1446. An active Scottish Episcopal church today,[1] it stands on College Hill in the midst of beautiful Roslin Glen, with the North Esk River below and the Pentland Hills nearby. Many believe the chapel harbors a long-lost secret. The Ark of the Covenant, the mummified head of Christ, the Holy Grail, lost scrolls from the Temple of Jerusalem, the Templar Order's treasures, Scotland's missing crown jewels, a Black Madonna, and more have been thought to lie within its vaults. Some understandably remain skeptical, saying that until the vaults are excavated no one can say anything for sure. With a subject as complex as Rosslyn, history and myth, fact and legend are intertwined.

Many have quested here, drawn by, among other things, the belief that Rosslyn Chapel has special connections to the Holy Grail and the Knights Templar. Lewis Spence says: "Nothing can shake my conviction that Rosslyn was built according to the pattern of the Chapel of the Grail as pictured in Norman romance, and that William St. Clair had in his poet's mind a vision of the Chapel Perilous when he set hand to the work."[2] Rosslyn has long been a beacon for creative luminaries—William and Dorothy Wordsworth, Sir Walter Scott,

Dr. Samuel Johnson, James Boswell, Robert Burns, and others are known to have visited it. Without question, it continues to inspire seekers as a place of worship, pilgrimage, and exploration.

"An elegant structure at Rosslyn"

The Earl of Rosslyn in his recent guidebook, *Rosslyn Chapel*, notes that the chapel was originally designed as part of a much larger building with a tower at its center. Work on the chapel, which took forty years, was completed in 1486. The founder, Sir William St. Clair, the third and last St. Clair Prince of Orkney, directed the entire process. He personally inspected each carving in wood before he allowed it to be carved in stone. That he took such loving care assures us that nothing in Rosslyn Chapel is there by accident.[3] Scottish historian Walter Bower, who updated Fordun's *Chronicle of the Scottish Nation* in 1447, wrote: *Willelmus de Sancto-Claro est in fabricado sumptuosam structuram apud Roslyn*—"Sir William St. Clair is erecting an elegant structure at Rosslyn."[4]

One of the best-known sources on Rosslyn Chapel and the St. Clair family is an extensive work by Father Richard Augustine Hay, Canon of St. Genevieve in Paris and Prior of St. Piermont. The Earl writes that Hay "examined historical records and charters of the St. Clairs and completed a three-volume study in 1700, parts of which were published in 1835 as *A Genealogie of the Saintclaires of Rosslyn*. His research was timely, since the original documents subsequently disappeared."[5] Father Hay comments on Sir William's great dedication to the building process:

> Prince William, his age creeping up on him, came to consider . . . how he was to spend his remaining days . . . That he might not seem altogether unthankful to God for the benefices he received from Him, it came into his mind to build a house for God's service, of most curious work . . . He caused artificers to be brought from other regions and foreign kingdoms and caused daily to be abundance of all kinds of workmen present as masons, carpenters, smiths, barrowmen, quarriers . . . First he caused draughts [plans] to be drawn upon eastland boards [imported Baltic timber] and he made the

carpenters carve them according to the draughts [plans], and he gave them for patterns to the masons.[6]

The identity of these "foreign kingdoms" and "other regions" from which the builders came is still debated. Sir William's family motto was "Commit Thy Work to God," and Rosslyn Chapel was a major focus of his dedicated efforts.

Sir William and chivalric Orders

Contrary to common assumption, Sir William St. Clair was neither a Templar nor a Freemason. To begin with, he lived in the fifteenth century; the Templar Order was officially dissolved by papal bull in May of 1312, and the Grand Lodge of England did not officially start until 1717, the Grand Lodge of Scotland not until 1736. Sir William was, however, a member of the Order of Santiago and the Order of the Golden Fleece.

By 1390, the idea of maintaining an elaborate knightly Order dedicated to the promotion of chivalry had fallen out of favor in most European courts. The Order of the Golden Fleece was started at Bruges in the early fifteenth century as part of a "medieval Renaissance:" "The year 1430 saw the proclamation in the court of Burgundy of a new monarchical order on the old, neo-Arthurian model, explicitly restricted to knights and calculated to promote chivalrous values and behaviour: . . . the 'Order of the Golden Fleece.'"[7] Founded by Philip the Good, Duke of Burgundy, the Order of the Golden Fleece was "perhaps in its time, the most prestigious Order of Knighthood in Europe."[8] The original Order consisted of a Grand Master (the sovereign Duke) and twenty-three knights. The membership was later increased to thirty-one and then to fifty-one.[9] A worldwide Order of the Golden Fleece still exists, although it is now structured somewhat differently, with two major divisions, the Spanish and the Austrian. On 8 September 1953, Austria recognized the Order as a Hapsburg institution, and King Juan Carlos is now the recognized head of the Spanish Order.[10]

In his *Genealogie* Father Hay mentions an Order of the Cockle, by which he no doubt means the Order of the Couquille St. Jaques—that is, the Order of Santiago:

> The "Order of San Jago di Compostella," better known as "The Knights of Santiago," [was] founded with strong Templar connections in the 12th century. At the time that Sir William belonged, novices were obliged to spend six months aboard ship! After the Templar suppression of 1307, many fugitive Templars joined this particular Order. A Scottish membership of this body would certainly suggest that the incumbent had completed the pilgrimage to Santiago de Compostella. Like so many other Scots of that time.[11]

The Order of Santiago "appears to have had close links with the Order of Alcantara and may have drawn its membership from the Friars of Caceres ... As the Order grew, its influence spread, particularly throughout France, Italy (and to a lesser extent England and Hungary) as well as in the Holy Land."[12] The Order of Santiago was closely related to the Order of St. James and the Sword; in fact, historians debate whether or not the two were identical. Like other Orders of the time, they took in refugee Templars after 1312.

The cathedral of St. James at Santiago was reputedly built over St. James's relics and is famous for the large number of pilgrims who visit it, even today. St. James is also the patron of pilgrims. Walter Stein states: "St James is the patron of all pilgrims who make their pilgrimage by land or sea. When Portuguese travellers and heroes of discovery went to India, St James was their patron ... We find the pilgrimage of St James leading as far south as India, and also to the north, to a chapel situated near Edinburgh ... Rosslyn Chapel."[13]

The emblem of St. James was the scallop shell, which pilgrims brought back from Santiago as tokens of the pilgrimage. Stein suggests that these shells were used in the mortar of Rosslyn Chapel when it was being built.

Devastating effects
of the Reformation

Sir William had generously endowed Rosslyn Chapel land for dwellings and gardens, and his grandson (also Sir William) did the same in 1523. But the Reformation, which took hold in the sixteenth century in Scotland, devastated Rosslyn. The Sinclairs remained Catholic, and Catholic churches, altars, and furnishings were deemed "idolatrous" and "Popish:" "Oliver St Clair was repeatedly warned to destroy the altars in the chapel and in 1592 was summoned to appear before the General Assembly and threatened with excommunication if the altars remained standing after August 17, 1592. On August 31st . . . 'the altars of Roslene were haille demolishit.' From that time the Chapel ceased to be used as a house of prayer, and soon fell into disrepair."[14]

In 1650, Cromwell's troops, under General Monck, attacked Rosslyn Castle, and the general used the chapel to stable his horses. On 11 December 1688, a Protestant mob from Edinburgh plus villagers from Roslin pillaged and burned Rosslyn Castle and further damaged the chapel. It remained abandoned until 1736, when, encouraged by Sir John Clerk of Penicuik, James St. Clair glazed the windows for the first time, repaired the roof, and relaid the floor with flagstones. Notably, 1736 is the year when the Grand Lodge of Scotland was founded, and Clerk was a prominent Freemason.

Rosslyn Chapel, Templar Wood,
and Roslin Glen

The area surrounding Rosslyn Chapel itself reflects Templar connections. Only a few miles away is the village of Temple—in medieval times known as Balantradoch, the medieval headquarters of the Scottish Knights Templar. The ruined Temple church still stands today. Templar Wood is also nearby; viewing it from the air, one sees it is shaped in the splayed cross of the Knights Templar—similar to the engrailed cross of the Sinclairs, which is found all over Rosslyn Chapel.[15] Moreover, Templar Wood, the village of Temple, and Rosslyn

Chapel seem placed in relation to each other according to precise geometric measurements—a point that a number of researchers and professional surveyors are currently studying. Gifted dowsers say important ley lines, or pathways of geophysical energy, intersect at the chapel's location, which may be significant geomantically.

Ancient Roslin Glen is known to have been settled by the Bronze Age. "It is also the largest surviving tract of ancient woodland in Midlothian, in which over two hundred species of flowering plants and sixty species of breeding birds have been recorded. Several of the plant species are rare."[16] The glen, along with the nearby castles of Rosslyn and Hawthornden, has long had literary associations. In the early seventeenth century William Drummond of Hawthornden, said to be the first Scottish poet to write in pure English, was visited by Ben Jonson, poet laureate of England. The Earl of Rosslyn relates an anecdote about this famous meeting:

> He was visited there [Hawthornden, adjacent to Rosslyn], in 1618 by Ben Jonson . . . who had made the journey from London to Edinburgh on foot. Drummond is said to have been sitting under a tree when his guest arrived and to have risen to greet him with the words: "Welcome, welcome, royal Ben," to which, not to be outdone in courtesy or craft, Jonson replied, "Thank ye, thank ye, Hawthornden."[17]

Roslin Glen is famous in Scottish history as a hideout. The entire Rosslyn-Hawthornden complex reputedly contains a network of underground caverns, and several caves have rooms large enough to hide sixty or seventy persons. The most famous, Wallace's Cave, is named for William Wallace, who apparently sought refuge there during the Battle of Roslin in 1302. Sir Alexander Ramsay hid there from the English army that captured Edinburgh in 1338, and "Bonnie Prince Charlie," Prince Charles Edward Stuart, was sought but not found there in 1746. Some caves under Hawthornden Castle contain Pictish carvings, which Queen Victoria came to view.[18]

In May of each year up until the Reformation in the mid-sixteenth century, the Sinclairs sponsored an annual festival held in Roslin Glen. A variety of plays, in particular, *Robin Hood and Little John*, were performed by gypsies. Rosslyn Castle had two towers, one named

Robin Hood and the other Little John; Sir William would have been well acquainted with this tradition before beginning work on Rosslyn Chapel in 1446. On 20 June 1555, the Scottish Parliament passed severe legislation against the gypsies, including a ban on the play *Robin Hood and Little John*. Sir William Sinclair (not the founder, but his descendant) was Lord Justice General of Scotland at the time, and as he did not agree with such draconian laws against the gypsies, he defied the ban and allowed the plays to continue in Roslin Glen.

In some places in Europe, the gypsies found sympathetic Christians who did not condone the various persecutions against gypsies. On Corpus Christi Day in 1584, a number of gypsies, fleeing arrest as heretics, sought refuge with the Knights of St. James of Santiago de Compostela. Convinced of the gypsies' Christian convictions, the knights accepted and protected them. Compostela is a major pilgrimage center even today; and we have seen that Rosslyn Chapel's founder, Sir William St. Clair, was a member of the Order of Santiago.[19]

St. Sara is the patron saint of the gypsies and is still celebrated today, especially in southern France. In Catholic tradition, Sara was said to be the black assistant who accompanied the three Marys from the Holy Land to France—Mary the sister of the Virgin, Mary the mother of James and John, and Mary Magdelene. In gypsy tradition, Sara was a gypsy woman (some say Egyptian) who helped the three Marys land safely in southern France after the Crucifixion.[20]

Rosslyn's exquisite carvings

A 1930s guidebook likens Rosslyn Chapel to a Bible in stone and says it resembles the Temple of Jerusalem: "Like Solomon's Temple, for which David, his father, made such ample provision, the 'Collegiate Church of St Matthew' was intended to be 'exceedingly magnificent, of fame and glory throughout all countries' (1 Chron. 22:5) and such it has proved to be through the centuries."[21] Many biblical scenes are depicted on Rosslyn's walls and pillars, yet the chapel also contains a fair amount of imagery that is not explicitly Christian. We know the Christian Fathers and later Christians adopted symbols of the earlier pagan wisdom traditions and reinterpreted them in a Christian light. So it is not surprising to find such a wide variety of imageries in many

Gothic cathedrals and chapels, including Rosslyn. Some of the more enigmatic figures include an image of Moses with horns, Christ with his right hand raised in blessing, an angel holding a scroll, a devil with a kneeling couple beside him, an angel with the engrailed (Sinclair) cross, musician angels with various instruments, and a fox dressed as a priest preaching to a flock of geese. Other carvings represent the seven deadly sins, the seven virtues, and, popular in medieval times, the Dance of Death. Templar, Masonic, Rosicrucian, and Christian symbolism and iconography are woven throughout the chapel in a rich tapestry of stone. In many ways, the carvings at Rosslyn Chapel are about the interplay of opposites and complements: the divine and the everyday, light and dark, male and female, life and death.

Carvings of New World plants, such as North American agave cactuses (some say aloe) and corn (maize), in the chapel may support the theory, discussed later in this chapter, that Prince Henry Sinclair voyaged to the New World at the end of the fourteenth century—before the chapel was built, and before Columbus.

The Green Man

One such symbol with pagan roots is the archetypal Green Man, of which Rosslyn Chapel has more carvings than any other medieval chapel in Europe. There are 103 carved images of the Green Man inside the chapel alone, and more on the exterior of the building. The Green Man is usually portrayed as a head with foliage growing profusely from the mouth, which represents fertility. The faces of the Rosslyn Green Men range from full and beaming with health to decidedly skeletal. Some experts propose that they symbolize collectively the four seasons of nature. In a Christian context, the Green Man symbol is often said to represent death and resurrection.

Although people often assume it is mainly a Celtic motif, this is not so; the Green Man is a universal symbol with very early roots: "Heads from Lebanon and Iraq can be dated to the 2nd century AD, and there are early Romanesque heads in 11th-century Templar churches in Jerusalem. From the 12th to 15th centuries heads appeared in cathedrals and churches across Europe."[22] Green Man carvings are also found in ancient Eastern temples—for instance, in the Apo Kayan area of Borneo, where he is perceived as the Lord God of the Forest;

in the chapels of Dhankar Gompa, high in the Indian Himalayas; in the temples of Kathmandu, Nepal; and in the Jain temples of Ranakpur. They are also reminiscent of vegetation gods who died and rose again, such as Tammuz or Osiris. Generally, the Green Man motif did not make its way into western Christian church carvings until around the sixth century. British Folklore Society scholar Jeremy Harte comments that "for all their differences in mood, these carvings give a common impression of something—someone—alive among the green buds of summer or the brown leaves of autumn. Green Men can vary from the comic to the beautiful, although often the most beautiful ones are the most sinister."[23]

Sir William no doubt included the Green Man in his late-medieval chapel to acknowledge both the Celtic traditions of the area and the chapel's beautiful natural setting. Indeed, the chapel may have been placed where it is because of the surrounding glen. The prolific Green Man symbols seem to acknowledge the aliveness of the earth and the processes of nature, conveying the message throughout Rosslyn Chapel: the power and wonder of nature are everywhere.

Several other originally pagan customs and symbols that have been incorporated into Christian festivals, including Easter egg hunts, Easter bunnies, and the Christmas—or Yuletide—tree, involve the color green. In medieval times it was considered the color of St. John the Evangelist. It also signifies springtime, reproduction, initiation, gladness, abundance, and prosperity. Green is associated with Grail symbolism, and the Grail quest can be seen as an attempt to return to Paradise. Some believe Rosslyn's Green Man carvings represent Robin Goodfellow—"Jack 'o the Green" or, in popular folklore, Robin Hood.

The Apprentice Pillar

One of the most famous carvings at Rosslyn Chapel is the exquisitely worked, stunningly beautiful Apprentice Pillar. A variety of authors, including Christian pastors, theologians, Freemasons, modern-day Templars, Rosicrucians, and Hermetic scholars, have written about this pillar's extraordinary beauty, symbology, and associated legends.

Around the bottom of the pillar are carved eight dragonlike beasts gnawing at the roots of a tree. In Scandinavian myth, the eight dragons of Neifelheim are said to lie at the base of Yggdrasil, the great ash tree that binds together heaven, earth, and hell. They keep the fruit of knowledge from growing on the Tree of Life. The theme of spiritual knowledge being withheld from humankind due to human igno-rance—represented by the serpent-dragons—recurs in many Western philosophical traditions, including Rosicrucianism, Hermeticism, Gnosticism, alchemy, the Templar tradition, and Freemasonry. In Christian terms, this imagery signifies the ongoing conflict between good and evil.

The Murdered Apprentice carving

Among the several legends associated with the Apprentice Pillar, one—the story of the Murdered Apprentice—is uniquely its own. This tale is referred to in a 1677 account, but some believe it may have originated earlier:

> The Master Mason, having received from the Founder the model of a pillar of exquisite workmanship and design, hesitated to carry it out until he had been to Rome . . . and seen the original. He went abroad and in his absence an apprentice, having dreamt that he had finished the pillar, at once set to work and carried out the design as it now stands, a perfect marvel of workmanship. The Master Mason on his return, seeing the pillar completed, instead of being delighted at the success of his pupil, was so stung with envy that he asked who had dared to do it in his absence. On being told that it was his apprentice, he was so inflamed with rage and passion that he struck him with his mallet, killed him on the spot and paid the penalty.[24]

The legend was recorded by Thomas Kirk, a Yorkshire man who traveled through Scotland in 1677. After a brief stop at St. Catherine's Well on Edinburgh's outskirts, Kirk approached Rosslyn:

> Two miles further we saw Roslen Chapel, a very pretty design, but was never finished, the choir only and a little vault. The roof is all stone, with good imagery work; there is a better man at exact descriptions of the stories than he at Westminster Abbey: this story he told us that the master builder went abroad to see good patterns,

but before his return his apprentice had built one pillar which exceeded all that ever he could do or had seen, therefore he slew him; and he showed us the head of the apprentice on the wall with a gash in the forehead and his masters head opposite to him.[25]

Indeed, there is a carving in a northern corner of the chapel dubbed "the Murdered Apprentice" that is said to represent the poor young mason.

A similar tale is familiar to Freemasons worldwide. Hiram Abiff, King Solomon's gifted master of works and builder of Solomon's Temple, was approached by three jealous masons who attempted to extort master mason's secrets from him. When Hiram refused, they treacherously murdered him. The death of the principal architect of Solomon's Temple, and the issue of the Temple being left incomplete, are not specifically mentioned in the Bible. Notably, the theme of a temple remaining unfinished due to the murder of a builder is also present in other traditions. For these and other topics relating Rosslyn Chapel to Rosicrucianism and Freemasonry see my previous book, *The Quest for the Celtic Key* (2002), cowritten with Scottish Masonic researcher Ian Robertson.

The Murdered Apprentice carving appears to have been modified at some point. Researcher Keith Laidler comments:

> Robert Brydon, whom I was fortunate to meet, was again able to offer confirmation of this identification. He told me that the face of the Apprentice is not what it seems to be. An American Templar, on a visit to Rosslyn, had examined the face of the "Apprentice" in detail. The carving has been very carefully altered: it originally possessed a beard and moustache, but these have been painstakingly removed (I was able to confirm this myself later, with the aid of high-power binoculars). This was a highly significant discovery. In medieval times, an apprentice stone mason was not allowed to sport a full beard and moustache. Facial hair was reserved for those who had completed their initiation into the mysteries of the craft. In other words, the head on the plinth at Rosslyn was not the head of the Apprentice, but the head of the Master.[26]

This leaves us with a question: Did someone alter this, and possibly other, carvings at Rosslyn? If so, this carving probably no longer appears as it was designed and approved by Sir William. Perhaps the original carving, or the legend associated with it, was unusual enough that someone would take the trouble to change it. And if the Murdered Apprentice carving was altered, who was it originally supposed to represent? A murdered master, perhaps? In ancient and much of medieval times, only master masons were allowed to wear a full beard, so, the carving was probably not originally of an apprentice. Notably, the Knights Templar also had long beards, as they were allowed to cut their head hair but not their beards.

If this carving were originally of a master mason, it might be connected to the Masonic legend of Hiram Abiff. If so, one legend seems to have been purposely modified to appear as another; that is, the gifted master murdered by three jealous apprentices became the talented apprentice murdered by his jealous master.

Another possibility, of course, is that the original, bearded carving was not meant to be of a builder at all.

The Veil of Veronica carving

The well-known story of the lady Veronica tells how she compassionately wiped the face of Christ as he was carrying the cross through the streets of Jerusalem, on the way to his Crucifixion. It is said that as a reward for her kindness, an image of his face miraculously remained on the cloth. So powerful was the medieval cult that grew around this scene, that the incident became the sixth of the fourteen Stations of the Cross. Yet ironically, the story appears nowhere in the Gospels. The cloth, preserved as a relic, became known as the Veil of Veronica. Some historians have identified it with the Mandylion of Edessa, which disappeared in 1204 after the siege of Constantinople. Preserved in Rome as a matter of record since at least 1011 and venerated by pilgrims, the veil, "called the Veronica . . . was seen publicly very rarely, but one of those rare occasions was just a few years before the first appearance of the Lirey Shroud—in the Holy Year 1350—when it was displayed to a rapturous audience of pilgrims. It was the talk of Europe."[27] Papal records show that in the jubilee years 1300 and 1350, many people were trampled in the rush to look upon the veil, which was said to cure all ills, especially leprosy. So we know there was a medieval relic that the Vatican recognized as the Veil of Veronica. The Veronica story was also performed in Paris as a miracle play, traditionally under auspices of medieval guilds. The veil disappeared during Charles V's "sack" of Rome in 1527. The square medieval reliquary in which it had been kept is still in St. Peter's sacristy. In Russia a vigorous and rather mysterious cult of Veronica lasted until at least the nineteenth century.

The image of only a head on the Veil of Veronica is clearly *not* the same as the full-body image on the Shroud of Turin, believed by some to be a first-century burial shroud. However, some scholars note that the head on the Shroud seems disproportionate to the body, and there are unresolved issues about its dating.

A carving of the Veil of Veronica is present at Rosslyn Chapel, but like the Murdered Apprentice carving, it has been badly damaged. The head on the cloth is untouched, but the image of the person holding the cloth is unrecognizable. Whoever did this made certain not to damage the image of Christ's head on the cloth but to disfigure only the person holding it.

With "the Veronica" carving, two aspects immediately stand out. The image of the person holding the cloth has been badly damaged. The head has been removed and it is impossible to know whether the image represents St Veronica, or even if it is female. Robert Brydon, Laidler relates, is one of the most knowledgeable of all Rosslyn researchers, and "has examined the chapel in detail . . . He told me that he is convinced the damage in the chapel is 'very specific, not done by accident . . . Someone has deliberately damaged parts of it for a reason.' This puts a new slant on the removal of the head of 'St Veronica.' Everyone assumes that the head of the person holding the towel is female; however, if the head of the person holding the towel was that of a man, *this would change the meaning of the image utterly.*"[28]

If the person holding the veil were male, who would this be? This question has prompted a plethora of theories. Does this carving have something to do with the alleged Rex Deus families, supposedly descended from Christ and the House of David, of which the Sinclairs are said to have been a part? Did the Knights Templar have the Veil of Veronica or the Shroud of Turin as a treasured relic?

Templar-related carvings in Rosslyn Chapel

Certain symbols are considered "diagnostic signs of Templarism."[29] These include: (1) two brothers on a horse; (2) the Agnus Dei;

(3) a five-pointed star; (4) a stylized representation of the head of Christ; (5) a floriated cross; and (6) a dove in flight, carrying an olive branch in its beak. Rosslyn Chapel has all of these images, either exactly as stated or in some variation.

Two brothers on a horse. In the bottom left-hand corner of a window in the chapel's south aisle is a carving of a knight on horseback with a passenger seated behind him. Many consider it a variation on the medieval Templars' official seal, which featured two brothers on a horse. Another theory suggests "these figures may represent the legend of William 'the Seemly' St. Clair, who is said to have carried back a portion of the true cross, or 'Holy Rood,' to Scotland. It is after this relic that Holyrood Abbey and Palace are named."[30] Others believe it represents the knight Bartholomew Ladislaus, bodyguard of the queen and one of William St. Clair's companions when he brought the Holy Rood to Rosslyn; seated behind him is Queen Margaret, whose husband, King Malcolm Canmore, encouraged the St. Clairs to settle in Scotland.[31] As we saw earlier, the symbol of two knights or warriors on one horse probably goes back to Sumerian times.

The Agnus Dei seal. The image of the Agnus Dei is the Lamb of God, which symbolized Christ and appeared on many medieval Templar seals; for example, it shows up on one side of a 1304 seal of William de la More, Master of the Temple in England. Rosslyn Chapel has a carving that greatly resembles the Agnus Dei: "At its [a pillar's] top is an angel holding a seal depicting the Lamb of God, an emblem said to be associated with the Knights Templar."[32] The carving bears a cross with a banner and a lamb, with two exceptionally worn figures, believed to be angels, holding the seal at either side. In this case, the disfigurement is due to the weather; after the seventeenth century, the Sinclairs of Rosslyn worshipped in their private family chapel in the castle, so the chapel was left exposed to the elements, primarily due to lack of funds to maintain it. The theme of two hands holding something is repeated in other Rosslyn carvings, though none of the others are of the Agnus Dei.

A five-pointed star. The chapel's roof is the only example of a carved, barrel-vaulted solid stone medieval roof in Scotland. The ceiling in the interior of the chapel has detailed carvings of daisies, lilies, roses, and other flowers as well as numerous five-pointed stars. Each kind of symbol is carved on one section of the ceiling, which is divided into five parts. Throughout the ages, the number five has always been associated with Mary or some form of the Divine Feminine. The rose section of the roof is said to represent the five wounds of Christ and the five virtues of Mary; in medieval times the rose had only five petals. The lily section signifies Mary's purity, the Annunciation, and the Assumption.

The cult of the Virgin Mary reached a peak of popularity in the twelfth century, the first part of the Templar Order's existence and became more prevalent again in the fifteenth century, which is when Rosslyn Chapel was built. As we have seen, the Templars especially venerated Mary. She was the patroness of the Order, and they dedicated many chapels and cathedrals to her.

Some scholars believe the five-pointed star may also refer to Mary Magdalene. In ancient times the five-pointed star was associated with Venus and Isis, for example, and it also appears frequently on the ceilings of Egyptian temples. Adjacent to the carvings of stars on Rosslyn Chapel's ceiling are also images of the moon, the sun, four angels, a dove, and, barely visible, the face of Christ with his right hand raised in blessing.

A stylized head of Christ. The stylized head of Christ appears in the Veil of Veronica carving, discussed above. Numerous rumors in medieval times intimated that the Templars had a special cloth with the head of Christ on it—perhaps the Shroud or the Veil of Veronica. Some historians wonder whether this could be the alleged head called Baphomet that the inquisitors, during the trials, accused the Templars of worshipping. Some researchers state outright that this carving at Rosslyn "signifies the true heresy of the Templars—the Veil of Veronica."[33] Historian Andrew Sinclair, in *The Discovery of the Grail*, comments: "The two 'Grails' of the Templars—the containers of the Holy Shroud and the Holy Veil from Constantinople—may have reached the vaults of Rosslyn with the flight of the French knights to Scotland with their treasures and their records."[34]

A floriated cross. Also in Rosslyn Chapel is what is believed to be the burial stone of Sir William St. Clair (1297–1330), son of Henry Sinclair, who died in Spain while attempting to fight the Saracens. This granite slab, only three feet long, bears a chalice with a long stem carved along one side of it, and a sword on the other. Within this chalice, at the top, is a floriated cross—an octagon design with a rose at the center. This octagon design is a part of the eight-pointed cipher the Templars were known to have used.

Floriated crosses are also found at other churches nearby. A tombstone at Melrose, even smaller than the Rosslyn burial stone, features a small eight-pointed cross fleury within a large eight-pointed cross. Other Templar-related symbols on gravestones at Melrose include floral crosses within a circle or disk-head and a boss of the five-petalled rose, a symbol of the Virgin Mary. Other Melrose gravestones are carved with scallop shells, indicating that one had made the arduous pilgrimage to Compostela. A grave stone at Corstorphine Church in Edinburgh has a cross fleury inside a circle and a stem within leading down to the steps of Calvary and the Temple of Solomon, with a crusader sword etched by its side.[35]

A dove in flight, carrying an olive branch. On the chapel ceiling, in the section with the five-pointed stars, is carved a dove in flight carrying an olive branch. This symbol, well known from the biblical story of Noah and the Ark, also signifies Christ's love for humanity. It also sometimes represents Mary or the Holy Spirit. In Wolfram's *Parzival*, the *Templeisen*'s shields bear a turtle dove, a sign of God's unconditional love.

Other Templar-related carvings. Other carvings at Rosslyn may have Templar connotations. According to Niven Sinclair, devoted patron of Rosslyn, the Madonna and Child at Rosslyn may be linked with the Black Madonna pilgrimage tradition. The Templar banner, the *beauseant*, with its black-and-white checkered pattern, may be cleverly included as a chessboard on a pair of Victorian-era stained glass windows; St. Maurice is depicted on one and St. Longinus on the other. Both of these saints are associated with the Precious Blood of Christ, so some believe their portrayal here alludes to the Rex Deus theory with reference to the Sinclairs of Rosslyn. I also believe there are others with alchemical symbolism that are Templar related.

The Grail and
Rosslyn Chapel

Although many Grail traditions are associated with other countries, some do pertain to Scotland. One geomantic observation is that the layout of Scottish sacred sites, such as Iona, Scone, and Rosslyn Chapel, have a "Grail energy" that forms a special spiritual matrix in the landscape. But most recent Grail speculations concerning Scotland have centered on Rosslyn. One carving in the chapel is of the high priest Melchezidek holding a chalice—which some consider an image of the Grail. One author notes the solid stone roof appears as "literally a stone fallen from heaven—the *lapis exilis* of *Parzival* which was called the Grail."[36] Stein comments on possible links between Rosslyn Chapel and the Grail:

> There are two spiritual traditions which found each other and united in Rosslyn Chapel. These two traditions appear also in the history of the Holy Grail ... The microcosmic aspect follows the story of Joseph of Arimathea who took away with him the saviour's blood. Whenever the Holy Blood is worshipped, this microcosmic tradition is found ... The other, the macrocosmic tradition, was used as the source for another story of the Holy Grail by Wolfram of Eschenbach, who shows the connection of the Holy Grail with astrology ... That these two traditions have united in Rosslyn Chapel can be seen in the symbols there ... which indicate both paths: how man can strive to become Divine, and how the Divine became flesh. Christ as the cornerstone of cosmic and human evolution is shown in the chapel ... The master who built the chapel has conveyed many secrets of evolution to those who study, not only what is portrayed, but how it is portrayed.[37]

The Apprentice Pillar and the Grail

One of the most persistent legends about Rosslyn Chapel says that the Grail, in the form of a silver platter or perhaps a chalice, is hidden in the elegantly carved Apprentice Pillar. Well-known Grail researcher Trevor Ravenscroft claimed in 1962, after twenty-some years of research all over the world, that his quest ended at Rosslyn Chapel. A number of years ago, his wife, certain of the Grail's presence in the

Apprentice Pillar, chained herself to it in "a vain attempt to force the authorities to X-ray it and discover the Grail. Later radar researches, carried out by Tony Wood and Greg Mills, operating Groundscan radar equipment, have detected no metal object within."[38] The pillar has not been X-rayed since then, so the legend remains unproved. Some point out that the Grail object may not be metal, in which case radar would not detect it. Others believe the legend may be true anyway. As has been said, the power of an idea doesn't depend on whether it is literally true or not; what counts is whether people *believe* it is true.

The wooden bowl at Rosslyn Chapel

Author Andrew Sinclair found a simple oak bowl—a Grail—in the vaults of Rosslyn Chapel while assisting Niven Sinclair and his associates in conducting groundscans of the chapel:

> Evidence of lower chambers revealed by the process bore out ancient drawings and medieval tales of buried St Clair knights in vaults below the chapel floor. The radar pulses also detected reflectors, which indicated metal, probably the armour of the buried knights. Particularly exciting was a large reflector under the Lady Chapel, which suggested the presence of a metallic shrine there, perhaps that of the Black Virgin, which still marks so many holy places on the pilgrim route to Compostela, a sacred way that has one of its endings in Rosslyn Chapel.[39]

However, it was difficult to reach the vaults:

> The groundscan had shown two stairways leading beneath the slabs. Laboriously, one set of flagstones was lifted, rubble was cleared, and indeed, three steep stone steps were found to lead to a vault below. I was the first to squirm into this secret chamber. It was small, comprising the space between the foundations of two pillars. It was arched with stone, but access to the main vaults beyond had been sealed by a thick wall of stone masonry . . . The soggy wood from three coffins had been stacked in front of the blocking wall. Sifting through the debris below the broken coffins, I found human bones and the fragments of two skulls, two rusty Georgian coffin handles, a mason's whetstone, and a simple oak bowl, left there by

a mason from his meal along with his flint for sharpening the tools of his craft.[40]

Sinclair notes that a plain wooden bowl "is what the original Grail from the Last Supper would have been—a wooden platter passed by Jesus Christ in His divine simplicity to His poor Apostles...Such a simple workman's bowl, perhaps as old as the late Middle Ages when this chapel was designed as a Chapel of the Grail, was a Grail as good as any other, the container of God's bounty on earth."[41] For that matter, any bowl or cup can symbolize the Grail, if one thinks of it as a material object shaped as a cup.

Though the team tried to drill deeper into the vaults, the drill bit jammed continuously, and much dust and debris kept blocking their way: "After a week of work, we were defeated. The vaults of this Chapel of the Grail would keep their secret shrine. The St Clair knights would not be disturbed in their tombs. Perhaps that is how it should be. They had been buried beyond the reach of intruders. They would only reappear on the Day of Judgment, when the stone slabs would crack open."[42] So, the mystery of the Grail at Rosslyn is likely to remain an enigma for some time to come.

The barons of Roslin

In his famous poem *The Lay of the Last Minstrel*, Sir Walter Scott wrote about twenty barons of Roslin buried in full knightly armor, beneath Rosslyn Chapel:

> Seem'd all on fire that chapel proud,
> Where Roslin's chiefs uncoffin'd lie,
> Each Baron, for a sable shroud,
> Sheathed in his iron panoply...
> There are twenty of Roslin's barons bold
> Lie buried within that proud chapelle...
> And each St Clair was buried there
> With candle, with book and with knell.[43]

John Slezer, in a 1693 account of the chapel, says of the barons: "The last lay in a vault so dry that their bodies have been found intire after Fourscore Years, and as fresh as when they were first buried. There goes a tradition, that before the death of any of the family of Roslin, this Chapel appears all in Fire."[44]

In the eighteenth century Robert Forbes, bishop of Caithness, surveyed the grounds and interior of Rosslyn Chapel, including at least some part of the extensive area underneath the chapel. He reported what he saw in *An Account of the Chapel of Roslin* (1774). He refers to ten barons of Roslin being buried in the vaults of the chapel but does not mention any treasure. Some who believe the Sinclair knights would have been buried with Rosslyn's reputed treasures critique Forbes for possibly withholding information. Others point out that treasure or scrolls may be stored elsewhere or there may be other vaults under the chapel or in the surrounding kirkyard that Forbes did not see. Until Rosslyn's vaults are actually excavated, nothing can be said for certain.

The Holy Rood and Scotland's lost crown jewels

Mary of Guise—Queen Regent of Scotland and mother of Mary, Queen of Scots—in a 1546 letter to Lord William St. Clair of Rosslyn refers to being shown "a great secret within Rosslyn." What she saw is as yet unknown and unexplained. Authors Hopkins, Simmans, and Wallace-Murphy comment:

Her attitude is a complete reversal of what one would expect. She swears to be a "true mistress" to him and protect him and his servants for the rest of her life in gratitude for being shown *a great secret within Rosslyn*, the nature of which is not disclosed. The general tone of the letter is more like that of someone subservient to a superior lord than that of a sovereign to her vassal. This is simply due to the deference shown by a senior representative of a senior branch of the Rex Deus dynasty, namely, Mary of Guise, to the leading member of the principal dynasty of the group, Lord William of Roslin.[45]

A number of experts believe she was shown the Sinclair knights in effigy. Others believe she saw more precious things as well: the lost crown jewels of Scotland and the Holy Rood—a piece of the True Cross. Two passages, dated 21 March 1545, from the official "Acts of the Lords of Council in Public Affairs," imply that the crown jewels and the Holy Rood were entrusted to William St. Clair and were never returned. Since these passages predate Marie of Guise's letter to Lord

William by about a year, they support the idea that she may have seen these priceless objects:

> The lords ordain William St. Clair of Roslin to produce within three days all jewels, vestments and ornaments of "the abbay and place of Halyrudhous...put and ressavit within his place" so that the Cardinal and administrator may see them and that they may be "usit in the solempnyt tyme not approchand, to the honour of God"...
> The laird of Craigmillar protested by his procurator that he should be assoilzied in the matter against the laird of Roslin for detaining the Holyrood jewels.[46]

The Holy Rood and some of the Scottish crown jewels have never been found. Are they perhaps in Rosslyn Chapel's vaults? If Lord William was a senior member of the European Rex Deus families, could this be partly why he chose not to return them, as Wallace-Murphy and others suggest? Are these precious items, and perhaps others, lying in wait until the correct moment for them to be brought forth—a time known only to a select group—as some speculate? Could any of this relate somehow to the Kingdom of Jerusalem, the historical succession of those said to be the blood descendants of Christ? In any case, Marie of Guise's remains inexplicable by scholars—an enigma of Scottish history.

Will there be an excavation?

The question of what may be hidden at Rosslyn Chapel has become a modern-day myth in the making, much like the Templar mythos. Maybe nothing is there. But many think the chapel does hold something of value, and they want to know what that is. Will the vaults of Rosslyn Chapel ever be excavated? Or, *should* they ever be excavated? Some believe they are best left alone. Others are adamant that if the vaults hold something important for all humanity, such as the Jerusalem Temple scrolls, it should be brought to light and made known to all.

The decision whether or not to excavate is of course up to the Earl of Rosslyn and his family and to the Rosslyn Chapel Trust, the current administrators of the chapel. Moreover, as there are important burial sites around Rosslyn Chapel, the Right of Sepulchre law, which prohibits disturbance of existing graves and churchyards, applies to Rosslyn. Stuart Beattie, director of Rosslyn Chapel Trust, explains: "Due to the Scottish law of the 'Right of Sepulchre,' a rather lengthy legal procedure would have to be followed, in order to secure the necessary permission to dig on the church grounds by the authorities. Meanwhile, the focus is on *preservation* of the building, and not on excavation, at this time."[47] Beattie says the Trust *may* in the future challenge the Right of Sepulchre to obtain legal permission to begin a professional excavation, but this is not likely any time soon. In the meantime, saving the chapel from further damage and preserving it for posterity is obviously the Trust's first priority.[48]

James Simpson, architect of the extensive conservation projects at Rosslyn, states:

> It may be 2010 before the programme of conservation and development currently envisaged is completed. Fifty or so years of decline will have been followed by thirty years of making up the deficit. Nor will that be the end of the matter; managing and caring for a site like Rosslyn never ends. It is in the very nature of "heritage" that responsibilities, as well as rights, are passed on from generation to generation.[49]

Rosslyn Castle as
a medieval scriptorium

Few today are aware that Rosslyn Castle was once an important medieval scriptorium, where manuscripts were manufactured with great care and skill. Among the many produced at Rosslyn are the five St. Clair manuscripts, each bearing one or more St. Clair signatures, which are now in the National Library of Scotland. In the booklet *Rosslyn: A History*, Robert Brydon explains:

> One of these is a giant compendium mostly written by James Mangnet in 1488. Commissioned by William St Clair (for his inscription appears as that of first owner), the 1,000 hand-written pages contain significantly: GUILD LAWS, FOREST LAWS, and "THE LAWIS

AND CUSTUMIS OF YE SCHIPPIS." Legalities all vital to the Scottish Operative Guilds! A work also necessary for the legal guidance of their hereditary Patrons, Protectors and Arbitrators; the St Clairs of Rosslyn.[50]

This text, called the Rosslyn-Hay manuscript, is the earliest extant work in Scottish prose.[51] In addition to the guild, forest, and shipping laws it contains a section titled *The Buk of the Order of Knighthede* (*The Book of the Order of Knighthood*).

According to its inscription, Gilbert Hay, knight, carried out the translation and produced the three part folio on the instructions of William Sanctclare of Rosslyn. A small panel (PATRICUS LOWES ME LIGAVIT), integral to the leather binding, indicates that the binder was Patrick de Lowis, a burgher of Rosslyn who died in 1466. The heavily worked leather binding is recognised as the most important example of its kind in the British Isles.[52]

The St. Clairs of Rosslyn appear to have had relationships with certain medieval guilds in Edinburgh and with certain Orders of knighthood. Brydon asks, regarding the contents of the Rosslyn-Hay manuscript: "As hereditary judges, or 'Grand Masters' administering Guild Laws, did the hereditary St Clair mandate extend over other Orders or fraternities such as those of Knighthood? This has always remained an unanswered question."[53]

Among the other manuscripts made at Rosslyn Castle is one, recently identified as made at Rosslyn, in the Bodleian Library at Oxford University. Brydon continues: "Paper-makers, translators, and scribes . . . were certainly part of the manuscript manufactory attached to the great library at Rosslyn Castle which was looted in the 17th century. It is now understood that in the translation and reproduction of important manuscripts, Rosslyn could be compared with Anjou in France. (Some of the works produced at Rosslyn are known to have originated at Anjou)."[54] Rosslyn's connections with the illustrious House of Anjou would be a fascinating subject in its own right.

According to one local tale, a great fire gutted Rosslyn Castle in 1441. Sir William was apparently beside himself, thinking his precious books and scrolls were destroyed. To his relief, his trustworthy chaplain had lowered a trunk full of manuscripts from the window, thus saving them for posterity. A nineteenth-century account relates:

The news of this fire coming to the Prince's ears, through the lamentable cries of the ladies and gentlewomen, and the sight thereof coming to his view . . . upon the College Hill (the site of the chapel) he was sorry for nothing but the loss of his Charters and other writings; but when the Chaplain, who had saved himself by coming down the bell-rope tied to a beam, declared how his Charters and writs were all saved, he became cheerful, and went to recomfort his princess and the ladies . . . and rewarded his chaplain very richly. Yet all this stayed him not from the building . . . neither his liberality to the poor, but was more liberal to them than before, applying the safety of his Charters and writings to God's particular Providence.[55]

Many speculate that the chapel's purpose, among other things, was to house Sir William's manuscripts, but whether scrolls or manuscripts are safeguarded under the chapel remains to be seen.

Many medieval castles are rumored to contain buried treasure, and Roslin Castle is no exception. A persistent local legend speaks of an enormous treasure whose hiding place will not be revealed until the day a trumpet blast wakes up from her long sleep "a certain Lady of the ancient house of St. Clair." Yet someone with a profound knowledge of Templarism, British historian Michael Bentine, during a 1994 interview at Rosslyn, dismissed the tales of treasure. In his view, Rosslyn's real treasure is the spirituality that can be felt there. He is convinced, however, that the Templars had access to great secrets and that someday when Rosslyn's vaults are opened, important documentation connected with the Templars will be disclosed.[56]

Indeed, perhaps the treasure isn't a material treasure at all. Perhaps it is—and has always been—spiritual in nature; for the spiritual aspects of the quest, not the material, are most important. Even if a material treasure, such as the Holy Rood or valuable scrolls, is eventually found, an important question will still be: What is its spiritual significance?

The New World and Prince Henry Sinclair

According to members of the Sinclair family and a growing number of experts, even before Rosslyn Chapel was built, the Sinclairs were involved in the search for the New World. Prince Henry Sinclair, Earl of Orkney, set off on a voyage of discovery for a great new country in 1398 and dropped anchor in Guysborough Harbor, Nova Scotia, on 2 June of that year. The document said to describe his voyage, the Zeno Narrative, was written in 1558—160 years later—in Venice, by Nicolo Zeno, the famous Venetian admiral. His brother was the famed Venetian naval war hero, Carlo Zeno; another key player in this story is Antonio Zeno. So, the Zeno family name was synonymous with great renown on the high seas. The Zeno Narrative contains Nicolo Zeno's Map of the North, which many believe referred to Prince Henry's journey to the New World. Though contested by some historians in the past, other academic experts now believe that the Zeno Narrative is genuine. Remarkably, this particular map appears to accurately describe aspects of Greenlandic and Nova Scotian geography not known in Europe in 1558. Supporters naturally say this proves the expedition did get to Nova Scotia; otherwise, how could its coastline have been mapped so precisely?

Professor Hugh Purcell of Vienna claims Prince Henry Sinclair met with Carlo Zeno at the Danish court in Copenhagen some thirty-four years before his purported 1398 journey:

> The Venetians, including Carlo Zeno, accompanied by King Peter [Peter I of Cyprus] when he visited the court of Denmark in 1364— where they would certainly have met Prince Henry, as well as Paul Knutsson, who had just returned from a voyage to the New World, where he had been sent by King Magnus of Norway to find out what had happened to the settlers from Greenland who had emigrated to mainland North America and had apparently "gone native." King Magnus was anxious to bring them back to the Catholic faith.[57]

From Nova Scotia, Prince Henry is believed to have also gone on to Massachusetts—fueling a fiercely growing controversy today about pre-Columbian voyages to the New World. In fact, Columbus "must certainly have known about Prince Henry's voyage from one of Prince Henry's grandsons, when he was resident on the islands of Porto Santo and nearby Madeira in the 1470s," according to Professor Purcell.[58]

Zeno's Map of the North is not the only early map depicting parts of North America and the northern polar regions, however. On 29 July 2002 in a joint press release the U.S. Brookhaven National Laboratory, the University of Arizona, and the Smithsonian Center for Materials Research and Education announced the latest research on the "Vinland Map." Using carbon-dating technology, scientists from these institutions determined the date of the map to be approximately 1434, which is almost sixty years before Columbus sailed to the West Indies:

> Housed in Yale University's Beinecke Rare Book and Manuscript Library, the map shows Europe (including Scandinavia), Northern Africa, Asia and the Far East, all of which were known by 15th-century travelers. In the northwest Atlantic Ocean, however, it also shows the "Island of Vinland," which has been taken to represent an unknown part of present-day Labrador, Newfoundland, or Baffin Island . . . The map, drawn in ink and measuring 27.8 x 41.0 centimeters, surfaced in Europe in the mid-1950s, but had no distinct record of prior ownership or provenance in any famous library . . . The map . . . was purchased in 1958 for $1 million by Paul A. Mellon, . . . and, at Mellon's request, subjected to an exhaustive six-year investigation . . . Beginning in 1995, . . . [researchers] undertook a detailed scientific study of the parchment . . . They were allowed to trim a 3-inch-long sliver off the bottom edge of the parchment for analysis [and with a spectrometer] determined a precision date of 1434 A.D. plus or minus 11 years. The unusually high precision of the date was possible because the parchment's date fell in a very favorable region of the carbon-14 dating calibration curve. This new analysis of the map parchment reaffirms the association with the Council of Basel since it dates exactly to that time period, and makes a strong case for the map's authenticity. [59]

The lead Brookhaven researcher on the project commented: "Many scholars have agreed that if the Vinland Map is authentic, it is the first known cartographic representation of North America, and its date would be key in establishing the history of European knowledge of the lands bordering the western Atlantic Ocean. If it is, in fact, a forgery, then the forger was surely one of the most skillful criminals ever to pursue that line of work."[60]

If one early map that includes North America has been scientifically dated to before 1492, there may be others, proponents of the Sinclair theory maintain. The Zeno Narrative map may be one example.

Andrew Sinclair comments on Prince Henry and his voyage:

> He was also the Lord of Orkney and the Shetlands, the axis of transatlantic trade . . . In 1398, Prince Henry St Clair set out with a large expedition of soldiers and monks to establish two colonies in the New World; one at Louisburg in Nova Scotia . . . and another at Newport, Rhode Island. The notorious round tower on a hill there, with its 8 arches in the manner of the original Church of the Holy Sepulchre could never have served as the colonial windmill that some claim it to be.[61]

Newport was settled in 1639, and earliest mention of the famous stone tower there is in the will of Governor Benedict Arnold, dated 1677. Yet according to the Sinclair theory, the Newport Tower may have been standing there for more than two hundred years when the English arrived. It has no parallel in colonial New England, and its unique features continue to puzzle the experts today. It is built in Norman-Romanesque style, with eight columns and arches, two floors, a fireplace with two flues, and several double-splayed windows. Sinclair family members believe it was inspired by the architecture of the Holy Sepulchre in Jerusalem, a concept the crusaders had brought back to Europe.

There are two major "camps," often in bitter disputes with each other, about the origins of the Newport Tower: those who believe Governor Arnold built it and those who believe Viking explorers built it. Critics of the Arnold theory point out that although records say Arnold owned a stone mill, they do not say he built it. Critics of the Viking theory say that the evidence isn't sufficient to support that thesis.[62]

In recent years, however, experts have noted that certain architectural features of the Newport Tower are also found in Scotland or Orkney. Moreover, historian Andrew Sinclair as well as several architects have confirmed that the one measure unique to the Newport

Tower is the Scottish "ell," which equals 37 inches or 93.98 cm—not the English "foot." Also, the tool marks on the stones are unlike those on other colonial stonework; rather, they generally match tools manufactured before 1400. On this basis, the tower's origin is estimated as sometime between 1150 and 1400. Some architectural experts say the original tower was precolonial, and in colonial times the pillars' bases were strengthened, possibly to use the tower as a windmill.[63] Nothing certain can be concluded at this point, but research continues.

At Westford, Massachusetts, is a worn carving that some experts believe is a medieval knight in effigy that dates to the later half of the fourteenth century. Historian Frederick Pohl, in *Prince Henry Sinclair*, describes the Westford knight carving: "The long sword with large wheel pommel is of a late fourteenth-century type. It is a Scottish claymore of 1350–1400 . . . Armorial scholars say that the basinet is of a form that was in fashion for only twenty-five years, from 1375 to 1400."[64] Since this period *precedes* Columbus's voyage in 1492, the date of the carving is of course hotly debated today. What, then, is it doing in Massachusetts? And who does it represent?[65]

Sir William St. Clair, founder of Rosslyn Chapel, was concerned about the burning of books and the destruction of learning in his day and so was inspired to build something to last for posterity. His chapel can be viewed as the expression of a universal wisdom tradition with many aspects to it, all codified in stone for posterity. History has shown that Sir William was right—yes, there *were* attempts to destroy Rosslyn Chapel, yet it still survives.

In the present day we are so used to consulting books and the printed word that we forget how important the world of symbol was in medieval times. Niven Sinclair has pointed out: "History can more accurately be found: in the face of the land, in the faces of the people we meet, in the language(s) we speak, in our customs, traditions, and superstitions"[66] than in the printed word alone. In the Middle Ages only a privileged few could read or write, yet many were able to contemplate the symbolism expressed in the carvings of such monuments as Rosslyn Chapel or Chartres Cathedral, for example. The skilled craftsmen who built these extraordinary medieval buildings, and the learned ones who sponsored and assisted them, have left us a silent, spiritual message to decipher. Robert Brydon writes in *Rosslyn: A History:* "Over the years the Guilds, the Templars, the Rosicrucians, and the Masons have all recognised something of their own mystery teaching in the complex allegory presented by Rosslyn Chapel. An arcanum, a book in stone. An unfinished labour of love that lasts forever."[67]

Appendix 1

Chronology of Events During Templars' Era (1119–1314)

Templar events are in bold. Other events and people relating to the Church, Grail manuscripts, and the Crusades are included when relevant to this book.

1118–31	Reign of Baldwin II, King of Jerusalem
1119	**Official public emergence of the Order of the Temple; nine knights, led by Hugh de Payn, the first Templar Grand Master, present themselves to Baldwin II in Jerusalem**
1119	Cistercian Order constitution, *Carta Caritatis*, presented to Pope Calixtus II
1119–27	**First nine Templar knights remain in the Holy Land**
1124	Christian Franks control Tyre and occupy entire coast, except for Ascalon, which remains under Muslim control
1126	Death of Hughes de Champagne, recorded at Chartres
1127	**(Autumn) The early Templars return from the Holy Land; beginning of the Order's unprecedented rise in power and influence**
1128	First Cistercian house established in Britain (Waverley, Surrey)
1129	**(January) Council of Troyes; Rule of the Templar Order established**
1129	William of Malmesbury completes *De Antiquitate Glastonie Ecclesie*
1130	**Bernard of Clairvaux completes *In Praise of the New Knighthood***
1131–43	Reign of Fulk of Anjou, King of Jerusalem
1132	Construction of the western facade and front nave of St. Denis Cathedral begins
1134	Construction of the north tower of Chartres Cathedral begins
1135	Council of Pisa

1136	Geoffrey of Monmouth brings Arthurian literature to the world's attention with his Latin text, *History of the Kings of Britain*
1136–37	**Templars established in the Amanus March (north of Antioch)**
1137	Zangi, Muslim ruler of Aleppo and Mosul, captures Fulk, King of Jerusalem, then releases him
1138–42	Byzantine confrontation with crusader principality of Antioch
1139	**Templar Castles in the Holy Land completed: Baghras, Darbask, Destroit, La Roche, de Roussel, Port Bonnet**
1140	Alliance of Jerusalem and Damascus against Zangi, Muslim ruler of Aleppo and Mosul
1140	Council of Sens
1143	Death of Fulk of Anjou, King of Jerusalem
1144	Zangi wins control of Edessa on Christmas Eve; sparks the Second Crusade
1145	(December) Pope Eugenius III proclaims the Second Crusade
1146	Bernard of Clairvaux travels extensively and preaches the Second Crusade
1146	Murder of Zangi, Muslim ruler of Aleppo and Mosul; his son, Nur al-Din, succeeds him
1147–49	Second Crusade
1147–70	Peak of career of Bernard de Ventadorn, renowned Languedoc troubadour favored in Eleanor of Aquitaine's court; influenced not only the Occitan tradition, but also French and German poetry
1148	Council of Reims
1148	(July) Louis VII of France, Queen Eleanor of Aquitaine, and Emperor Conrad III go to the Holy Land (Second Crusade)
1149	Baldwin III, with consent of the Patriarch of Jerusalem, gives Dietrich of Alsace the relic of Holy Blood collected by Joseph of Arimathea
1149–50	**Gaza granted to the Templars**
1151	Death of Abbot Suger of St. Denis (1081–1151)
1150–1300	General time frame of the Cathars and Albigensians

1153	**Death of Bernard of Clairvaux**
1153	Construction of Notre Dame Cathedral, Paris, begins
1153	Ascalon falls to the Franks
1154	Nur al-Din takes control of Damascus in the Holy Land
1160	**Grand-scale Templar round church founded in Tomar, Portugal, by Gualdim Pais, Templar Grand Master**
mid-1160s	**Hierarchical statutes added to the Templar Rule**
late 1160s	**Statutes on daily monastic life, chapter meetings, and penances added to the Templar Rule**
1163–69	Nur al-Din's lieutenant, Shirkuh, wins control of Egypt; he dies two months later and is succeeded by his nephew, Saladin
1163–74	Reign of Amaury, King of Jerusalem
1170	Murder of St. Thomas à Becket, Archbishop of Canterbury
1171	Saladin proclaims overthrow of the Fatimid caliphate; as master of Egypt, finds himself in conflict with Nur al-Din
1174	Death of Nur al-Din; Saladin wins control of Damascus
1174	Canonization of Bernard of Clairvaux
1174–85	Reign of Baldwin IV, King of Jerusalem
1183	Saladin wins control of Aleppo
1185–86	Reign of Baldwin V, King of Jerusalem
1186–94	Reign of Guy of Lusignan, King of Jerusalem
1187	Battle of Hattin; Jerusalem falls to Saladin
1189–92	Third Crusade
1190–1220	Various Grail manuscripts written in France, Wales, England, Germany, and Spain
1190	Formation of the Teutonic Knights of St. Mary's Hospital at Jerusalem
1190	Chrétien de Troyes (Champagne) brings the Holy Grail, Perceval, and Lancelot to the attention of the world with his Grail romance, *Perceval*
1190	Pope Alexander III pronounces the Cathars "anathema"
1190–92	Richard I arrives in Holy Land; Christians recover several cities, but not Jerusalem, from the Muslims
1191	**Templar headquarters in the Latin East moved to Acre**
1191	Richard I ("the Lionheart") meets Saladin at Battle of Arsuf

1191	Announcement of discovery of King Arthur's tomb in Glastonbury Abbey cemetery
1191–92	**Templars occupy Cyprus**
1192	Joachim of Fiore, monastic scholar and mystic, founds the Florensian Order
1192	Richard I departs from Holy Land with his entourage, said to include Templars
1192	**Richard I captured on way home from Crusade by the troops of Austrian Duke Leopold V, with whom he had quarreled; imprisoned and held for ransom by German Emperor Henry VI; privileges in Richard's dominions, including English Templars' privileges, suspended during this time**
1193	Saladin dies at age 55 in Damascus; succeeded by his brother al-Adil
1201	Fourth Crusade begins
1204	Franks victorious at Constantinople
1205	Beginning of Cathar massacres by the Inquisition
1206	St. Francis of Assisi begins his mission
1208	(10 March) Pope Innocent III calls for a crusade against the Albigensians
1209	Start of the Albigensian Crusade, Beziers, France
1209	Franciscan Order Rule approved by Innocent III
1217–21	**Building of Atlit (Pilgrims' Castle), a major Templar fortress in Holy Land**
1218–21	Fifth Crusade
1220	Dominican Rule confirmed
1223	Second Franciscan Rule confirmed by papal bull
1224/5–74	Lifespan of St. Thomas Aquinas, theologian, natural philosopher, and poet
1228–89	Crusade of Frederick II
1233	Beginning of the Inquisition; Pope grants right to proceed to Dominican Order
1233–1315	Lifespan of the Blessed Ramon Lull, scholar, philosopher, and alchemist
1239–40	Crusade of Theobald of Champagne
1240–41	Crusade of Richard of Cornwall

1241	Hospitallers negotiate the return of Jerusalem to Christian control
1241	Albertus Magnus (Albert the Great), Dominican, sent to Paris to study theology; intellectual, translator of texts, and alchemist; made Bishop of Regensburg in 1260; teacher of Thomas Aquinas; died in 1280
1244	Franks lose Jerusalem in Holy Land
1244	(16 March) final siege of Montsegur; 225 Cathars massacred
1245	Oxford-based Roger Bacon, pioneer-teacher of the "new" Aristotle, science, and metaphysics, goes to Paris to teach; became a Franciscan c. 1250; wrote his *Opus Maius* in 1267
1248–54	Crusade of St. Louis
1250	Battle of Mansurah
1252	King Henry III of England accuses the Templars of "excessive pride"
1257–67	**Additional penances added to the Templar Rule**
1260–1327/8	Time of Meister Eckhart, Dominican theologian, philosopher, mystic
1265–1308	Time of Johannes Duns Scotus, Scottish Franciscan theologian and developer of Aristotle's arguments
1265–1321	Lifespan of Florentine Dante Alighieri, author of *The Divine Comedy*
1266	Safed falls to the Turks
after 1268	**Catalan Rule of the Templars created**
1271	Languedoc comes under rule of French crown
1271–72	Crusade of Edward of England
1273	Rudolf of Habsburg elected king of Germany
1274	Council of Lyon
1274	Death of St. Thomas Aquinas
1277	Maria of Antioch sells her rights to the throne of Jerusalem to Charles of Anjou
1285	Council of Constantinople (Second Synod of Blachernae) discusses and rejects pro-western interpretation of the Trinity as enunciated by the Patriarch John XI Bekko
1291	**(August) Acre falls to the Mamluks; Templars evacuate Atlit and Tortosa**

1302	Loss of Ruad and massacre of the Templar garrison there
1305	Clement V becomes Pope
1307	Head of St. Euphemia kept in a silver reliquary in the house of the Temple, Nicosia
1307	(13 October) Dawn arrests of the Templars in France
1307	(27 October) Pope orders all Christian kings to arrest Templars
1308	Pope Clement suspends Inquisition of the Templars in France
1308	(August) About sixty Templar officials, including Grand Master Jacques de Molay and four other high officials, interrogated at Chinon Castle and plead guilty, hoping to be reconciled with the Church
1309	(August) Papal commission begins in France
1310	(February) Templar trial begins
	(April) Philip de Marigny, brother of King Philip IV's chief minister of finance, installed as Archbishop of Sens
	(May) Provincial church council under Archbishop Marigny orders fifty-four Templars burned at the stake as "relapsed heretics"
	(May) Papal commission adjourned for five months
	(November) Templar defense collapses
1311	Council of Vienne; Templar Order formally dissolved by Pope's first bull, *Vox in excelso*, but charges against the Order "not proven"
1312	Pope's second bull, *Ad providam*, transfers Templar property to the Hospitaller Order
1314	(March) Last Templar Grand Master, Jacques de Molay, and preceptor of Normandy, Geoffroi de Charney, burned at the stake; both publicly retracted their confessions and were executed the same day in Paris
1314	(April) Death of Pope Clement V
1314	(24 June, St. John's Day) Battle of Bannockburn (Scotland)
1314	(November) Death of Philip IV, king of France
1319	Order of Christ founded in Tomar, Portugal
1571	Ottomans destroy much of the central Templar archive in Cyprus

Appendix 2

Grand Masters of the Knights Templar

1119–1136	Hugh of Payns
1136–1149	Robert of Craon
1149–1152	Everard des Barres
1153	Bernard of Tremelay
1154–1156	Andrew of Montbard
1156–1169	Bertrand of Blancfort
1169–1171	Philip of Nablus
1171–1179	Odo of Saint–Amand
1181–1184	Arnold of Torroja
1185–1189	Gerald of Ridefort
1191–1192/3	Robert of Sable
1194–1200	Gilbert Erail
1201–1209	Philip of Plessis
1210–1218/9	William of Chartres
1219–1230/2	Peter of Montaigu
1232–1244/6	Armand of Perigord
1247–1250	William of Sonnac
1250–1256	Reginald of Vichiers
1256–1273	Thomas Berard
1273–1291	William of Beaujeu
1291–1292/3	Theobald Gaudin
1293–1314	James of Molay

Source: M. Barber, *The New Knighthood: A History of the Order of the Temple* (Cambridge: Cambridge University Press, 1994), xxiii.

Note: Other accounts include Richard de Bures, 1227–1245.

APPENDIX 3

Templar Sites of England and Wales

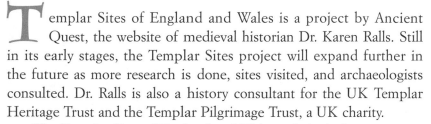

Ancient Quest

Templar Sites of England and Wales is a project by Ancient Quest, the website of medieval historian Dr. Karen Ralls. Still in its early stages, the Templar Sites project will expand further in the future as more research is done, sites visited, and archaeologists consulted. Dr. Ralls is also a history consultant for the UK Templar Heritage Trust and the Templar Pilgrimage Trust, a UK charity.

The Templar Sites of England and Wales website is the gateway to a public database of historical and visitor information on sites associated with the Knights Templar (1119–1312). It assists the traveler, pilgrim, or researcher in learning more about the sites and, where appropriate, visiting them. The website features such sites as the magnificent Temple Church in London, Temple Rothley, Temple Ewell, and the painting at Templecombe Church in Somerset, all of which can still be viewed today.

For full details and more information, please see:

www.ancientquest.com

The project was begun by Karen and Jon Ralls in late 2001 to contribute to Templar history and to complement publication of *The Templars and the Grail*. Dr. Karen Ralls gives talks at international conferences on subjects discussed in this book, such as the Knights Templar, Rosslyn Chapel, the Grail journey, or Celtic sites. To contact Karen to arrange lectures and workshops, slide presentations, tours to Templar sites, or film consultancy about *The Templars and the Grail*, please see:

www.karenralls.com

Knowledge comes, but Wisdom lingers . . .
—Alfred Lord Tennyson

Appendix 4

Illustrations

The illustrations that follow include exterior and interior photographs of Rosslyn Chapel and photographs of some of its magnificent stone carvings. They are presented here with the kind permission of Rosslyn Chapel Trust, current administrators of the chapel. Dubbed by experts the "architectural gem" of medieval Scotland, Rosslyn Chapel is certainly worth a visit, not only for its extraordinary architectural features but also for its beautiful natural environment—the trio of chapel, castle, and glen.

Also included here are photographs of items from the Brydon Collection, the private family collection of Robert Brydon, Scottish Templar historian. Part of this collection has been on display for the past several years as part of the Rosslyn Chapel Museum exhibition. This collection is in process of being cataloged and photographed; hopefully in the future other items will also be on display.

ABOVE: Exterior view of Rosslyn Chapel. The foundation stone was laid on St. Matthew's Day, 21 September 1446. The chapel's orientation is due east/west, marked out as the sun's ray fell that day, the fall equinox. The original plans, or records of them, have never been found. Nineteenth-century excavations revealed the foundations for a much larger nave; the chapel we see today was originally intended to be a more extensive, cruciform building with a tower at its center. *(copyright: Antonia Reeve/Rosslyn Chapel Trust)*

ABOVE: View from the choir section looking east towards the main altar of Rosslyn Chapel. Behind the altar are the three famous pillars—on the left, the Mason's Pillar, in the middle, the Journeyman's Pillar, and to the right, the Apprentice Pillar—said to represent Wisdom, Strength, and Beauty, respectively. The stained glass windows high above the altar depict the Resurrection; the statue of the Virgin Mary holding the infant Jesus directly above the main altar is a later Victorian addition. *(copyright: Antonia Reeve/Rosslyn Chapel Trust)*

ABOVE: Legend says the ornately carved Apprentice Pillar was created by a gifted apprentice who was later murdered by his jealous master. Parallels have been drawn between the story of the Apprentice Pillar and the Masonic story of Hiram Abiff, the Master Mason of Solomon's Temple in Jerusalem. At the pillar's top is a representation of the biblical story of Abraham and Isaac; at its base are eight dragons, from whose mouths emerge the vines that spiral around the pillar. They portray the eight dragons of Neifelheim from Scandinavian mythology who lie at the base of Yggdrasil, the great ash tree that binds together heaven, earth, and hell. The founder's Nordic heritage and connection with Orkney are believed to have inspired this symbolism. *(copyright: Antonia Reeve/Rosslyn Chapel Trust)*

RIGHT: The Mason's Pillar, although less elaborate than the ornate Apprentice Pillar, is beautifully carved. The two together may represent the pillars of Boaz and Joachim, which stood at the inner porch entrance to Solomon's Temple in Jerusalem. Carvings at the top of the Mason's Pillar include a number of musician angels and an angel holding a Bible, proclaiming the good news of Christ's birth. *(copyright: Antonia Reeve/Rosslyn Chapel Trust)*

ABOVE: View of the exquisite fifteenth-century Lady Chapel carvings in
Rosslyn Chapel, including altars dedicated to St. Matthew, the Blessed Virgin,
St. Andrew, and St. Peter; stained glass windows of the twelve apostles; and a
view of the Journeyman and Apprentice pillars. The Lady Chapel is fifteen
feet high and extends the whole thirty-five-foot width of the chapel.
(copyright: Antonia Reeve/Rosslyn Chapel Trust)

RIGHT: At the top of the three pillars in the Lady Chapel are numerous portrayals of angels singing or playing musical instruments. They represent the heavenly host praising God, as described in Luke 2:13. This carving, of an angel playing the bagpipes, is at the top of the Mason's Pillar, and two Green Man carvings can be seen on either side of him. *(copyright: Antonia Reeve/Rosslyn Chapel Trust)*

LEFT: One of the finest examples of a Green Man carving within Rosslyn Chapel. Inside the chapel a total of 103 Green Man carvings have been counted, with additional examples on the outside of the building. An ancient fertility symbol with strong Celtic associations, the Green Man also has connections to the legends of Robin Hood and Little John, which were featured in the popular plays performed in Roslin Glen. *(copyright: Antonia Reeve/Rosslyn Chapel)*

ABOVE: A Green Man master pattern piece, the final project of a Scottish apprentice coppersmith, late eighteenth century or early nineteenth century. *(copyright The Brydon Collection)*

RIGHT: Nineteenth-century sculpture of the head of St. Sara, carved in jet, from Santiago de Compostela, Spain. Every 24th of May, gypsies from all over the world converge at Saintes-Maries-de-la-Mer in southern France to honor St. Sara, their patron saint. Every May and June, gypsy plays were performed in Roslin Glen. *(copyright: The Brydon Collection)*

LEFT: An angel holding a shield with an engrailed cross, the coat of arms of the Sinclair family. Also found on the coat of arms of the earls of Rosslyn, this symbol is repeated throughout Rosslyn Chapel, including on the fronts of the Lady Chapel altars and on the ceiling of the sacristy. *(copyright: Antonia Reeve/Rosslyn Chapel Trust)*

BELOW RIGHT: A knight on horseback armed with a spear, and a figure holding a cross seated behind him. These figures may represent the legend of William "the Seemly" St. Clair, carrying back a portion of the true cross, or Holy Rood, from Jerusalem to Scotland. Alternatively, the passenger may be Queen Margaret and the knight Bartholomew Ladislaus, a companion of William St. Clair on that journey. Others believe this carving stands for the medieval Templar seal: two Templar brothers on one horse. *(copyright: Antonia Reeve/Rosslyn Chapel Trust)*

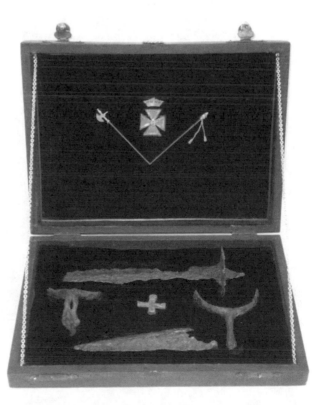

ABOVE: A burial stone said to be that of the William St. Clair who died fighting the Moors in Spain in 1330, while attempting to escort the heart of Robert the Bruce to the Holy Land. This stone was originally located at the site of an earlier church, southwest of the present chapel, in what is now a village graveyard. Carved on it is a floriated cross.
(copyright: Antonia Reeve/Rosslyn Chapel Trust)

RIGHT: Western European crusader artifacts found during a British excavation under the Temple in Jerusalem in 1912, including a lead Templar cross and remnants of a sword, a spur, and a lance. These items have been dated to the medieval period by experts.
(copyright: The Brydon Collection)

ABOVE: Painting of a Scottish Knight Templar at Rosslyn Chapel, first half of the nineteenth century. *(copyright: The Brydon Collection)*

RIGHT: An example of one of the angel carvings in Rosslyn Chapel in a pose that has specific relevance to Freemasonry. (*copyright: Antonia Reeve/Rosslyn Chapel Trust*)

LEFT: A carving concerning the archetypal theme of good and evil—a devil with an angry and disappointed expression and a couple looking away from him toward a nearby carving of an angel with a cross. (*copyright: Antonia Reeve/Rosslyn Chapel Trust*)

Notes

Introduction

1. U. Eco, "Dreaming the Middle Ages," in *Travels in Hyperreality*, translated by W. Weaver (New York: Harcourt Brace, 1986), 61–72.

Chapter 1: Warrior-Monks of the Middle Ages

1. M. Barber, *The New Knighthood: A History of the Order of the Temple* (Cambridge: Cambridge University Press, 1994), 44.

2. Ibid., 45.

3. H. Nicolson, *The Knights Templar: A New History* (Stroud: Sutton Publishing, 2001), 12.

4. S. Runciman, *The Eastern Schism: A Study of the Papacy and the Eastern Churches during the Eleventh and Twelfth Centuries* (Oxford: Oxford University Press, 1955), 105.

5. J. Prawer, *The Crusader's Kingdom* (London: Phoenix Orion, 1972), 253.

6. N. Smart, *The Religious Experience* (New York: Macmillan, 1996), 47.

7. J. F. O'Sullivan, *Studies in Medieval Cistercian History* (Spencer, Mass.: Cistercian Publications, 1971), 186.

8. M. Deansley, *A History of the Medieval Church 590–1500* (London: Routledge, 1925), 110.

9. A. H. Bredero, *Bernard of Clairvaux: Between Cult & History* (Edinburgh: T. & T. Clark, 1966), 267.

10. J. Wasserman, *The Templars and the Assassins: The Militia of Heaven* (Rochester, Vt.: Inner Traditions, Rochester, 2001), 130–31.

11. Ibid., 64.

12. A. Butler and S. Dafoe, *The Templar Continuum* (Bellevue, Ont.: Templar Books, Thevou Publishing Group, 1999), 73.

13. Ibid.

14. Nicolson, *Knights Templar*, 190.

15. Barber, *New Knighthood*, 267.

16. A. Butler and S. Dafoe, *The Warriors and the Bankers* (Bellevue, Ont.: Templar Books, Thevou Publishing Group, 1998), 73.

17. Nicolson, *Knights Templar*, 162.

18. Barber, *New Knighthood*, 271.

19. Nicolson, *Knights Templar*, 161.

20. Ibid., 166.

21. Ibid., 164.

22. E. Lord, *The Knights Templar in Britain* (Harlow: Pearson Education Ltd., 2002), 161–2.

23. Nicolson, *Knights Templar*, 185.

24. Ibid.

25. Butler and Dafoe, *Continuum*, 75.

26. Nicolson, *Knights Templar*, 183.

27. Barber, *New Knighthood*, 262.

28. C. Walford, *Fairs: Past and Present: A Chapter in the History of Commerce* (London: Elliot Stock, 1883), 271.

29. Nicolson, *Knights Templar*, 191.

30. Barber, *New Knighthood*, 262.

31. Butler and Dafoe, *Continuum*, 74.

32. Nicolson, *Knights Templar*, 192.

33. Ibid., 193.

34. Ibid.

35. H. Finke, *Papsttum und Untergang des Templerordens*, Vatican document Reg. Aven. no. 305, vol. 564 (Munster, 1907), 52–63 and 121–22. See also M. Barber, "The Templars and the Turin Shroud," *Catholic Historical Review* 68 (1982), 212.

Chapter 2:
Origins of the Order

1. A. Forey, "The Emergence of the Military Order in the Twelfth Century," *Journal of Ecclesiastical History* 36 (1985), 176.

2. M. Barber, "Origins of the Order of the Temple," *Studia Monastica* 12 (1970), 220.

3. J. Richard, "Hospitals and Hospital Congregations in the Latin Kingdom during the First Period of the Frankish Conquest," in *Outremer Studies in the History of the Crusading Kingdom of Jerusalem presented to Joshua Prawer*, edited by B. Kedar, H. Mayer, and R. Smail (Jerusalem: Yad Izhak Ben-Zvi Institutem, 1982), 89–100.

4. Forey, *Emergence*, 175; M. L. Bulst-Thiele, *Sacrae domus militiae Templi Hierosolymitani magistri: Untersuchungen zur Geschichte des Templeroordens 1118/9–1314* (Göttingen: Vandenhoeck & Ruprecht, 1974), 20–21.

5. M. Barber, "The Charitable and Medical Activities of the Hospitallers and Templars, 11th to 15th Centuries" (The Whichard Lecture, Greenville, N.C., 23 March 2000), 6.

6. Ibid.

7. Nicolson, *Knights Templar*, 23.

8. S. Runciman, *A History of the Crusades* (Harmondsworth: Penguin, 1978), 2: 477.

9. M. Baigent, R. Leigh, and H. Lincoln, *The Holy Blood and the Holy Grail* (London: Random House Arrow Books, 1982), 61.

10. Nicolson, *Knights Templar*, 26.

11. J. Upton-Ward, trans. and ed. *The Rule of the Templars: The French Text of the Rule of the Order of the Knights Templar* (Woodbridge, Suffolk: Boydell Press, 1992), 3.

12. Barber, *New Knighthood*, 8.

13. Guillaume de Tyre, *A History of Deeds Done beyond the Sea,*

translated by E. A. Babcock and A. C. Krey (New York: Octagon Books, 1976), 1: 39.

14. Nicolson, *Knights Templar*, 31.

15. Barber, *Origins*, 222.

16. N. H. Mazet, *Daggers*, part 1: *The Templars*, 2001, p. 20. (See also www.tsj.org).

17. Ibid. 20–21; emphasis mine.

18. Ibid.

19. Butler and Dafoe, *Continuum*, 64.

20. Ibid.

21. Barber, *Origins*, 222.

22. J. Riley-Smith, *The First Crusaders, 1095–1131* (Cambridge: Cambridge University Press, 1997), 76.

23. A. C. Krey, *The First Crusade: The Accounts of Eyewitnesses and Participants* (Princeton: Princeton University Press, 1921), 48–52.

24. I. Wood, *The Merovingian Kingdoms 450–751* (Harlow: Pearson Education Ltd., 1994), 233.

25. Baigent, Leigh, and Lincoln, *Holy Blood and Holy Grail*, 264–65.

26. D. C. Munroe, "Urban and the Crusaders," in *Translations and Reprints from the Original Sources of European History*, vol. 1:2 (Philadelphia: University of Pennsylvania, 1895), 20.

27. John France, *Victory in the East: A Military History of the First Crusade* (Cambridge: Cambridge University Press, 1994), 286–87, 315.

28. N. Cohn, *Pursuit of the Millennium* (Oxford: Oxford University Press, 1970), 66.

29. R. Rohricht, *Regesta Regni Hierosolymitani* (Innsbruck, 1893), 19 no. 83.

30. Ibid., 25 no. 105.

31. Runciman, *History*, 1: 292.

32. M. Bennett, "Jerusalem's First Crusader King: Godfrey de Bouillon," *BBC History Magazine* (London) May 2001: 50.

33. Butler and Dafoe, *Continuum*, 63.

34. Riley-Smith, *First Crusaders*, 154.

35. Butler and Dafoe, *Continuum*, 63.

36. G. Coppack, *The White Monks: The Cistercians in Britain 1128–1540* (Stroud: Tempus, 1998), 17.

37. A. Forey, *The Military Orders from the Twelfth to the Early Fourteenth Centuries* (Basingstoke: Macmillan, 1992), 231–33.

38. Nicolson, *Knights Templar*, 22.

39. Ibid.

40. Mazet, *Daggers*, part 1, p. 18.

41. J. Dodds, *Architecture and Ideology in Early Medieval Spain* (University Park: Pennsylvania State University Press, 1990), 113.

42. Barber, *New Knighthood*, 12.

Chapter 3:
Organization and Beliefs

1. Nicolson, *Knights Templar*, 113.

2. Barber, *New Knighthood*, 185.

3. M. Barber, "Supplying the Crusader States," in *The Horns of Hattin,* edited by B. Z. Kedar (Jerusalem: Yad Izhak Ben-Zvi; Aldershot: Ashgate Variorum, 1992), 186.

4. Ibid.

5. Ibid.

6. Ibid., 187.

7. Nicolson, *Knights Templar,* 114.

8. Ibid., 116.

9. Barber, "Supplying the Crusader States," 317.

10. Ibid.

11. Barber, *New Knighthood,* 188.

12. Ibid.

13. Barber, *New Knighthood,* 188.

14. Ibid.

15. Nicolson, *Knights Templar,* 119.

16. Barber, *New Knighthood,* 190.

17. Ibid.

18. Ibid.

19. Ibid.

20. Ibid.

21. Ibid.

22. Ibid., 193.

23. J. Robinson, *Born in Blood* (London: Random House Arrow Books, 1989), 125.

24. Nicolson, *Knights Templar,* 116.

25. Upton-Ward, *Rule of the Templars,* 11.

26. Ibid., 12.

27. Ibid.

28. Barber, *New Knighthood,* 182.

29. Butler and Dafoe, *Continuum,* 58.

30. Ibid.

31. Ibid.

32. Mazet, *Daggers,* Part I, p. 17. See also www.tsj.org.

33. Nicolson, *Knights Templar,* 141.

34. Walter Map, *De nugis curialium,* edited and translated by M. R. James, C. N. L. Brooke, and R. B. Mynors (Oxford: Oxford University Press, 1983), 58–60.

35. J. Prawer, *Crusader Institutions* (Oxford: Clarendon Press, 1980), 214.

36. Butler and Dafoe, *Continuum,* 56.

37. Ibid.

38. Ibid.

39. J. Wilkinson, J. Hill, and W. F. Ryan, eds., *Jerusalem Pilgrimage 1099–1185* (London: Hakluyt Society, 1988), 294.

40. G. Hancock, *The Sign and the Seal: The Quest for the Lost Ark of the Covenant* (New York: Crown Publishers, 1992), 101.

41. Upton-Ward, *Rule of the Templars,* 91.

42. R. van den Broek, and W. J. Hanegraaff, eds., *Gnosis and Hermeticism: From Antiquity to Modern Times* (Albany: State University of New York Press, 1998), viii.

43. Piers P. Read, *The Templars* (London: Weidenfeld & Nicolson, 1999), 136.

44. M. Barber, *The Trial of the Templars* (Cambridge: Cambridge University Press, 1978), 254.

45. E. Begg, *The Cult of the Black Virgin* (Harmondsworth: Penguin, [1985] 1996), 25.

46. Ibid., 103.

47. Ibid., 26.

48. Finke, *Papsttum und Untergang des Templersordens.* (2 vols.) Muntster, 1907, Vatican doc. Reg. Aven. No. 305, vol. 564.

49. D. Selwood, *Knights of the Cloister: Templars and Hospitallers in Central-Southern Occitania c.1100/c.1300* (Wood-bridge, Suffolk: Boydell Press, 1999), 30.

50. P. Mullen, *Shrines of Our Lady* (London: Piatkus, 1998), 69–70.

51. L. Picknett and C. Prince, *The Templar Revelation* (New York: Touchstone Books, Simon & Schuster, 1997), 105.

52. A. Baring and J. Cashford, *The Myth of the Goddess: Evolution of an Image* (Harmondsworth: Viking Penguin, 1991), 645.

53. Nicolson, *Knights Templar*, 131.

54. Ibid.

55. Ibid.

56. A. Forey, "Women and the Military Orders in the 12th and 13th centuries," *Studia Monastica* 29 (1987), 66.

57. Nicolson, *Knights Templar*, 131.

Chapter 4: The Downfall of the Order

1. S. Dafoe, "The Fall of Acre—1291," *Templar History Magazine* 1 (2) (Winter 2002), 23. Dafoe is Grand Historian for the Sovereign Great Priory of Canada Knights Templar and publisher of this new journal out of Belleville, Ontario, Canada.

2. M. Barber, "The Trial of the Templars Revisited," in *The Military Orders: Welfare and Warfare*, edited by H. Nicolson (Aldershot: Ashgate, 1998), 333.

3. Nicolson, *Knights Templar*, 204.

4. Barber, *Trial*, 45.

5. Wasserman, *Templars and Assassins*, 224.

6. Barber, *Trial*, 47.

7. Ibid., 49.

8. Ibid.

9. P. Partner, *The Knights Templar and Their Myth* (Rochester, Vt.: Destiny Books, 1990), 70.

10. Lord, *Knights Templar in Britain*, 184.

11. Wasserman, *Templars and Assassins*, 224.

12. Barber, *Trial*, 59.

13. Wasserman, *Templars and Assassins*, 224.

14. Barber, *Trial*, 53.

15. Wasserman, *Templars and Assassins*, 224.

16. Ibid., 225.

17. Barber, *Trial*, 62–63.

18. M. Barber, "James of Molay, the last Grand Master of the Order of the Temple," in *Crusaders and Heretics: 12th–14th Centuries*, Variorum Collected Studies Series (Aldershot: Ashgate, 1995), 114. (Originally published in *Studia Monastica* 14 [1972].)

19. Wasserman, *Templars and Assassins*, 226.

20. Ibid, 227.

21. Ibid, 228.

22. M. Barber, "The World Picture of Philip the Fair," in *Crusaders and Heretics: 12th–14th Centuries*, Variorum Collected Studies Series (Aldershot: Ashgate, 1995), 26. (Originally published in *Journal of Medieval History* 8 [1982].)

23. Wasserman, *Templars and Assassins*, 228.

24. Partner, *Knights Templar and Their Myth*, 60.

25. Nicolson, *Knights Templar*, 216.

26. Lord, *Knights Templar in Britain*, 187.

27. Ibid.

28. Barber, *Trial*, 248–50.

29. H. C. Lea, *A History of the Inquisition of the Middle Ages*, 3 vols. (1888; reprint, New York: Russell and Russell, 1955).

30. R. Kieckhefer, *European Witch Trials: Their Foundation in Learned and Popular Culture, 1300–1500* (London, 1976), 10–14, 108–12. See also R.

Keickhefer, *Magic in the Middle Ages* (Cambridge: Cambridge University Press, 2000, 188.

31. M. Barber, "Lepers, Jews and Moslems: The Plot to Overthrow Christendom in 1321," *History* 66 (1981), 1–17.

32. M. Lambert, *Medieval Heresy* (Oxford: Blackwell, 1992), 180.

33. J. Henderson, *The Construction of Orthodoxy and Heresy* (Albany: State University of New York Press, 1998), 123.

34. W. Wakefield and A. Evans, *Heresies of the High Middle Ages* (New York: Columbia University Press, 1969), 2.

35. E. Burman, *Supremely Abominable Crimes: The Trial of the Knights Templar* (London: Allison & Busby, 1994), 79.

36. Ibid., 81.

37. Ibid., 82.

38. Wasserman, *Templars and Assassins*, 231.

39. Ibid., 231–32.

40. Nicolson, *Knights Templar*, 220.

41. Wasserman, *Templars and Assassins*, 232.

42. Ibid., 234.

43. Ibid.

44. Ibid., 238.

45. Barber, *New Knighthood*, 304.

46. Partner, *Knights Templar and Their Myth*, 82.

47. Baigent, Leigh, and Lincoln,

Holy Blood and Holy Grail, 76.

48. R. Owen, "Vatican File Shows Pope Pardoned Massacred Knights," *London Times*, 30 March 2002.

49. Ibid.

50. Ibid.

51. Ibid.

52. P. Byrne, *Templar Gold: Discovering the Ark of the Covenant* (Nevada City, Calif.: Blue Dolphin Publishing, 2001), 55.

53. Ibid., 55.

54. Ibid., 55, 57.

55. Ibid., 54.

56. Ibid.

57. Ibid., 54–55.

58. Ibid., 105.

59. Barber, *New Knighthood*, 311.

60. Burman, *Supremely Abominable Crimes*, 259.

61. Barber, *Trial*, 211–13.

62. Wasserman, *Templars and Assassins*, 236.

63. Nicolson, *Knights Templar*, 231.

64. Barber, *Trial*, 214.

65. Ibid., 215.

66. Ibid., 216.

67. Ibid.

68. Nicolson, *Knights Templar*, 238.

69. Butler and Dafoe, *Warriors and Bankers*.

70. Lord, *Knights Templar in Britain*, 191.

71. J. Parker, *The Knights Templar in England* (Tucson: University of Arizona Press, 1965), 92.

72. Lord, *Knights Templar in Britain*, 192.

73. Ibid.

74. Ibid., 194.

75. Ibid.

76. Ibid.

77. Barber, *Trial*, 198.

78. Ibid., 199.

79. Ibid.

80. Lord, *Knights Templar in Britain*, 200.

81. Ibid., 202.

82. Ibid., 203.

83. Ibid., 200–1.

84. M. Baigent and R. Leigh, *The Temple and the Lodge* (New York: Little Brown & Co., 1989), 18.

85. Ibid., 33.

86. Ibid.

87. Personal communication from Robert Brydon, FSA Scot., Edinburgh, December 1999.

88. J. Maidment, *A Rental of all the annual rents and Templar lands founded throughout the whole Kingdom of Scotland beginning from the Boundaries towards England and so descending through the whole kingdom from the said Boundaries all the way to the Orkneys*, MS. c. 1823, 1839, and undated (Edinburgh: National Library of Scotland, no. acc. 8090).

89. J. Maidment, *Templaria* (Edinburgh, 1828–30).

90. Baigent and Leigh, *Temple and Lodge*, 97.

91. Lord, *Knights Templar in Britain*, 201.

92. E. Haagensen and H. Lincoln, *The Templars' Secret Island: The Knights, the Priest and the Treasure* (Moreton-in-March, Gloucestershire: Windrush Press, 2000), inside jacket.

93. Ibid., 94.

94. Wasserman, *Templars and Assassins*, 237.

95. Nicolson, *Knights Templar*, 237.

96. Ibid.

97. Barber, *Trial*, 219.

Chapter 5:
Legends of the Grail:
The Chivalric Vision

1. J. Matthews, *Elements of the Grail Tradition* (Shaftesbury: Element, 1990), 1.

2. J. Wood, "The Holy Grail: From Romance Motif to Modern Genre," *Folklore* 3 (2) (London, October 2000), 171.

3. Ibid.

4. Ibid., 172.

5. J. Markale, *The Grail* (Rochester, Vt.: Inner Traditions, 1999), 133.

6. R. Barber, *The Knight and Chivalry* (Woodbridge, Suffolk: Boydell & Brewer, [1970] 1995), 97.

7. N. Goodrich, *The Holy Grail* (New York: Harper Collins, 1992), 218.

8. W. J. Stein, *The Ninth Century: World History in Light of the Holy Grail* (London: Temple Lodge Press, 1991), 184.

9. Ibid., 184.

10. Ibid., 186.

11. J. Michell and C. Rhone, *Twelve-Tribe Nations* (London: Thames and Hudson, 1991), 13.

12. Ibid., 14.

13. Goodrich, *Holy Grail*, 24.

14. A. Sinclair, *The Discovery of the Grail* (London: Random House, 1998), 124.

15. E. Begg and D. Begg, *In Search of the Holy Grail and the Precious Blood* (London: Harper Collins, 1995), xvi.

16. W. J. Stein, *The Ninth Century: World History in Light of the Holy Grail* (London: Temple Lodge Press, 1991), 137.

17. Ibid.

18. L. Gardner, *Bloodline of the Holy Grail* (Shaftesbury: Element, 1996), 250.

19. Begg and Begg, *In Search of the Holy Grail*, xvii.

20. Ibid.

21. T. Ravenscroft, *The Spear of Destiny* (York Beach, Maine: Samuel Weiser, 1973), 8.

22. Begg and Begg, *In Search of the Holy Grail*, xvii.

23. Ibid., 206.

24. Matthews, *Elements*, 52–53.

25. Markale, *Grail*, 133–34.

26. H. Nicolson, *Love, War, and the Grail: Templars, Hospitallers and Teutonic Knights in Medieval Epic and Romance 1150–1500*, History of Warfare Series, vol. 4 (Leiden: Brill, 2001), 108.

27. N. Bryant, trans., *The High Book of the Grail, A Translation of the Thirteenth-Century Romances of Perlesvaus* (Cambridge, U.K.: D. S. Brewer, 1978).

28. R. S. Loomis, *The Grail: From Celtic Myth to Christian Symbol* (Princeton: Princeton University Press), [1963] 1991, 193–94.

29. Bernard of Clairvaux, "Sermon 1:1," in *On the Song of Songs*, trans. Kilian Walsh (Kalamazoo, Mich.: Cistercian Publications, 1971), 1: 1.

30. D. Merkur, *The Mystery of Manna* (Rochester, Vt.: Park Street Press: 2000), 106.

Chapter 6: A Mythos in the Making

1. Prawer, *Crusaders' Kingdom*, 268–69.

2. Barber, *New Knighthood*, 8.

3. Hancock, *Sign and Seal*, 390.

4. K. Kenyon, *Digging Up Jerusalem* (London: Ernest Benn Ltd., 1974), 14.

5. Ibid., 16.

6. N. A. Silberman, *Digging for God and Country: Archaeology and the Secret Struggle for the Holy Land, 1799–1917* (New York: Knopf, 1982), 89–99.

7. Ibid., 180–88.

8. Haagensen and Lincoln, *Templars' Secret Island*, 98–99.

9. Hancock, *Sign and the Seal*, 391.

10. Haagensen and Lincoln, *Templars' Secret Island*, 98.

11. Ibid.

12. Hancock, *Sign and Seal*, 393.

13. Ibid.

14. Ibid.

15. Kenyon, *Digging Up Jerusalem*, 31.

16. Ibid.

17. Haagensen and Lincoln, *Templars' Secret Island*, 101.

18. Kenyon, *Digging Up Jerusalem*; see also QEDEM—*Monographs of the Institute of Archaeology*, Hebrew University, Jerusalem, no. 35, 1996.

19. M. Ben-Dov, *In the Shadow of the Temple*, trans. I. Friedman (New York: Harper & Row; Jerusalem: Keter Publishing House, 1985), 347.

20. R. Y. Nijem, "Archaeological Excavations in Jerusalem," p. 6. See: www.aqsa.org.uk.

21. T. Sagiv, "Solomon's Stables and the Southern Gates," www.templemount.org (20 October 1996), 3.

22. Ibid., 5.

23. Johann of Wurzburg, "Descriptio Terrace Sanctae," in *Descriptiones Terrae Sanctae ex saec*, VIII, IX, XII et XV, edited by T. Tobler (Leipzig, 1874), ch. 5.

24. Sagiv, "Solomon's Stables," 6–7.

25. Hancock, *Sign and Seal*, 163.

26. Ibid.

27. Ibid., 164.

28. Ibid.

29. Ibid.

30. C. Beckingham, "An Ethiopian Embassy to Europe," in *Prester John: the Mongols and the Ten Lost Tribes*, edited by C. F. Beckingham and B. Hamilton (Aldershot: Ashgate Variorum, 1996), 198. See also C. Beckingham, "Prester John in West Africa," on pages 207–11 of the same work.

31. Hancock, *Sign and Seal*, 170.

32. G. Patton and R. Mackness, *Web of Gold: The Secret History of a Sacred Treasure* (London: Sidgwick & Jackson, 2000), 41.

33. Ibid., 42.

34. Ibid., 44.

35. Ibid.

36. Ibid., 45 and 265.

37. C. Knight and R. Lomas, *The Hiram Key* (London: Century, 1996), 266–67.

38. M. Baigent and R. Leigh, *The Dead Sea Scrolls Deception* (London: Jonathan Cape, 1991), 21.

39. Knight and Lomas, *Hiram Key*, 268–69.

40. Ibid.

41. R. Allan, *Diana, Queen of Heaven* (Kempton, Ill.: Pigeon Point/ Adventures Unlimited, 1999), 73. See also the website: www.rumormillnews.com.

42. Ibid.

43. Ibid.

44. Ibid.

45. Byrne, *Templar Gold*, 2001, 348–49.

46. Ibid.

47. Ibid.

48. Ibid., 381.

49. Ibid.

50. H. Bernstein, *Ark of the Covenant, Holy Grail* (Marina del Rey, Calif.: DeVorss & Co., 1998), 183.

51. Ibid., 186–87.

52. L. Fanthorpe and P. Fanthorpe, *The Oak Island Mystery* (Toronto: Hounslow Press, 1995), back cover.

53. Ibid., 88–89.

54. M. Bradley, *The Columbus Conspiracy* (Willowdale, Ont.: Hounslow Press, 1991), 139.

55. Ibid., 135.

56. Ibid.

57. Ibid., 131.

58. M. H. Hall, *America's Assignment with Destiny*, The Adepts Series, vol. 5 (Los Angeles: Philosophical Research Society, 1951), 54–55.

59. P. Falaradeau, *Societes Secretes en Nouvelle-France* (Quebec: Louise Courteau editrice, 2002); also, correspondence from author.

60. Ibid.

61. Ibid.

62. Ibid.

63. Barber, *New Knighthood*, 334.

Chapter 7:
Rosslyn Chapel:
Wisdom in Stone

1. R. Forbes, *Account of Roslin Chapel* (Edinburgh, 1774), 1.

2. L. Spence, "Mystical Roslin," photocopy of article from an SMT magazine, Scotland (May 1952), 29.

3. Earl of Rosslyn, *Rosslyn Chapel*, Official Guidebook (Roslin, Midlothian: Rosslyn Chapel Trust, 1997), 2.

4. *Proceedings of the Society of Antiquaries* 12 (Edinburgh, 1877–78), 223.

5. Ibid.

6. Ibid.

7. D'A. J. D. Boulton, *The Knights of the Crown: The Monarchical Orders of Knighthood in Later Medieval Europe 1325–1520* (Woodbridge, Suffolk: The Boydell Press; New York: St. Martin's Press, 1987), 357.

8. R. Brydon, *Rosslyn: A History of the Guilds, the Masons, and the Rosy Cross* (Roslin, Midlothian: Rosslyn Chapel Trust, 1994), 9.

9. Boulton, *Knights of the Crown*, 357.

10. C. Waters, *Of Days and Knights, A Chronological History of the Crusades, the Templars and Similar Orders* (Whitby, U.K.: published by author, 2002), 16.

11. Brydon, *Rosslyn: A History*, 9.

12. Waters, *Days and Knights*, 25.

13. W. J. Stein, *The British, their Psychology and Destiny* (London: Temple Lodge Press, 1990), 28.

14. Earl of Rosslyn, *Rosslyn Chapel*, 2.

15. Ibid., 11.

16. Ibid.

17. Ibid.

18. Ibid.

19. Chev. Robert Brydon, personal communication, 1995.

20. Ibid.

21. W. Grant, *Rosslyn: Its Chapel, Castle, and Scenic Lore* (Edinburgh, 1936), 37.

22. M. Harding, *A Little Book of the Green Man* (London: Aurum Press, 1998), 58.

23. J. Harte, *The Green Man* (Andover, Hampshire: Pitkin Unichrome Ltd., 2001), 1.

24. Earl of Rosslyn, *Rosslyn Chapel*, 27.

25. T. Kirk and R. Thoresby, *Tours in Scotland 1677 and 1681*, edited

by P. Hume Brown (Edinburgh, 1892), 41–42.26. K. Laidler, *The Head of God* (London: Weidenfeld & Nicolson, 1998), 276.

27. L. Picknett and C. Prince, *Turin Shroud: In Whose Image?* (London: Corgi Books, 2000), 97.

28. Laidler, *The Head of God*, 263; emphasis mine.

29. M. Hopkins, G. Simmans, and T. Wallace-Murphy, *Rex Deus* (Shaftesbury: Element, 2000), 177.

30. Earl of Rosslyn, *Rosslyn Chapel*, 31.

31. Ibid.

32. Ibid., 18.

33. Hopkins, Simmans, and Wallace-Murphy, *Rex Deus*, 177.

34. Sinclair, *Discovery of the Grail*, 248.

35. Ibid., 120.

36. A. Sinclair, *The Secret Scroll* (London: Sinclair-Stevenson, 2000), 155.

37. Stein, *The British*, 29–30.

38. Begg and Begg, *In Search of the Holy Grail*, 23.

39. Sinclair, *Secret Scroll*, 155–6.

40. Ibid.

41. Ibid.

42. Ibid.

43. Earl of Rosslyn, *Rosslyn Chapel*, 37.

44. J. Slezer, *Theatrum Scotiae* (London, 1693), 63.

45. Hopkins, Simmans, and Wallace-Murphy, *Rex Deus*, 235.

46. *Acts of the Lords of Council in Public Affairs 1501–1554,* selections from the *Acta Domiorum Concili*, introductory to the Privy Council of Scotland, edited by Robert Kerr Hannay (Edinburgh, 1932), 540.

47. Mr. Stuart Beattie, Rosslyn Chapel Trust director, personal communication, No-vember 2000.

48. The conservation and extensive restoration projects at Rosslyn are in need of funding. If you would like to assist with this worthwhile effort, contact the Rosslyn Chapel Trust. See the Rosslyn Chapel website: http://www.rosslynchapel.org.uk.; or write to Mr. Stuart Beattie, Director, Rosslyn Chapel Trust, Rosslyn Chapel, Roslin, Midlothian, EH25–9PU, United Kingdom.

49. J. Simpson, "The Conservation of Rosslyn: An Unfinished Story of Decline and Recovery," in *Rosslyn: Country of Painter and Poet* (Edinburgh: Trustees of the National Galleries of Scotland, 2002), 84. This book accompanied the 2002 Rosslyn exhibition at the National Gallery of Scotland, Edinburgh.

50. Brydon, *Rosslyn: A History*, 5.

51. Ibid.

52. Ibid.

53. Ibid., 18.

54. Ibid.

55. Fr. R. A. Hay, *Genealogy of the*

Sinclairs of Roslin (Edinburgh, 1835), 27–28.

56. T. Wallace-Murphy and M. Hopkins, *Rosslyn: Guardian of the Secrets of the Holy Grail* (Shaftesbury: Element, 1999), 198.

57. Hugh D. Purcell, Vienna, Austria, 2001, "Third Article," 7. (Mr. Niven Sinclair provided me with some of Professor Purcell's unpublished research in June 2002.)

58. Ibid., 14.

59. U.S. Department of Energy Brookhaven National Laboratory, press release on their website: http://www.bnl.gov/bnlweb/pubaf/pr/2002/bnlpr072902a.htm.

60. Ibid.

61. Sinclair, *Discovery of the Grail*, 247.

62. Niven Sinclair, personal communication, June 2002.

63. Ibid.

64. F. J. Pohl, *Prince Henry Sinclair: His Expedition to the New World in 1398* (Halifax, Nova Scotia: Nimbus, 1969), 163.

65. For more information on the Westford knight carving, see the Clan Sinclair website: www.clan-sinclairusa.org.

66. Niven Sinclair, personal communication, December 1999.

67. Brydon, *Rosslyn: A History*, back page.

BIBLIOGRAPHY

Acts of the Lords of Council in Public Affairs 1501–1554. Selections from the *Acta Domiorum Concili*, introductory to the Privy Council of Scotland. Edited by Robert Kerr Hannay. Edinburgh, 1932.

Addison, C. G. *The Knights Templars*. London, 1842.

Allan, R. *Diana, Queen of Heaven*. Aptos, Calif.: Adventures Unlimited/Pigeon Point Publishing, 1999.

Anderson, F. *The Ancient Secret: In Search of the Holy Grail*. London: Victor Gollancz Ltd., 1953.

Arnold, B. *German Knighthood: 1050–1300*. Oxford: Clarendon Press, 1985.

Ashe, G. *The Discovery of King Arthur*. New York: Henry Holt & Co, 1985.

Baigent, M., and R. Leigh. *The Temple and the Lodge*. New York: Little Brown and Co., 1989.

———. *The Dead Sea Scrolls Deception*. London: Jonathan Cape, 1991.

———. *The Inquisition*. Harmondsworth: Penguin Books, 1999.

Baigent, M., R. Leigh, and H. Lincoln. *The Holy Blood and the Holy Grail*. London: Jonathan Cape, 1982.

Barber, M. "Origins of the Order of the Temple." *Studia Monastica* 12 (Barcelona, 1970).

———. *The Trial of the Templars*. Cambridge: Cambridge University Press, 1978.

———. "The Templars and the Turin Shroud." *Catholic Historical Review 68* (1982).

———. "Supplying the Crusader States." In *The Horns of Hattin*, edited by B. Z. Kedar. Jerusalem: Yad Izhak Ben-Zvi Institute; Aldershot: Ashgate Variorum, 1992.

———. *The Two Cities: Medieval Europe 1050–1320*. London and New York: Routledge, 1992.

————. *The New Knighthood: A History of the Order of the Temple.* Cambridge: Cambridge University Press, 1994.

————. "The World Picture of Philip the Fair." In *Crusaders and Heretics: 12th–14th Centuries.* Variorum Collected Studies Series. Aldershot: Ashgate, 1995. (Originally published in *Journal of Medieval History* 8, [Amsterdam, 1982].)

————. "James of Molay, the Last Grand Master of the Order of the Temple." In *Crusaders and Heretics: 12th–14th Centuries.* Variorum Collected Studies Series. Aldershot: Ashgate, 1995. (Originally published in *Studia Monastica* 14 [Barcelona, 1972].)

————. "Lepers, Jews and Moslems: The Plot to Overthrow Christendom in 1321." *History* 66 (1981).

————. "The Trial of the Templars Revisited." In *The Military Orders: Welfare and Warfare*, edited by H. Nicolson. Vol. 2. Aldershot: Ashgate, 1998.

————. "The Charitable and Medical Activities of the Hospitallers and Templars, 11th to 15th Centuries." The Whichard Lecture, Greenville, N.C., 23 March 2000.

Barber, R. *The Figure of Arthur.* London: Longman, 1972.

————. *The Knight and Chivalry.* Woodbridge, Suffolk: Boydell & Brewer, [1970] 1995.

Barber, R., and J. Barker. *Tournaments.* Woodbridge, Suffolk: Boydell Press, 1989.

Begg, E. *The Cult of the Black Virgin.* Harmondsworth: Penguin Books, [1985] 1996.

Begg, E., and D. Begg. *In Search of the Holy Grail and the Precious Blood.* London: Harper Collins, 1995.

Ben-Dov, M. *In the Shadow of the Temple.* Translated by I. Friedman. New York: Harper & Row; Jerusalem: Keter Publishing House, 1985.

Bennett, M. "Jerusalem's First Crusader King: Godfrey de Bouillon." *BBC History Magazine* (London), May 2001.

Bernard of Clairvaux. "De laude novae militiae ad milites Templi liber." In *Sancti Bernardi Opera*, edited by J. Leclercq et. al., vol. 3. Rome, 1963.

————. "In Praise of the New Knighthood." In *The Works of Bernard of Clairvaux, vol. 7, Treatises*, 3, translated by C. Greenia. Cistercian Fathers Series, vol. 19. Kalamazoo, Mich.: Cistercian Publications, 1977.

————. *On the Song of Songs*. Translated by Kilian Walsh. Vol. 1. Kalamazoo, Mich.: Cistercian Publications, 1971.

Biddle, M. *King Arthur's Round Table*. Woodbridge, Suffolk: Boydell Press, 2000.

Boulton, D'A. J. D., *The Knights of the Crown: The Monarchical Orders of Knighthood in Later Medieval Europe 1325–1520*. Woodbridge, Suffolk: Boydell Press; New York: St. Martin's Press, 1987.

Bradley, M. *Holy Grail across the Atlantic*. Toronto: Hounslow Press, 1988.

Bredero, A. H. *Bernard of Clairvaux: Between Cult and History*. Edinburgh: T&T Clark, 1966.

Bryant, N. trans. *The High Book of the Grail: A Translation of the Thirteenth-Century Romances of Perlesvaus*. Cambridge, U.K.: D. S. Brewer, 1978.

Brydon, R. *Rosslyn: A History of the Guilds, the Masons, and the Rosy Cross*. Roslin, Midlothian: Rosslyn Chapel Trust, 1994.

Bulst-Thiele, M. L. *Sacrae domus militiae Templi Hierosolymitani magistri: Untersuchungen zur Geschichte des Templeroordens 1118/9–1314*. Göttingen: Vandenhoeck & Ruprecht, 1974.

Burckhardt, T. *Chartres and the Birth of the Cathedral*. Ipswich: Golgonooza Press, 1995.

Burman, E. *Supremely Abominable Crimes: The Trial of the Knights Templar*. London: Allison & Busby, 1994.

Butler, A., and S. Dafoe. *The Warriors and the Bankers*. Belleville, Ont.: Templar Books, Thevou Publishing Group, 1998.

————. *The Templar Continuum*. Belleville, Ont.: Templar Books, Thevou Publishing Group, 1999.

Butler, E. M. *The Myth of the Magus*. Cambridge: Cambridge University Press, 1948.

Byrne, P. *Templar Gold: Discovering the Ark of the Covenant*. Nevada City, Calif.: Blue Dolphin Publishing, 2001.

Carley, J. "Arthur in English History." In *The Arthur of the English*, edited by W. R. J. Barron. Cardiff: University of Wales, 1999.

Cavendish, R. *King Arthur and the Grail*. London: Weidenfeld & Nicolson, 1978.

Cohn, N. *Pursuit of the Millennium*. Oxford: Oxford University Press, 1970.

Coppack, G. *The White Monks: The Cistercians in Britain 1128–1540*. Stroud: Tempus, 1998.

Dafoe, S. "The Fall of Acre–1291." *Templar History Magazine* 1:2 (winter) 2002.

Deansley, M. *A History of the Medieval Church 590–1500*. London: Routledge, 1925.

Dodds, J. *Architecture and Ideology in Early Medieval Spain*. University Park: Pennsylvania State University Press, 1990.

Earl of Rosslyn. *Rosslyn Chapel*. Roslin, Midlothian: Rosslyn Chapel Trust, 1997.

Falaradeau, P. *Societes Secretes en Nouvelle-France*. Quebec: Louise Courteau Editrice, Inc., 2002.

Fanthorpe, L., and P. Fanthorpe. *The Oak Island Mystery*. Toronto: Hounslow Press, 1995.

Finke, H. *Papsttum and Untergang des Templeordens*. Vatican document Reg. Aven. no. 305, vol. 564. 2 vols. Munster, 1907.

Forbes, R. *Account of Roslin Chapel*. Edinburgh, 1774.

Forey, A. "The Emergence of the Military Order in the Twelfth Century." *Journal of Ecclesiastical History* 36 (1985).

———. "Women and the Military Orders in the 12th and 13th Centuries." *Studia Monastica* 29 (Barcelona, 1987).

———. *The Military Orders from the Twelfth to the Early Fourteenth Centuries*. Basingstoke: Macmillan, 1992.

France, J. *Victory in the East: A Military History of the First Crusade*. Cambridge: Cambridge University Press, 1994.

Fulcanelli. *The Dwellings of the Philosophers*. Boulder: Archive Press, 1999.

Gardner, L. *Bloodline of the Holy Grail*. Shaftesbury: Element, 1996.

Goetinck, G. *Peredur: A Study of Welsh Tradition in the Grail Legends*. Cardiff: University of Wales Press, 1975.

Goodrich, N. *The Holy Grail*. New York: Harper Collins, 1992.

Green, M., and R. Howell. *A Pocket Guide to Celtic Wales*. Cardiff: University of Wales Press, 2000.

Haagensen, E., and H. Lincoln. *The Templars' Secret Island: The Knights, the Priest and the Treasure*. Moreton-in-Marsh, Gloustershire: Windrush Press, 2000.

Hall, Manly P. *The Adepts in the Western Esoteric Tradition: Orders of the Quest*. Los Angeles: Philosophical Research Society, 1949.

———. *America's Assignment with Destiny*. The Adepts Series, vol. 5. Los Angeles: Philosophical Research Society, 1951.

Hancock, G. *The Sign and the Seal: The Quest for the Lost Ark of the Covenant*. New York: Crown Publishers, 1992.

Harding, M. *A Little Book of the Green Man*. London: Aurum Press, 1998.

Hay, Fr. R. A. *Genealogy of the Sinclairs of Roslin*. Edinburgh, 1835.

Henderson, J. *The Construction of Orthodoxy and Heresy*. Albany: State University of New York Press, 1998.

Hopkins, M., G. Simmons, and T. Wallace-Murphy. *Rex Deus*. Shaftesbury: Element, 2000.

Housley, N. *The Italian Crusades: The Papal-Angevin Alliance and the Crusades against Christian Lay Powers 1254–1343*. Oxford: Clarendon Press, 1982.

Jarman, A. O. H. "The Merlin Legend and the Welsh Tradition of Prophecy." In *The Arthur of the Welsh*, edited by R. Bromwich, A. O. H. Jarman, and B. F. Roberts. Cardiff: University of Wales Press, 1991.

Jung, E., and M-L. von Franz. *The Grail Legend*. Translated by C. G. Jung Foundation. 2d ed. Princeton: Princeton University Press, 1970.

Kaeuper, R. W. *Chivalry and Violence in Medieval Europe*. Oxford: Oxford University Press, 1999.

Kaeuper, R. W., and E. Kennedy. *The Book of Chivalry of Geoffroi de Charny: Text, Context, and Translation*. Philadelphia: University of Pennsylvania Press, 1996.

Keen, J. *Chivalry*. New Haven and London: Yale University Press, 1984.

Kenyon, K. *Digging up Jerusalem*. London: Ernest Benn Ltd., 1974.

Kieckhefer, R. *European Witch Trials: Their Foundation in Learned and Popular Culture 1300–1500*. London: Routledge, 1976.

————. *Magic in the Middle Ages*. Cambridge: Cambridge University Press, 2000.

Kirk, T., and R. Thoresby. *Tours in Scotland 1677 and 1681*. Edited by P. Hume Brown. Edinburgh, 1892.

Knight, C., and R. Lomas. *The Hiram Key*. London: Century, 1996.

Krey, A. C. *The First Crusade: The Accounts of Eyewitnesses and Participants*. Princeton: Princeton University Press, 1921.

Laidler, K. *The Head of God*. London: Weidenfeld & Nicolson, 1998.

Lambert, M. *Medieval Heresy*. Oxford: Blackwell, 1992.

————. *The Cathars*. Oxford: Blackwell, 1998.

Lea, H. C. *A History of the Inquisition of the Middle Ages*. 3 vols. 1888; reprint, New York: Russell and Russell, 1955.

Leff, G. *Heresy in the Later Middle Ages*. Manchester: Manchester University Press, 1967.

Lincoln, H. *Key to the Sacred Pattern*. Moreton-in-Marsh, Gloustershire: Windrush Press, 1997.

Lively, P., and Kerven, R. *The Mythic Quest*. London: British Library, 1996.

Loomis, R. S. *The Grail: From Celtic Myth to Christian Symbol*. Princeton: Princeton University Press, [1963] 1991.

Lord, E. *The Knights Templar in Britain*. Harlow: Pearson Education Ltd., 2002.

Lynch, M. *Scotland: A New History*. London: Pimlico, 1991.

Maalouf, A. *The Crusades through Arab Eyes*. London: Al Saqi Books, 1984.

MacKenzie, K. *Royal Masonic Cyclopaedia*. 1877. Wellingborough: Aquarian, 1987.

Maidment, J. *A Rental of all the annual rents and Templar lands founded throughout the whole Kingdom of Scotland beginning from the Boundaries towards England and so descending through the whole kingdom from the said Boundaries all the way to the Orkneys*, MS. c. 1823, 1839, and undated. Edinburgh: National Library of Scotland, no. acc. 8090.

———. *Templaria*. Edinburgh, 1828–30.

Map, W. *De nugis curialium*. Edited and translated by M. R. James, C. N. L. Brooke, and R. B. Mynors. Oxford: Oxford University Press, 1983.

Markale, J. *King of the Celts: Arthurian Legends and Celtic Tradition*. Rochester, Vt.: Inner Traditions, 1977.

———. *Merlin*. Rochester, Vt.: Inner Traditions, 1995. Originally published as *Merlin L'Enchanteur*, 1981.

———. *The Grail*. Rochester, Vt.: Inner Traditions, 1999.

Matthews, J. *Elements of the Grail Tradition*. Shaftesbury: Element, 1990.

———. *Gawain*. London: Harper Collins, 1990.

———. *The Mystic Grail: The Challenge of the Arthurian Quest*. New York: Sterling Publishing, 1997.

Matthews, J., and C. Matthews. *Ladies of the Lake*. London: Harper Collins, 1992.

Merkur, D. *The Mystery of Manna*. Rochester, Vt.: Park Street Press, 2000.

Michell, J. and C. Rhone. *Twelve-Tribe Nations*. London: Thames and Hudson, 1991.

Molin, K. *Unknown Crusader Castles*. London: Hambledon and London, 2001.

Munroe, D. C. "Urban and the Crusaders." In *Translations and Reprints from the Original Sources of European History*. vol. 1:2. Philadelphia: University of Pennsylvania, 1895.

Nasr, S. H., ed. *Ismaili Contributions to Islamic Culture*. Tehran: Imperial Iranian Academy of Philosophy, 1977.

Newby, P. H. *Saladin in His Time*. London: Faber & Faber, 1983; New York: Dorset Press, 1992.

Nicolson, H. *The Knights Templar: A New History*. Stroud: Sutton Publishing, 2001.

———. *Love, War, and the Grail: Templars, Hospitallers and Teutonic Knights in Medieval Epic and Romance 1150–1500*. History of Warfare Series, vol. 4. Leiden: Brill, 2001.

O'Sullivan, J. F. *Studies in Medieval Cistercian History*. Spencer, Mass.: Cistercian Publications, 1971.

Parker, T. W. *The Knights Templar in England*. Tucson: University of Arizona Press, 1965.

Partner, P. *The Knights Templar and Their Myth*. Rochester, Vt.: Destiny Books, [1981] 1990. Originally published as *The Murdered Magicians* (Oxford: Oxford University Press, 1981).

Patton, G., and R. Mackness. *Web of Gold: The Secret History of a Sacred Treasure*. London: Sidgwick and Jackson, 2000.

Picknett, L., and C. Prince. *The Templar Revelation*. New York: Touchstone Books, Simon & Schuster; London: Bantam Press, 1997.

———. *Turin Shroud: In Whose Image?* London: Corgi Books, 2000.

Pohl, F. J. *Prince Henry Sinclair: His Expedition to the New World in 1398*. Halifax, Nova Scotia: Nimbus, 1969.

Prawer, J. *The Crusader's Kingdom*. London: Phoenix Orion, 1972.

———. *Crusader Institutions*. Oxford: Clarendon Press, 1980.

Ralls, K., *Music and Celtic Otherworld*. Edinburgh: Edinburgh University Press, 2000.

Ralls, K., and I. Robertson. *The Quest for the Celtic Key*. Edinburgh: Luath Press, 2002.

Ravenscroft, T. *The Spear of Destiny*. York Beach, Maine: Samuel Weiser, 1973.

Richard, J. "Hospitals and Hospital Congregations in the Latin Kingdom during the First Period of the Frankish Conquest." In *Outremer Studies in the History of the Crusading Kingdom of Jerusalem presented to Joshua Prawer*, edited by B. Kedar, H. Mayer, and R. Smail. Jerusalem: Yad Izhak Ben-Zvi Institutem, 1982.

Riley-Smith, J. *The Knights of St. John in Jerusalem and Cyprus 1050–1310*. London: Macmillan; New York: St. Martin's Press, 1967.

———. *The Crusades: A Short History*. London: Athlone Press, 1987.

———. *The First Crusaders, 1095–1131*. Cambridge: Cambridge University Press, 1997.

———. *Hospitallers: The History of the Order of St. John*. London: Hambledon, 1999.

Roberts, B. "Culhwch ac Olwen, the Triads, Saints' Lives." In *The Arthur of the Welsh*, edited by R. Bromwich, A. O. H. Jarman, and B. Roberts. Cardiff: University of Wales Press, 1991.

Robinson, J. *Born in Blood*. London: Random House Arrow Books, 1989.

———. *Dungeon, Fire and Sword: The Knights Templars in the Crusades*. New York: M. Evans & Co., 1991.

Rohricht, R. *Regesta Regni Hierosolymitani*. Innsbruck, Austria, 1893, 19, no. 83.

Runciman, S. *The Eastern Schism: A Study of the Papacy and the Eastern Churches during the 11th and 12th Centuries*. Oxford: Oxford University Press, 1955.

———. *A History of the Crusades*. 3 vols. Harmondsworth: Penguin, 1978.

Selwood, D. *Knights of the Cloister: Templars and Hospitallers in Central-Southern Occitania c.1100/c.1300*. Woodbridge, Suffolk: Boydell Press, 1999.

Seward, D. *The Monks of War*. Harmondsworth: Penguin Books, [1972] 1995.

Silberman, N. A. *Digging for God and Country: Archaeology and the Secret Struggle for the Holy Land, 1799–1917*. New York: Knopf, 1982.

Simon, E. *The Piebald Standard*. London: Cassell, 1959.

Simpson, J. "The Conservation of Rosslyn: An Unfinished Story of Decline and Recovery." In *Rosslyn: Country of Painter and Poet*. Edinburgh: Trustees of the National Galleries of Scotland, 2002.

Sinclair, A. *The Discovery of the Grail*. London: Random House, 1998.

———. *The Secret Scroll*. London: Sinclair-Stevenson, 2000.

Sire, H. J. A. *The Knights of Malta*. New Haven and London: Yale University Press, 1994.

Slezer, J. *Theatrum Scotiae*. London, 1693.

Smart, N. *The Religious Experience*. New York: Macmillan, 1996.

Sora, S. *The Lost Treasure of the Knights Templar: Solving the Oak Island Mystery*. Rochester. Vt.: Destiny Books, 1999.

Spence, L. "The Arthurian Tradition in Scotland." *Scots Magazine* (Edinburgh and Glasgow), April 1926.

Stein, W. J. *The Ninth Century: World History in Light of the Holy Grail*. London: Temple Lodge Press, 1991.

Tennyson, Lord Alfred. *Idylls of the King (1859–91)*. London: Penguin, 1988.

Thiede, C. P., and M. D'Ancona. *The Quest for the True Cross*. London: Weidenfeld & Nicolson, 2000.

Turner, R. V., and R. Heiser. *The Reign of Richard the Lionheart*. Harlow; Pearson Education, 2000.

Ullendorff, E., and C. F. Beckingham. *The Hebrew Letters of Prester John*. Oxford: Oxford University Press, 1982.

Upton-Ward, J. M., trans. and ed. *The Rule of the Templars*. Woodbridge, Suffolk: Boydell Press, 1992.

van der Broek, R., and W. J. Hanegraaff. *Gnosis and Hermeticism: From Antiquity to Modern Times*. Albany: State University of New York Press, 1998.

Waite, A. E. *The Hidden Church of the Holy Grail*. London: Rebman Ltd., 1909.

Wakefield, W. L., and A. P. Evans. Heresies of the High Middle Ages. New York: Columbia University Press, 1969.

BIBLIOGRAPHY

Walford, C. *Fairs: Past and Present: A Chapter in the History of Commerce.* London: Elliot Stock, 1883.

Wallace-Murphy, T., and M. Hopkins. *Rosslyn: Guardian of the Secrets of the Holy Grail.* Shaftesbury: Element, 1999.

Wasserman, J. *The Templars and the Assassins: The Militia of Heaven.* Rochester, Vt.: Inner Traditions, 2001.

Waters, C. *Of Days and Knights, A Chronological History of the Crusades, the Templars and Similar Orders.* Whitby, U.K.: published by author, 2002.

Weston, J. L. *From Ritual to Romance.* Princeton: Princeton University Press, [1920] 1993.

Wilkinson, J., J. Hill, and W. F. Ryan, eds. *Jerusalem Pilgrimage 1099–1185.* London: Hakluyt Society, 1988.

Wood, I. *The Merovingian Kingdoms 450–751.* Harlow: Pearson Education Ltd., 1994.

Wood, J. "The Holy Grail: From Romance Motif to Modern Genre." *Folklore* 3 (2) (London, October 2000), 171.

Index

QUEST BOOKS
are published by
The Theosophical Society in America
Wheaton, Illinois 60189-0270,
a worldwide, nonprofit membership organization
that promotes fellowship among all peoples of the world,
encourages the study of religion, philosophy, and science,
and supports spiritual growth and healing.

Today humanity is on the verge of becoming, for the first
time in its history, a global community. The only question is
what kind of community it will be. Quest Books strives to fulfill
the purpose of the Theosophical Society to act as a leavening;
to introduce into humanity a large mindedness, a freedom from
bias, an understanding of the values of the East and West; and
to point the way to human development as a means of service,
both for the individual and for the whole of humankind.

For more information about Quest Books,
visit **www.questbooks.net**
For more information about the Theosophical Society,
visit **www.theosophical.org**,
or contact **Olcott@theosmail.net**,
or (630) 668-1571.

*The Theosophical Publishing House is aided by
the generous support of the KERN FOUNDATION,
a trust dedicated to Theosophical education.*